Mourning into Dancing:

Vivid, captivating, and full of hope. Walter Wangerin is at his story-telling best. Through powerful personal stories, Wangerin explains the core of biblical faith in a gripping, strengthening way.
—Ronald J. Sider

A spellbinding demonstration of grief, grace, and godly love.
—J. I. Packer

I can't decide what moved me most in this book—the thrilling stories or the sharp, surprising insights. The title says it all: Walt Wangerin leads us through the valley of shadows, and somehow we come out on the other side dancing. The last enemy has been disarmed, the last fears put to rest.
—Philip Yancey

Walter Wangerin has given us another incomparable gift. His stories, his people, his wisdom, his whimsy bring the reader gently into wondrous truth. What grace is here, and so graciously given, yet with the fire and smoke of earth, of sorrow, of triumph! Everything we expect from this superb writer!
—Lewis B. Smedes

Walter Wangerin has a great ability to help us focus on the ultimate question of life and make it interesting.
—Senator Paul Simon

Wangerin does not instruct us; he encounters us. . . . Death comes to our dances, and if we dance at all, it must be in her forbidding presence. But the wondrous conclusion to which Walt brings us is that we who must die, must dance, and that both are our destiny, and neither dying nor dancing is missing from the whole of life.
—Calvin Miller

Walter Wangerin explores the many aspects of death with a kind of bold grandeur. His writing, more than ever, gives me hope for the state of Christian letters. After reading *Mourning into Dancing*, I want to write again, to write about terror and beauty and pain—and to write well.
—Karen Mains

Life at its heart is love in belonging; it is joy in relationship; it is the victory of spirit in adversity. Walter Wangerin's *Mourning into Dancing* is experience-reading, for the author engages the reader in felt identification. To read this book is to share a "happening" of grace.
—Myron S. Augsburger

MOURNING INTO DANCING

WALTER WANGERIN, JR.

ZondervanPublishingHouse

Grand Rapids, Michigan

A Division of HarperCollins*Publishers*

Mourning into Dancing
Copyright © 1992 by Walter Wangerin, Jr.

Requests for information should be addressed to:
Zondervan Publishing House
Grand Rapids, Michigan 49530

Library of Congress Cataloging-in-Publication Data

Wangerin, Walter.
    Mourning into dancing / Walter Wangerin, Jr. ·
       p.   cm.
    ISBN 0-310-54880-2 (alk. paper)
      1. Grief—Religious aspects—Christianity. 2. Death—Religious aspects—Christianity. 3. Consolation. I. Title.
    BV4905.2.W36   1992
    248.8'6—dc20   92-9180
                                                      CIP

Published in association with the literary agency of Alive Communications, P.O. Box 49068, Colorado Springs, CO 80949.

Printed in the United States of America

92 93 94 95 96 97 / DH / 10 9 8 7 6 5 4 3 2 1

This edition is printed on acid-free paper and meets the American National Standards Institute Z39.48 standard.

For my father
my senior forever

Contents

MOURNING
INTO
DANCING

I
THE COSMIC DRAMA: LIFE AND DEATH

Personal Stories

1   The Guest

U ninvited, unappreciated. Feared, in fact. Abhorred! There comes to any party, at any time, one who causes such dismay and hatred that the people respond by not responding at all: they ignore her.

They know they can't command her. The silent part of their souls knows that she controls, and she is not kind. She'll do as she pleases. So they pretend that she isn't there, that she's not anywhere. That she is not. And this is the marvelous thing: they succeed! Though she continues to stand beside them, breathing against their necks, they dance their fervid, grinning dances, by motion alone denying her presence until she touches them, one by one or two by two, and the game is up, and the dance is done, and none can refuse her. None. And then her name is on the lips of those whose dancing she destroyed.

Her name is—

❦

For her sixteenth birthday my daughter decided to give herself a surprise party.

I guess she got tired of waiting.

This child is the youngest of four, adopted by her mother and me in August 1974, when she was eight months old. Her birthday is January 9. Her name is Talitha.

Her mother said, "I'll help you."

The child sighed. "I can handle it," she said.

She can handle anything. She's in high school.

Her mother said, "At least let's work on the guest list together."

"The what?"

"The guest list. The invitations. I'll save you time by writing the invitations for you."

Talitha rolled her eyes. I could have predicted that. A parent gets only so much credit per month per teenager, and Thanne had used up all her credit since Christmas. She'd have to earn more before this child would admit the authority or wisdom of her mother again.

"Ain't gonna *be* no guest list," said Talitha, much exasperated by parental intrusions. "Ain't gonna *be* no invitations," she said. "You just put the word out: *It's a party at Talitha's, Saturday night,* and kids come."

Poor Thanne. So dumb and so helpless. "But how do you plan? How do you know who's coming, then?"

"That," said Talitha, "is the surprise. *Surprise* party? Get it?" The kid pronounced this wonderful pun without a hint of humor. She actually meant it.

Besides, parents are distinctly unfunny, the teenager's burden.

Thanne said, "But what if strangers come?"

"Ain't no one here I don't know."

"What about liquor? What about thieves? I don't want anyone strolling through my house with plans to come back at night."

"Ain't nothing we can't handle, Kenya and me." Kenya is Talitha's girlfriend, stronger than she and as certain. "Relax, Mom. Me and Kenya can handle anyone and anything. Any *thing.*"

She believed it.

I believed it. Talitha is as bold as they come. When she was an infant, I said her skin was the color of caramel and she as soft. Now I say the color is brass.

Ain't nothing we can't handle, Kenya and me.

Truly, truly: for example, midway into evening, three girls and a boy rang the doorbell, none of whom I'd seen before. When I opened the door they marched past me in single-file, saying: "Bosse." That's the name of the high school. "Bosse. Bosse," dead-faced, as if handing me their tickets. They marched, without my greeting, without my direction, straight down to the basement. Within two minutes, while yet I stood in the doorway, they marched up again, single-file and dead-faced, straight out of the house, Talitha and Kenya immediately behind them like prison guards with truncheons. "You," they called after the boy, "can come back whenever you wanna. Leave your sisters behind!" Absolutely no embarrassment in their voices. None.

To me, before they returned downstairs to the dance, they said, "Them girls'd steal us blind. No one would find their purses tonight."

Me and Kenya can handle anything.

I believed it.

Until there came the guest they had not anticipated, one whom they scarcely conceived of, whom they absolutely could not comprehend nor ever would control.

But they prepared for that party in a sweet, self-confident oblivion.

They sent me to the store. I didn't argue. Talitha said, "Get twelve big-bottle Cokes and eight pizzas." I didn't discuss the figures or the choices. I didn't argue. "Oh," she said, "and two black lights." No, I didn't dispute the lighting: I was saving the little credit with I had my teenager for more serious issues—especially since her mother had spent all *her* credit, and one parent, at least, ought to seem a little bit wise in the world, somewhat in authority.

Thanne heard the "black light" thing. Thanne said, "Talitha, I refuse to let you dance in a room too dark to see in!"

Talitha rolled her eyes and sighed, but said nothing.

I could have told Thanne that her parental word was weak, that it had spent its force for the month.

Three weeks earlier, by a single word, she revealed the deficit with her teenager. After a night out, we, bland parents, entered the kitchen to find Talitha sweating, Talitha rolling out the most enormous hunk of dough I've ever seen: it drooped down all four sides of the butcher's block.

Casually Thanne said, "What are you making?"

Talitha, laboring: "Coffee cake."

Thanne, smiling with genuine humor, unaware of the importance of the conversation: "Oh! Well, that's three coffee cakes for sure."

She said, "Three."

And Talitha, freezing above a blob of dough the size of a bean-bag chair, said: "The recipe says *one* cake. This is *one* coffee cake."

If Thanne had said nothing, that much dough would certainly have become three cakes. But the single maternal word, *three,* made it *one,* one absolutely, one as a statement of teenage independence. One!

See? Thanne's credit was clearly exhausted.

Talitha (*ain't nothing I can't handle*) covered her dough with butter and sugar and cinnamon. She turned it over on itself, then brought the ends around in the shape of a croissant as huge as a human hug. She removed all the grates but the lowest one from the stove, and stuffed the oven with her cake. She baked it at low heat for nearly two hours, grimly, with a droop to her eye that declared a magnificent self-assurance and contempt for mothers, generally.

And it worked.

That is to say, the coffee cake—greater and grander, more glorious than the thrones of many parents—baked clear through. Now, finally, Talitha cut it in three parts. With one she fed the marching band of her high school. With one she fed her family through a month of breakfasts. And one she froze—which we have since eaten in various manifestations. We have had french-toast-coffee-cake by Talitha, a victor who gloats long in victory.

When, therefore, she asked for two black lights, I let her mother do the fussing, let her mother remonstrate, while I myself—I did not argue. I went forth and bought, failing *black* lights, two dim bulbs, one blue and one green.

And thus was the basement lighted.

And I was not altogether surprised by the effect. Talitha had been right: once one's eyes adjusted, one could see. Dimly, to be sure. Dramatically, the faces emerging from deep shadow. But I stood downstairs in the midst of the music, at the edge of the dancing, and I could see, and I began for a moment to wonder:

Perhaps the girl, so smart in few things, was smart in many. Perhaps, as she declared in her own swaggering manner, there was nothing she could not handle.

I watched her. For nearly an hour I watched the dancing in our basement, and I was moved by the beauty of our children, and I loved them, truly.

They seemed so easily to find a harmony and the rhythm of the evening, all leaping together, soaring from the floor together, a single mind by this one music, a single body, complex and confident and cool. (*Ain't nothing we . . .*)

They did not hold one another, nor, so far as I could see, did they dance in pairs. They were communal. At odd moments, by signals I never discovered, one dancer took a central attention and then, though all the dancers still were dancing, this one accomplished astonishing moves. He floated. He seemed to stay aloft impossibly long, whirling his feet in the process, describing designs with the points of his shoes, intricate patterns, delicate pictures, all in the air, all gone the moment he hit the floor with weight and rhythm, the kick, the imperial, absolute stomp—so sure of himself! So beautiful. And all the dancers were singing the song that the tape recorder was playing, over and over: "Boom! I got your girlfriend. Boom! I got your girl." And all of the dancers maintained an expression of thoughtful calm and self-assurance, smiling delight for the best moves, sometimes barking an outright laugh for the best of the best—moves that defied the natural laws. "Boom! I got your *boy*-friend. Boom! I got your *man!*"

I tell you truly: in that moment, affected by the craft and the talent, the marvelous unity, the utter confidence, the allegiance and the strength of this communion of children, I was inclined to believe Talitha. I almost wept with the glad perception: *yes, yes, you shall survive, bold child. There is nothing, there is no one you and your friends can't handle together.*

I was, I say, inclined that way—till that guest came whom no one controls, against whom no party nor any person is ever safe.

Thanne came down to the basement and touched my shoulder and whispered, "A phone call. I think you better take it."

She has an accurate instinct, Thanne does. She can sense the request that should be turned aside and the one that must be met. And since my writing has gained a certain notoriety in these latter years, she has had to make this decision often.

"Who is it?" I asked as we went upstairs. The music diminished beneath us, but the drumbeat and laughter came through the floor.

"Don't know. She said she lives in Iowa."

"What does she want?"

Thanne simply looked at me as I lifted the phone receiver to my ear, then she turned and left me alone.

"Hello?"

Silence. I thought perhaps the woman had disconnected during the time it took me to answer.

"Hello? This is Walt Wangerin."

"Yes." A quiet voice. A pause. Then: "I just wanted to say goodbye to someone kind." Silence again. Breathing.

It was the voice of a younger woman—younger than I am. Twenties or thirties.

"Hello? I'm sorry. I don't know what you mean."

After silence: "I can't take this anymore. I'm tired. I am so tired." In fact, she sounded slurred with weariness. "So I called you. To say goodbye. To someone kind."

All at once I felt terribly alert.

I said, "What is your name?"

Soft laughter. No answer.

"Can you be more clear for me? What do you mean, 'Goodbye'?"

In the background I heard an inarticulate whine. The phone was removed from the woman's mouth. Through muffling I heard: "Go back to bed. Leave mommy alone. Go!" And then to me a sudden rush of language, low and intense: "I never did anything when he hit me, but when he started to hit my oldest boy I couldn't take it anymore, and I divorced him. I divorced him. I divorced him. And when I was divorcing him, then I started to remember. . . ."

She stopped.

We both were silent a moment.

Downstairs, the beat: *Boom! I got your girlfriend. Boom! I got your*—

Upstairs I drew the phone very close to my mouth, pacing my study as I spoke. "Listen, please. You need to talk to someone. Not me. Someone there where you are. Who can you talk to?"

"I'm so tired, so tired." Her voice trailed away.

"Someone," I said, raising my voice, "must be near you in Iowa—"

Soft laughter. "Ohhh, I'm not in Iowa. I covered my tracks well."

"Who can you call? Who is a friend? Please, you have to call someone now."

Silence.

"Well, what about your lawyer? Surely, you had a lawyer for the divorce? Can you call the lawyer?"

"Divorce," she said, so much distance in her voice, farther and farther away from me. She spoke without passion. "When I was divorcing him I remembered. That my father. Well, my father was a preacher. And everyone loved him. Abused me. Well. Raped. Me, I am so tired. I just wanted to say goodbye to someone kind, and I thought you wouldn't mind. You write such kind things."

"Please, please," I spoke with a restrained desperation. I tried not to let my emotion rush through the phone. "Please tell me your name. I'll call someone for you. What will your children think if they find you dead tomorrow?"

"My children?" It seemed a mysterious issue, *children*. "They're not here," she said distantly. "They won't know."

"Yes, they are there," I fairly cried, I whispered. "I heard a child—"

"Oh, my *babies*. Oh. Well. My children are at school. The third grade. I teach . . . But you mean my . . . Oh."

The woman was truly fading. I was holding my left arm out to the air, my whole hand open with appeal, as if the gesture could smash space and time and find her. I brought it to my forehead and bowed my head. (*Boom, I got your boyfriend. Boom*—)

I said, "Listen. I cannot think that I will go to bed tonight while someone is dying somewhere, but I talked with her just before she died. Are you listening to me?"

"Yes."

"And you have my telephone number. And you know my name. Do you have a pencil?"

There was a long pause. Then, softly, "Yes."

"Now, then, write down my address. Are you ready? This—" The silence deepened at the other end. "Are you listening? Are you ready?"

"Yes."

"This is my address. Write it down." I gave it to her very slowly. "Okay? Do you have it? Please!"

"Yes."

"Then do this for me. Tomorrow is Sunday. Tomorrow I will go to church. I don't want to sit in church and think that you are dead and your babies are looking at you. So, tomorrow morning write me a note. You don't have to tell me your name. Don't reveal anything. Just write this, *Dear Walt, I woke up*. That's all. Just that. Will you do that?"

A very long silence.

And then she said, "Goodbye."

And she hung up.

And I stood in my study paralyzed in every joint, helpless, my hand still on my forehead, the telephone at my ear.

Uninvited, unappreciated, feared and despised, the terrible guest had come to my daughter's party, though my daughter did not know. The guest had not yet touched Talitha directly. Not yet. But she was here.

She comes in a hundred forms, ten of which, at least, she wore that night, January 9, the first day of the sixteenth year of my youngest child's life. Abuse is one such form. Divorce is another. The division of children and parents, by wounding or by the merest neglect or even by the natural independence of teenagerhood, as with Talitha, is a third. Sheer, fearsome anonymity is a fourth. Self-despising and despair and the cruelty of human loneliness and suicide, even in the contemplation of suicide, suicide by any means, emotional and physical—these are her forms. Did I say there were a hundred? She comes as variously as humans have both the imagination and the sin to accomplish the evil of their hearts. But her collective name is singular and familiar, even for those who would deny her.

Her name is Death.

Now when I went down into the basement for my daughter's party, I couldn't help but cry. For a choking frustration. For enormous pity. Pity. I was thinking of this nameless woman; I was thinking of these self-confident children around me. Beautiful they were; but their beauty, their dance, their strength and their sweet communion all were so fragile before the fatal guest. No, there was absolutely no protection in this silly song and its mindless denial: "Boom! I got your—" Nor was there truth in my daughter's bold declaration of power and wit and self-sufficiency. Not she alone, not she with Kenya, nor she and all her loyal friends and all the people in all the world with every invention, every magic, every insight since the world first fell to sin—no one, no one could "handle it."

Not when "it" is Death.

I cried for my daughter's outrageous ignorance. I cried for the danger into which she was by nature born. Already Death companioned her, as Death companions everyone. There is no party Death does not crash. There is no time she does not shadow. And the only way we blunt and cover her presence is by dancing a blind denial. She is here. Wherever there is life, Death walks the boundaries. She is here even now. And she will work her will despite the dances, all the dances, every dance save one.

I stood in the basement and mourned for the children, who delighted in youth and in movement, who laughed and applauded each other, who ate pizza and drank Cokes and considered the world a trifle less powerful than their own arms, their own strong hearts, their Fellowship of Smartness. I stood in the basement saying nothing. They did not need to know, yet, the guest that danced among them, breathing on the small hairs of their necks.

Once more the telephone rang.

Thanne came downstairs. "The woman from Iowa," she whispered.

I rushed upstairs and grabbed the receiver: "Hello!"

"I'm scared," the woman said. "I'm scared."

Good!—the roaring in my heart. I was so grateful to hear her voice again. Out loud, bowing my head as if I had never stopped this conversation, I said, "Why are you scared?"

"I," she said. She tried to speak. "I . . . Please, am I going to Hell?"

She had asked a true and horrible question, concerning the last and the deepest Death. But she gave me no time to answer. She said, "I'm scared they'll take my babies away! I'm scared they will put me in an institution."

Death, death, many forms of death, all terrifying.

She cried out, "Am I going to die?"

I cried back at her, "What is your name?"

Suddenly she was silent, breathing hard. She whispered, "See? This is what I mean. If I tell you my name, you will kill me, and I will die. See?"

Yes, a piece of me, in fleeting pictures, saw: If she were sundered from her babies, that would be death—not something *like* death, but death indeed, since this mother's motherhood would be destroyed within her; her identity, therefore, would be destroyed, some elemental part of her personal *self*.

For this is what Death is: Death is always suffered as separation. Because this is what life is: Life is always experienced in relationship. When the significant relationship breaks in fact and breaks for good, we die a death right there. That particular part of the self is no more, and the rest of the self feels pain for the loss.

Yes. At the edges of my attention I understood her ghastly whisper, how that I might be her killer if my action removed her children from her.

But I was filled with horror at the deeper death, the suicide she had initiated with pills and despair.

I said, "There's a worse way to lose your babies, and that's if they lose their mother from this world altogether and forever. That's if you die in bed tonight. Where are you?"

A very long pause, and then she spoke with a strange giggle in her voice. "I would ask my pastor if I am going to Hell. But," she paused and giggled again. "Oh, he is so young."

I took what I believed to be a hint. I said, "Listen, I have an idea." I spoke as carefully and as casually as I could. "Why don't I call your pastor? I could mention something about your situation. . . ."

Here are the exact words she spoke then: "Hmmm," almost girlish the contemplation, "we're on the same wavelength, aren't we, Walter?"

"Yes," I said. "But, if I am to call him, I'll need to know his telephone number."

Quietly, slowly, she gave it to me.

"Please don't be upset. Understand why I ask," I said. "I have to know his name. Or maybe he will just hang up when a stranger calls at this time on Saturday night."

After silence—all giggling gone, now—she whispered his name. I wrote it with the phone number in black pencil on my left palm.

Then I said, "How many members does your church have?"

Quieter and quieter, she whispered the figure.

"Please," I whispered back, afraid to break the string too soon, literally standing on tiptoe now, cradling the receiver between my shoulder and my jaw, holding the pencil in my right hand ready to inscribe the words upon the palm of my left: "Please, who shall I tell him is in trouble? There are so many people. What is your name?"

2 The Breaking, the Brokenhearted, and the Healing

W *hy art thou cast down, O my soul?"*
    The psalmist (Psalm 42) knows his sadness. When we are sad, we all know *that* we are sad. But we do not always know the source of the sorrow, and like the psalmist we have to ask, Why?

"Why art thou cast down, O my soul? And why art thou disquieted in me?"

What causes the sadness—even in seemingly good times?

Why, for example, does the mother of the bride, who truly desires best things for her daughter and who genuinely loves this son-in-law, weep at the wedding as though it were a funeral?

Well, because it is, in a sense, a funeral.

Or why, when a man has finally achieved the freedom of retirement and now can putter to his heart's content at things that give him greatest pleasure, does he sigh and descend to a sorrowful silence, as though his dearest friend had died?

Because a dear one *did* die.

Almost all our sadness has the same cause, though its forms are various in the actual events that we experience. Sometimes the form is outrageously evil, and then we forget it, if we do, only by severe and necessary effort: certain abuses in childhood, the beatings humans deliver to those they promised to love. But sometimes its form is that of the natural changes in human life, and so we scarcely recognize the cause at all. Yet all these, the causes of sadness, are at the core the same: the leave-taking of the children; the failure of one's soul-sustaining dream; betrayal, whether grand or gossipy, by a trusted friend; the surgery that took a breast; marital divorce; the loss of some beloved possession, the loss of a house by fire, or the invasion of thieves; the loss of a human function or of a significant role in society; the increasing loss of liberty with advancing age; the loss (and this is the paradigm of all our losses) of my dear one to the casket and the grave.

The details change, but the cause and the sorrow are always the same. The experience is universal. No one born to human flesh is ever exempt. Not one.

The cause of all our sadness is Death.

At its core, my daughter's fierce independence—this arch refusal to accept her mother's advice, this aggressive separation from the family that fed her, protected her, and never yet has ceased to love her, this second parturition, as it were, of every adolescent—is not unlike the multiple divorces suffered by the anonymous woman on the telephone. Since life itself is experienced only and always in relationship, the sundering of any real relationship *is* death, a little death or a death of traumatic consequence, but death. It's the sundering that's always the same.

And sadness follows.

And the name of our sadness, even the weeping at weddings, is grief. When we die, we grieve.

Death doesn't wait till the ends of our lives to meet us and to make an end. Instead, we die a hundred times before we die; and all the little endings on the way are like a slowly growing echo of the final *Bang!* before that bang takes place. It's like turning the record backward. Each lesser echo, each little death, has not only its own immediate sorrow; it draws fear and horror from the absoluteness of the last end, the real slamming of the door, the mortal and eternal BANG!

"Why art thou cast down, O my soul? And why art thou disquieted in me?" Thus the universal question.

And the psalmist's answer, also for us all, is this: he has suffered the break of significant relationships.

He has been severed from God ("Why hast thou forgotten me?"), which severing causes him palpable pain and grief: ("Why go I mourning because of the oppression of the enemy?") He has been broken from his God. The isolation is like a killing thirst, the parched, exhausted thirst of a hind chased into the wilderness, whose life can be restored only by cool water: "As a hart panteth after the water brooks, so panteth my soul after thee, O God. My soul thirsteth for God, for the living God."

But the access to God, the bridge of holy relationship, has itself broken down between them: "When shall I come and appear before God?" Alone, isolated, he must slake his thirst on salty sorrow only. He is grieving: "My tears have been my meat day and night."

Evidently, this is not only a spiritual separation, but one the psalmist has actually experienced in his daily life. He is no longer able to go to the house of God. He is divided from the multitude of worshipers with whom he joined his voice in joy and praise. He is cut off from kin and the singing community, from a gladness that once sustained him. But worst of all, perhaps, is the internal divorce, the breaking of himself from his self: for he had once led the throng in procession to the house of God. He had been a leader, whether by appointment or by the force of his personality; that was a part of his identity. He no longer leads. He is not what he has been—exactly as the anonymous woman on the telephone, should she lose her children and her motherhood thereby, would lose something of her self.

Number, then, his separations (all of which, though different, are the same), and note the scope of them altogether.

He is cut off from his own fond image of himself, his old role in the community, from the community too, from joy, from the house of God, and from the source of all life and goodness himself, from God. If he is, perhaps, even physically ill, broken in his body, then these separations are the sharper pains of that illness. If he is in some geographic exile, then he has, like the hart, been hunted indeed. Altogether, it is as though he were cut from the basic element of life, from water.

His most necessary relationships are broken.

What is such a condition? What shall we call it?

Listen to the terrible image wherewith he defines the experience, cool waters turned into crashing, murderous waters; then come to understand the mortal depth of it:

"Deep calleth unto deep at the noise of thy waterspouts: all thy waves and thy billows are gone over me." His brokenness makes him as helpless as a man sucked under the furious flood. His solitude feels like one whirled in the roaring horrors of chaos, drowning. These "waterspouts," these "cataracts," are not unlike the "fountains of the great deep" that, when they were opened, flooded the earth, swallowing all humankind. This is the name of the breaking of relationships: Death.

But his image is even more consuming than "simple" death. The *deep* that calls to *deep* is the Hebrew word *tehom*: these are the waters of Sheol, the abyss at the bottom of all existence into which the dead must sink and disappear. Worse yet, this is the *deep* of Genesis 1:2, when "the earth was without form and void, and darkness was upon the face of the *deep*." So extreme is his isolation, that it is like returning to the pre-creation void, the shroud of the perfect darkness that preceded Light. It feels to him as if the whole world were dissolving. For, sundered from the world, he can know no world, except in miserable memory: *"When I remember these things, I pour out my soul in me. . . ."*

"Why art thou cast down, O my soul?"

The psalmist not only names the cause; he communicates in powerful poetry how it feels to die.

To be "cast down," then, is no light thing. To be disquieted by such grief must feel, indeed, like drowning. The sound of the woman's more violent voice on the telephone, "I'm scared!" was like a cry across the waves: "Help! Help! Help!"

Does this news—of the long reach and the pervasiveness of death—distress you? Well, I can see that it might.

We spend a good deal of energy and intellect avoiding the notion of death altogether. It comforts us to banish our own dying to the distant, unthinkable future: later, ever later, never now—for what is to be is always not yet now. We really (even desperately) prefer the narrower definition of death, mere physical expiration, the *finis* to our personal dramas, because it flatters us to think that we are free until that final moment, the writers of these our private scripts, masters of our fate.

But consider how often grief overtakes us and bewilders us precisely because we don't understand either the sadness or the source—don't even know its name. It is always better to know its name, infinitely better to understand the process that shall continue to involve us, or else we will (like children) resist and fight as if against an enemy. In fact, grief is not an enemy. It hurts, to be sure. But it is the hurt of healing. Grief is the grace of God within us, the natural process of recovery for those who have suffered death, exactly as the slash in my arm, with scabs and pain and itchings, healed. Grief is itself the knitting of wounded souls, the conjoining again of brokenness.

Yes, there is an enemy stalking about, one so close to grief that it is easy to mistake them. But that's all the more reason to name and distinguish the two: not grief, *death* is the enemy!

But consider (again) how much of the Good News of Christ is devoted exactly to this, that we have victory over death.

If you think you can't endure the broader definition of death, the knowledge that it hazards every good relationship, daily striking things asunder (attending every party we poor humans plan), I would not argue. Nor would I call you weak. Such knowledge is intolerable. That's why the world simply ducks it, deluding itself, pretending by all means (from hedonism to folksy forms of philosophy to vague spirituality) that death is no horror, that death is not.

But you—you have a present Savior with whom to meet and wrestle a present death. Surely, in such company you need not ignore this enemy as the fearful world does. And the more you recognize death around you, the sweeter will seem the love of the Lord. You will know him better; you will realize the pragmatic and immediate power of his salvation—for wherever death is, there can also be the manifestation of his glorious victory. And you, child—you may stride with freedom, even *through* the difficulties, grief and the hard road, mourning and bereavement.

If the Gospel seems irrelevant to our daily lives, that is our fault, not the Gospel's. For if death is not a daily reality, then Christ's triumph over death is neither daily nor real. Worship and proclamation and even faith itself take on a dream-like, unreal air, and Jesus is reduced to something like a long-term insurance policy, filed and forgotten—whereas he can be our necessary ally, an immediate, continuing friend, the Holy Destroyer of Death and the Devil, my own beautiful Savior.

How else could the psalmist confront in such terrible detail his own dying, the sundering of vital relationships, and the grief that follows—except in the strength of the mighty Deity, yea, though that Holy One seem so distant?

> *Why art thou cast down, O my soul?*
> *And why art thou disquieted within me?*
> *Hope thou in God:*
> *for I shall yet praise him,*
> *who is my help*
> *and my God.*

3 Life Is Lived in Relationship

W here is there life without relationship?

I suppose the one eternal God once dwelt in an absolute nothingness, both solitary and complete. But in the instant when something began to exist besides God Alone, God became the Creator, and creation itself was never alone, therefore—was from the beginning related to its Creator.

God can. We can't.

For where is there life and not relationship?

The infant is conceived in relationship. Relationship prepares for its becoming. The intimate relationship of a man and a woman causes it to be. And tiny one cell, tiny two cells, this *self* begins and this *being* continues only so long as it finds a sweet, sustaining relationship within the womb of another.

The baby relationship may grow in hiding a while, its mother unconscious that company sleeps in her living room. But only for a while. The physical relationship develops, and the mother's body signals change. Soon she experiences a host of emotions not only regarding her "condition," her singular self, but also regarding this "other" within her. Now there are two; now there is a conscious relationship. And now, if all is well, even now in pregnancy, a woman loves an infant, and in such love is life indeed.

"Wally, look! Oh, look!"

Thanne lies on her back in our huge bathtub, nearly covered with water. Her womb is an island emergent, oval and white, surrounded by surf. Her head propped up, she smiles like morning sunshine at the round mountain that is herself but not herself alone.

She has spread her hands on either side of her great stomach. But she isn't touching it. There is awe in her gesture.

"Look," she whispers.

Suddenly I see a small bulge on the left side. While I watch, it moves. Smoothly, it crosses the meridian, left to right—and Thanne is giggling, now, high in her nose; her eyes glisten bright points of light.

"Do you see it?"

"Yes."

"The baby's turning. See it? See it? I think," she whispers, "that's the heel."

The bulge withdraws.

Thanne murmurs, "Ahhh."

But all at once the baby kicks. The bulge pops out so swiftly that it dashes the water and makes a little wave—and Thanne cries out. She utters one bark of laughter, and then her face crumples, and though she does not cease to smile, she is crying. She is crying.

"Are you okay, Thanne? Did that hurt?"

She can only shake her head. It didn't hurt. She is weeping because she loves the baby inside of her.

It hasn't a name. But it has place and love already; it has relationship so strong that this woman's heart would outdare all dangers to save it, this woman's heart already holds it dear: *it has life!*

The baby's mother's is the more manifest relationship; the baby's father's, at least at the start, is likewise obvious; but theirs are not the only relationships that the baby has.

"Thou didst form my inward parts," says the psalmist. "Thou didst knit me together in my mother's womb. . . . Thou knowest me right well!" Here is the third of three who, in relationship, cause a baby to be: the Creator. God.

For there is no life at all except in relationship with the Source of life, the Lord. "These," cries the psalmist, referring to every creature on earth, even from the lowly grass to noble humanity, "these all look to thee to give them food in due season. . . . When thou hidest thy face, they are dismayed; when thou takest away their breath, they die and return to their dust. When thou sendest forth thy Spirit, they are created; and thou renewest the face of the ground."

Where is there life in a perfect isolation, apart from relationship?

It is caused and sustained in relationship with God, Creator, Sustainer—and finally its Savior too. This is basic.

But life below the heavens, within creation—the life of the universe—*is* the mazy network of many relationships. No single thing can grow or flourish or know itself apart from other things. Nothing, says the psalmist, is created for itself alone; everything is created for the sake of something else: "Thou dost cause the grass to grow *for* the cattle, and plants *for* people to cultivate, that they may bring forth food from the earth." Plants for people; people for plants: a simple, irrevocable equation. Break it, and both die.

So the baby is born. Straightway he's a little Adam relating to nature, breathing in the air the plants breathed out. Nature feeds him and keeps him whom God commissions one day to "dress and till and keep" her in return. Little Adam, little farmer, little scientist, surgeon, something.

The baby is born, a tiny Eve now brought into relationship with another human being, receiving the hugs of her mother, bone of her bone, flesh of her flesh. Immediately there is the benefit of community, parental first, social thereafter. Adam and Eve each need the other as deeply as people and plants do, helpers "fit" for one another, folks who find themselves in the faces of the other. This *is* life: relationship.

The baby, I say, with a shock is born—and by the sudden distress of relationships does, to some degree, experience his being, feel his life and his self.

My son flew out of his mother. Or so it seemed to me. He flew out and up and over her, then dropped to her bosom; and all this terrified him, and it filled me with a fear on his behalf.

They said with excitement, "Look! The baby is crowning. Isn't it beautiful?"

I looked. I had to crane my head upward, since I was sitting beside Thanne's shoulders, holding her weight when she crunched to push with the mighty contractions. I looked up at a mirror affixed above the doctor. In it I saw a mud daub pressing against my poor wife's pale flesh. The baby's head. The baby's wet hair, I guessed. No, it didn't look beautiful.

"Yes," I said. "It's beautiful."

But Thanne strained until she was exhausted, sweating, tendrils of wet hair streaking her forehead. She worked so hard, enduring all dangers for her child—

The doctor said, "We'll have to do an episiotomy."

I watched in the mirror. I felt a sinking horror when a clean cut spilled blood so terribly red and the flesh was left a waxen yellow—

"Here it comes!"

And the baby slipped into the doctor's hands, blue, smeared, glistening, its fat face mashed shut. Immediately the nurses raised it up in a sweeping circle over its mother, aspirating the nose and mouth so swiftly, so skillfully, holding the child face upward, aloft—

"A boy!"

And there, right there, just as they lowered him to Thanne's bosom, I saw the fright, and deep in my father's bowels I understood.

His fat eyes popped open. He sucked air. He threw out his tiny arms as if to catch himself. *He was falling!*—he who had never fallen before. I gasped. All the relationships were changing so radically that it must have seemed for a moment that there were none, that he, at the moment of birth, was dying!

For until this instant his life was experienced in such close relationship to another that he had only to move to feel it, feel the walls of the womb that embraced him. And all sound must have been muffled by those walls, except the ordering, comforting beat of the heart–drum above. And the temperature had been temperate, and light was softened, and motion was rather like rocking.

All at once his body is assaulted. He discovers his nostrils by the jabbing in them. He feels chill wind on his skin. The light crashes his eyes. The sounds are hard and foreign—*and he's falling!*

Not gentle, though necessary, perhaps. Not appreciated, certainly. Nevertheless, these are relationships; and they declare unto the baby his being, that he *is*. The life that began nine months ago in conceptual relationship, apart from his own choosing, has just been shocked—not just by the world, but also by selfness. Some deep part of the infant begins dimly to know that he is here, he is a discrete being, he is alive, he *is*.

Oh, but this becoming is such hard work.

Soon he closes his eyes on his mother's bosom. Being is too much to consider just now. He sleeps.

But we look at one another, Thanne and I, his weary mother glad and beautiful indeed. And together we open relationship unto him. We too receive him. And within the trust and structure of *our* relationship we accord this infant his identity:

"Joseph," we whisper. "His name will be Joseph Andrew." And then, to signal the commitment of family, the place wherein this ego will grow, the people from whom he takes his potential, his person and his character, we confer upon him our own name as well: "Wangerin," we murmur. Joseph Andrew Wangerin. Our firstborn.

For no one develops even the self's identity except in relationship. Whether kind or crass or cruel, whether Godly and good or abusive and brutal, it is people-to-people that little Adam and tiny Eve discover themselves; in close community they are shaped.

Where is there life and not relationship?

Nowhere. No, not anywhere in all the grand cosmos of God.

Which is why, when any important relationship breaks, it is suffered as death.

And why, when it is renewed, we know it as resurrection.

Joseph was the oldest, born of our own loins. Four years later we received our fourth and last child by adoption. A daughter. She was eight months old when first we met her. And she was suffering something. To Thanne's quick eyes, she was suffering a death.

My little daughter lieth at the point of death. I pray thee, come and lay thy hands on her, that she may be healed; and she shall live.

In those first minutes it was Thanne who snatched up the child. I myself, I feared that I was the cause of her trouble. Thanne calmed her. And Thanne named her. From the beginning Thanne maintained marvelous faith on behalf of this infant.

While he yet spake, there came from the ruler of the synagogue's house certain which said, Thy daughter is dead; why troublest thou the Master any further?

As soon as Jesus heard the word that was spoken, he saith unto the ruler, Be not afraid, only believe.

And when he was come in to the house, he saith, Why make ye this ado, and weep? The damsel is not dead, but sleepeth. They laughed him to scorn. But when he had put them all out, he taketh the father and the mother and entereth in where the damsel was lying.

*And he took the damsel by the hand, and said unto her, Talitha cumi.
Damsel, arise.*

But I am getting ahead of myself. Let me tell the story more slowly. . . .

4 The Four Relationships of Life

I n fact, the adoption occurred with dizzy speed.

Joseph Andrew was four years old. Matthew Aaron, a chocolate-brown bomber, himself adopted, was three. Mary Elisabeth, plump as a strawberry, had just turned one. And Thanne began to feel maternal yearnings.

"Once more," she said, standing at the kitchen sink and gazing out the window. "Once more, to balance everything. Matthew shouldn't be the only one adopted. Mary should have a sister." There is order to all this woman doeth. There is also a sort of holy timing: a *Kairos*.

She wrote a letter to the same agency through which we had adopted Matthew three years earlier. In two days the agency telephoned: "We have a child now. Right now. A girl eight months old. Bi-racial."

Thanne, who initiates these things, can nonetheless be astonished by these things. She gaped at the floor in white silence, neither laughing nor crying nor breathing.

But the agency said: "This baby already responds to her name. The mother thought she could raise her, and she tried, but she can't. Do you understand that at this age the child would be wounded by a series of foster homes? The sooner she enters a permanent home, the better—"

Within two weeks of the letter, then, Thanne and I drove north to the city of the agency. We had a baby seat in the car; but it would not be used that day.

We were quiet. This wasn't a birthing, of course. But it was. It is possible, within an instant of time, with no particular knowledge or testimony or evidence, suddenly to love an infant—even if she is not the issue of one's own loins.

At the agency we were welcomed by the director, a short man named Ted Mikolon, for whom every new adoptive relationship was dramatic. A sentimental man.

He led us back to a small room. He entered first, then Thanne, then me. The only piece of furniture in the room was a crib to my right.

And in that crib, a peanut: a baby whose beauty I'll never forget until I die. She was sleeping on her back.

I crept to the crib and bent slowly over its rail. I smelled her. Her skin and her baby nostrils breathed forth a soft clean odor, absolute innocence. I came nearer, gazing in wonder. Her flesh was colored caramel. Her whole head was shaped like a light bulb, smooth everywhere, marvelously round with a scribble of black hair, narrow at the chin, narrower at the neck. Her eyes were closed but huge beneath their perfect brows, lashes long and glossy and luxurious. Her nostrils were neat punctures, whistling with the breathing. Her mouth made a cupid's bow. Her chin was almost missing.

I think I sighed. I made a sound.

It woke her.

She opened enormous eyes not five inches from my face, causing my own heart to leap and my moustache (I know) to lift in grinning.

She opened, I say, her eyes—wide and wider. And then her mouth. And then, in terror, the poor child screamed.

I jumped backward. She did not stop. Wildly—she jerked and turned and stared around the room, screaming, looking, looking for something.

I knew what she was looking for, and it broke my heart: she was seeking some familiar face, an old relationship to protect her. There weren't even tears, yet; the fright had come too suddenly. She saw Ted Mikolon, who was himself weeping. She saw me, sprouting a moustache, wearing massive glasses, some sort of brute.

This little baby was suffering the sundering from all that she had previously known—whatever that was, however good or ill. She was bereaved! *My little daughter lieth at the point of death.* A tiny soul in solitude.

But just as the tears began to rain down her poor, smashed countenance, Thanne stepped forward. Thanne picked her up. Immediately, with arms and legs and the heart's starvation, the baby seized the woman and held on and would not let go—no, did not let go, even as we drove home again through a hundred and seventy miles and four hours in another sort of silence altogether.

"Ow," the baby sobbed over and over. "Ow, ow, ow, ow—"

And the mother murmured in her infant ear, "I know, I know, I know. Talitha, I know—"

Thus it was that between the mother and the daughter a little life began, each in close relationship with the other, the baby rising truly in her mother's love.

But while he yet spake, there came from the ruler's house certain which said, Thy daughter is dead. Why troublest thou the Master any further?

But between me and Talitha was a distance, a gap, a deadness, not anything like a healthy life—though I did affect her by my presence, and so a painful sort of relationship, a difficult, wary life existed.

I loved her. I sent the thread of relationship toward her. But she did not accept it; and like an amputation, then, my love suffered the severance.

I loved her, and I desired with all my heart to shape her, to confer upon her an accurate identity (something very complicated when one's heritage is *both* Black and white), to prepare her, by a father's relationship, for a world not always kind to its minorities. *I wanted to name her with a true and powerful name.*

But she was afraid of me.

Every time I drew near, she widened her eyes in terror and began to scream. She would cry, then, with such deep grief that sometimes she fainted and slumped into a sudden silence. I could not touch—I could not extend relationship to—my daughter.

Moreover, she was in all things a completely passive child. She never initiated play; she showed no interest in rattles, jolly jumpers, toys; when alone, she lay perfectly still. She participated in the bare minimum of relationships, seldom smiling when her sister and brothers made frog-faces at her, never reaching toward them.

What went on within the child? What was her history? Had she been hurt? Left alone? Once, while she stood bare-butt in the bathroom, she happened to back up against the porcelain rim of the toilet; then she leaped away, shrieking, as if her flesh had been scorched. What had triggered so painful a reaction? What did she *think*? What memory, what name did she bring from her interrupted past into our household? Without relationship in its richer sense, I did not and could not know—and this death between us grieved me.

Her death was my death too.

Within the infant alone, life remains a mere potentiality. It is in relationship to others that life emerges and turns to actuality.

If life was to spark between my daughter and me, to join us together and bless us both, it could only be within the webbing of genuine relationship.

She needed me! But I needed, somehow, a safe access to her. We needed a language we both could understood without threat and without fear.

Now, when Jesus was come to the house of the ruler, and saw the tumult, and them that wept and wailed greatly, he saith, Why make ye this ado? The damsel is not dead, but sleepeth—

❧

Broadly, there are four areas for the borning—four kinds of significant relationships in which my daughter might arise, in which we all do live and move and have our being.

1. The first was the first from the beginning of things—when God breathed life into nostrils of a cold, grey clay, and this poor standing dirt became a living soul. Every breath I take is a token, a sign of the First Breath: for God was the Source of our lives, and God continues to be the Source of all life. Because every other relationship descends from this one, call our relationship with God the *Primal Relationship*.

2. And then the Creator provided a context for life and for the living of individual lives: time and space, forms whose voids he filled with light and land and seas; and these he dressed in growing things; these he crowded with swimming things and flying things, beasts and cattle and creeping things. God caused the abundant nature wherein we might act and eat and work and be. He gave us all *Natural Relationships*.

3. Again, from God came people for people. Adam had nothing to do with Eve's creation: his "deep sleep" proves him passive and no

partner in the divine act. And his "deep sleep" is also ours in this, that no human caused another; no human owns another; all are gifts to one another from the love of the Father of all. The third general category of relationships (like the second) remains whole and healthy so long as the first does, since it comes from the first. Call the myriad relationships among human beings *Communal Relationships*.

4. But then, each human being individually is an astonishing complex of relationships, systems fitted together, parts in dialogue with other parts. All living creatures, of course, required a balance of relationships within their physical beings: blood and breath and bone, nutrition, elimination.

But Adam was different. Adam knew Adam! He was the thinker *and* he was the thing he thought about—and from the beginning he liked what he saw. He knew his potential. He knew his purpose. And he was given, by God, to govern himself, since God gave him free will. Every other creature God limited by external restraints. Adam alone he asked to limit himself by his own obedient choice. Under God we were all accorded this same self-awareness, moral, physical, emotional, intellectual. We are created in God's image: we are granted the godly quality of a conscious relationship each with our self. This fourth relationship—embracing both the cognitive and the physiological sides of the human, mind and heart and spirit and body—we will call the *Internal Relationship*.

"And God saw everything that he had made, and, behold, it was very good."

Good was the fine interaction of all things, nothing separated from another thing. Good was the harmony of the cosmos. And *very good* the life experienced therein, the life sustained by an unbroken network of countless relationships. This wholeness was the intent of the Creator, the perfect will of God and perfect life for us. God desires the death of nothing.

And it will never be forgotten that this wholeness, springing first *from* God, is ever and only as healthy as the Primal Relationship. And this, in a word, is the health of that: Love. That God loved us in the abundance of his providence; and that we love God in the cheer of our obedience.

As love is the breath of the Primal Relationship, so love is the blood of the following three.

Love is the sweetest expression of life altogether.

5 Explaining the Four Relationships

I n a moment we'll lower our looking and watch the borning between my daughter and me—an awakening for both of us, a story I'll never grow tired of telling. But that's within the economy of Communal Relationships. And we cannot altogether understand life among humans unless we know the Source of Life and the relationship the Creator intended to keep with humankind.

This must receive our first attention, then: that relationship with God, by the kindness of God, is covenant.

THE PRIMAL RELATIONSHIP: COVENANT

Love is the very stuff of this relationship; an active love *is* its nature, its reality; where there is love between God and us there is relationship—and there, *there*, is life.

In my child's heart, the sweetest picture of such a love saw me and God from behind: me, a little Adam, and God, the Supernal Parent, strolling side by side between tomato plants, our heads bowed down in conversation, our hands clasped at our backs. It was after the work was done, after our showers, after supper in the easy evening, "in the cool of the day." I could imagine nothing so clean and kind and comforting as this, to walk with the God in the Garden.

But such love is not merely "good feelings," fondness, affection. Covenant defines love with a pragmatic clarity.

To those who had free will—the ability to choose and therein the ability to obey—God said: "You may freely eat of every tree of the garden; but of the tree of the knowledge of good and evil you shall not eat, for in the day that you eat of it you shall die" (Genesis 2:16–17 RSV).

On his own side of the covenant, God declares himself to be Providence, the Great Good Giver. The garden, the world itself, is the rich abundance of the Creator to his children, containing absolutely everything we need to support this body and life. This is his love, so simple no child can misunderstand it. God loves us by giving, by being the source of *all* things "pleasant to the sight and good for food." And he would give it freely, neither for payment in return, nor for some deserving on our part, purely out of fatherly, divine goodness and mercy. This is the measure and definition and business of his love.

On our side of the covenant, God asks merely that we obey. This isn't considered payment for his gifts; nothing from a finite creature could match the Infinite Creator's bounty. Obedience, rather, is free and willing, evidence that we acknowledge God to *be* God, wise and good, choosing ever the best for his children. (*Don't eat of that tree!*) Obedience, then, is worship. Obedience is the action and the expression of our love for him. It is how we love him.

But more: obedience actually shapes our lives by directing our behaviors. Our habitual action—much of what we *are*, therefore—is to be defined both by God's command and by our obedient response. Life is in this double loving!

Life is in what, then? Why, in our righteousness!

If ever righteousness should cease, if ever the children disobeyed their dear Father, if ever the healthy relationship should break (*for in the day you eat of it—*) life itself would cease (*—you shall die*).

This is exactly what Moses meant when he stood before the children of Israel, preparing them to enter the Promised Land. "Choose life!" he cried. This was not a figure of speech. This was life in fact. Israel could continue to *live* only in relationship with the Lord, and that relationship required their willing obedience. The alternative, horrible indeed, Moses declared as well, so that no one should be ignorant—either of the terms of life or of the cause of death.

"See," he cried, "I have set before you this day life and good." These two things are not unrelated; each is intrinsic to the other, since goodness, obedient and moral goodness, is the stuff of relationship and the shape of their lives. "I have set before you," Moses also cried, "death and evil." These things, too, are intimates; for evil *is* the breaking of relationship, which breaking is death.

How we live determines *whether* we live (yea, though the whole world deny this fundamental law of life: ignorance neither changes the law nor escapes it).

"If you obey the commandments of the Lord, loving the Lord, walking in his ways, then you shall live and multiply." Let children love by obeying; the Father will love by blessing. And out of this Primal Relationship the other three will continue to emerge: the Natural Relationship (for Moses declared that the land would be "abundantly prosperous in all the work of your hand"); the Communal (for "God will gather you again from all the peoples" and bless "the fruit of your body"); and the Internal ("for this means life to you and length of days"). The Primal Relationship initiates and governs life; the fullness of life is in all four.

"But if your heart turns away, and you will not hear, but are drawn away to worship other Gods and serve them, I declare to you this day, that you shall perish."

Death is the separation of essential relationships. And if the Primal should break first, then all that it governs weakens and begins to break. "Perish" is not a figure of speech. A people can scatter and vanish from the face of the earth.

Now, then, these three things are all the same thing: Love God. Obey him. Choose life. See how inextricably bound are "life" and "relationship" together? Here is our wholeness. And here is a marvelous paradox: that when we are in love and in life with the Infinite Creator, it doesn't matter a whit that we ourselves are tiny and finite. For by obedience we share his omnipotence! By obedience the least of us is in harmony with the stars, inhabitants of the vast pavilion of the universe (was ever "least" so large?)—and by cheerful obedience we soar: *we* are the emblems of the eternal God within this temporal world.

As long as we confess that God is God and we but creatures, not gods at all, we keep his image in our beings; we walk the world with his authority and weight and radiance. This is a wholeness as huge as heaven.

And this, Talitha, tiny child, is the life I desire for you. But how can you know it if I can't teach you?

And how can I teach you when there is no relationship between us, you and me, the father and the daughter?

Well, I will, by God, become the "helper fit" exactly for you!

THE COMMUNAL RELATIONSHIP: OUR NAMING

It is not good for anyone to be alone. Loneliness is brokenness. None but God is whole in himself. *I will make,* says he, indicating the fundamental pragmatism of human relationships, *I will make a helper fit for him.*

Perhaps it is here—people to people—that we experience life most immediately, continually, and intensely. If the relationship with God *is* life for us, then the complex network of relationships with other humans *completes* the individual life: the potential God breathes into us becomes, in human communion, actual. Here we come to know ourselves. Here, in the deepest sense, we realize our lives.

But here, as in the Primal Relationship, the health of the Communal Relationship is love—with this difference, that love to God, since it rises to One Unequal, is worship, while love to one another is equal and clearly utilitarian: not romantic so much as it is pragmatic.

Until there was an Eve, Adam could not know Adam. She, bone of his bone, was his mirror; in her face he saw one like his own, in her motion his own behavior; and in all her responses *to* him he could read his character, his goodness (when she beamed gratitude), his gruffness (when she withdrew to weep). Moreover, without an *other* the singular Adam could not accomplish the business of a whole humanity. The differences between people are, like the locks on puzzle pieces, the actual "fit" to make them one, helpers for each other. She was a woman with womanly features; he was a man with manly; this is a sign for the binding of beings, especially by the differences: in every sense, they *fit* together, and the happy fulfillment of such sweet fitting was life indeed, in the form of little babies.

People to people, then. The Communal Relationship: here the

soul receives its name and thereby its shape. As Eve gave Adam knowledge of himself, so Adam, exalting in the encounter, gave Eve (and himself as well, since relationship causes *all* to be moved by the motion of one) a name. "Flesh of my flesh!" he cried. "She shall be called Woman (*Ishshah*), because she was taken out of Man (*Ish*)." The classifying terms shout out relationship, declaring in a wonderful pun that neither is complete without the other.

Likewise, Eve gave names to her children, no name without its meaning. Scripture simply assumes that names reveal the character of a person, that names can establish identity. When one is named, he learns his purpose; (Abram becomes Abraham), she learns the quality of her relationships to all other beings; (Sarai becomes Sarah), they discover their places in human history and in the mind of God (Jacob becomes Israel, "Jesus" means "Yahweh is Salvation," and the murderous Saul becomes "small" Paul).

The life derived from the Primal Relationship, then, is defined and realized in the Communal Relationship: here, among us, must come to the child's completion.

For one alone is a fraction. Dying. She doesn't know how to produce her own food. Without her father, then—who cooks a slow and succulent stew, filling the house all day with its warm aroma— she'd perish. He is the helper fit for her. And this is how he loves her: he feeds her.

One alone is a fraction. The single thing in all the world she cannot see directly is herself. Her truest self shall remain a theory, a wish, a mystery, a dangerous fantasy, or an outrageous lie—until someone who knows her truly and who loves her well arrives to show her, truly and well, herself. Her father, perhaps. Her father could mirror her. He could name her.

But there must be between them the love of equals. If she loves him, she will suffer neither fear nor shame; she may be "naked" before him, hiding absolutely nothing of her genuine self so that he might see her, even to her spirit, truly. And if he loves her, he will not be frightening or threatful to her; he will not lie nor hurt nor yet pervert the "she" he sees, but in kindness will reveal this soul unto its self. Love permits the trust of one and the truth of the other. One alone is always a fraction. It takes at least two to make a whole *one*. How can the baby know her wonderful, dangerous beauty, except her father tell her? How can she, in action and in fact, *be*, except her father both name her and teach her the name?

Moreover, how can the father *be a father* apart from the child? His identity likewise depends upon her! This is the equality of Communal Relationships: each needs the other for the completion of the self. It is in his child that the father's fatherhood is born; with her it is exercised; by her being, in a real sense, he comes to be.

God made us and then commanded us to love.

But no created individual (except he sin the radical sin) can love himself alone. For love to be *love*, both real and active, it must have an object; there must be an other; and the other of every love is the central focus of the first. Always, in Communal Relationships, this is the fulfillment, the bloom, the finest expression and the sweetest experience of life: that two add up to one—and the loveliest one is ever the other one, so the first one feels an exquisite thanksgiving to God, the Giver of All Good Things.

This is living!

When all is well between us, when humans obey the Creator by loving each other, then no one's life will be ruptured or stunted. None will lack anything. No one will be useless. Rather, humankind will make a harmonious whole, a music of many individuals, the differences enriching everyone's life.

This, Talitha, is the living I longed to give you, whenever you might accept my invitation to enter the human community. . . .

🍂

There was a period when we feared that our tiny adopted daughter was deaf. We could clap behind her head and she wouldn't turn, would not so much as blink, so unresponsive was she to the stimulus. But that's all it was, after all: a pattern of unresponsive behavior, deep passivity. Little relationship to anything.

But she was so beautiful. A porcelain child with wide eyes and a smooth expanse of forehead, eyebrows dark as raven's wings, lashes that put me in mind of Egypt. I gazed always from a distance, my heart recoiling within me. Well, she was changing: she grew the softest tangle of ringlet hair. Her eyes shed forth an amber light. And her lips developed a delicate Negroid ridge.

Africa was in this child, the noble bone, the extravagant color, the generous blood of Africa. Now, to me this was an unspeakable richness. To her, of course, it was yet nothing, since she could not know it. But to the world around us, still criminal in its racism, this was going to be a problem.

When Thanne and this infant went forth into public, people shot them quizzical looks. Some turned a bold-faced loathing upon them. No matter that the child was beautiful: she was Black. No matter that she was also white: a little black is Black. And the mother is white? Here was a riddle whose answer the people detested: the husband and father must be Black! Unnatural!

Soon, soon the child would need to have a name, and to know her name, and by the name to know herself. For if we did not name her, the world would—and its name would wound her. Its name could kill her.

She needed a name that declared her worth, her beauty, her strength (in us, with us, and under God) before the violence of the world. She needed a *life* immune to its murders. But how could I name her if I could not speak to her? How could she become, who would not even be touched? That is why my heart recoiled and I suffered her growing beauty. The child knew not, knew nothing, knew neither the evils her beauty could trigger nor the beauty itself. She, as a singular "she," was not. Yet.

She still screamed when I came near to her. She shrank from my touch, forever keeping me away—

But love watches intensely the other. Love learns by every twitch and gesture. Love misses nothing, since love does not come fully to life apart from the other. Love learns because love yearns its own becoming—

I gazed always from a distance. I sat at one end of the dinner table, enacting fatherhood with three of my children, watching the fourth at the far end. Watching. If Joseph rocked back on his chair, I warned him of dangers and brought him down. If Matthew hid beans beneath his plate so that it rose on a small green mountain, I dropped the mountain and the boy together. If Mary sneezed, I wiped her nose and the right side of my face. If Talitha turned an entire bowl of oatmeal upside down on her beautiful head, I watched.

But during one such supper, in the darkness of winter, under a yellow kitchen light, oatmeal rolling in dollops all down her cheeks, the child glanced at me and, in meaningless spontaneity (I'm sure), flicked her eyebrows once, up and down, in my direction.

It looked as if the raven's wings had fluttered. It looked as if the sharp black brows had asked a question.

Immediately, compulsively—thoughtlessly, in fact, with no wisdom nor deep intent on my part—I flicked my eyebrows in return, up and down.

The child was transfixed, staring at me.

Slowly, slowly she raised her eyebrows so that both eyes widened. And slowly I did exactly the same.

She popped her eyebrows, up and down, up and down.

So did I.

She giggled! Talitha giggled.

I leaned forward with an intense expression on my face. I pursed my lips as if thinking a most solemn thought. And then I arched one eyebrow, all by itself, half-way up my forehead—

And my daughter burst out laughing.

I had just told a joke, and she got it.

Precious Jesus, I had discovered her tongue! The baby talked with eyebrows, a sort of sign-language, eyebrow-speech!

Bingo! In that instant we came to be, she and I, Talitha and me: life flowed warm and real and good between us. I screwed my eyebrows into a hundred configurations, and she answered, twitch for twitch. I said, *Pass the salt,* and my daughter laughed exactly as daughters do laugh at stupid daddies. I said, *You're covered with oatmeal, kid,* and she reached to rub the stuff with her fingers. I said, *I love you, Talitha.*

She said, *I know. I love you too.*

And so relationship began. And life therein.

I did not actually touch her yet. I took my time, now that there was a clear entrance to the child, a road by which to bring her out of solitude. By eyebrows first, by the whole face second, we wove ourselves together; by actual voices; by laughter and groanings and sobbings and cooing and sighing; and finally by the touch. By the side of my cheek and the side of her cheek. By hugging. And so my daughter graduated from her fractioned existence into wholeness. Life itself. Life.

He taketh the father and mother of the damsel, and entereth in where she was lying. And taking her by the hand, he said unto her, Talitha cumi; which is, being interpreted, Little girl, I say to thee, arise.

Talitha Michal Wangerin.

Hello, kid. Hello, my marvelous daughter.

As we became a "we" together, I became a father whose word she heard and honored; and so, slowly, I began to name her.

I taught all the children their selves, their immediate relationships, their various heritages. I told stories. On their birthdays each received the story that contained the child, and any time the child needed the reassurance of *self* and *worth* and love, she could come and ask, and in the evening I would tell the story again.

I nicknamed them, in celebration of difference. Joseph, the eldest and the palest, was "Vanilla." Matthew, so clearly Black in all his aspect, "Chocolate." Mary, for her quickness to blush in laughter and embarrassment, "Strawberry."

But the youngest of all, newly entered, fully enfranchised in this family—she who arose on the arch of an eyebrow—she could be nothing but the smoothest, sweetest, most beautiful "Caramel."

Her mother recalls the moment when she heard, from the living room, the sound of puzzle pieces dropping into place. But the three active children had left with me that morning. There was only she and Talitha in the house. Why, then—

Thanne crept to the doorway and peered in and began to cry. Talitha, yes. Talitha: earnest, squatting above a fat puzzle, making the picture come together. This was the first time ever that she had initiated play completely on her own. Thanne picked her up and hugged her and rained kisses on the astonished child.

And her father remembers a Sunday morning when, rushing into church, he found Ada Chester standing in a stairwell, holding the tiny Talitha at arm's length, scrutinizing her as if she were a cabbage. Ada Chester, Black woman, Black teacher retired, frightfully outspoken because (said the members) she had had brain surgery some years back and it had affected her—Ada Chester was studying the rim of Talitha's ears and the skin at the edge of her fingernails, just at the cuticle. "Pastor, wait!" She shut one eye and demanded: "Is this baby Black?"

I gave the simple answer, the truer one: "Yes."

Suddenly Ada clasped the child to her bosom, raised her face, closed both her eyes, and drew a deep breath. "Jesus," she hissed—and all at once I needed to be nowhere else but here, watching in a sacred silence. Even Talitha received the consecration with wide-eyed serenity.

"Jesus," whispered Ada Chester, "she's one of us, then. Lord, she is one of us."

❧

THE NATURAL RELATIONSHIP: OUR PLACE AND OUR LABOR

With the creation of light and dark, the day and the night, God caused *time* to be. (And in "time" events could now occur; history began.)

With the creation of a firmament to shape the world, to protect the cosmos from the wild waters of chaos above it, God caused *space* to be. (And in "space" things could now exist.)

By his mighty commands to things below the firmament, that the seas should keep their boundaries and the earth its various terrains, that every living thing should be fruitful and multiply according to the design of the Deity, God caused *place* to be, a viable environment, a living nature in which another sort of being might live and sustain its life.

Into a place precisely right for life, God put humankind.

And straightway, God ordained our relationship with all that had been created: "Replenish the earth, and subdue it: have dominion." For the male and the female together were the image of God in this place, God's signature (as it were) upon his stupendous work of art, God's emblem here, stewards of God over the possessions of God.

We did not then, and we do not now, "own" anything in creation. That's not the sort of relationship God intended; indeed, it's a murderous sort since possessors assume total rights over the possession; and the possession, having no control, can be used according to the whim of the owner—abused, misused, used *up*.

No: from the beginning the Creator retained ownership of creation. Our relationship, then—our "dominion"—was to serve God by preserving his world. We were to "keep" the garden in every sense, to be custodians of creation, to cultivate it so that it flourished in everlasting good health and conformed to God's designs for it. Adam did not make the animals; God did. Nonetheless, God offered Adam the high office of naming them, to understand God's handiwork with marvelous scrutiny and holy awe (as the finest scientists do today) and thus to see to the goodness of nature forever.

From the beginning, the Natural Relationship (a gift of God to us and ever dependent, therefore, upon the good health of the Primal Relationship) was meant to be mutual, a balanced exchange. It was meant to *be* relationship: we are here for creation, exactly as creation is here for us; and as long as both obey the Creator, each shall be the health and the glory of the other.

Creation is for us: it satisfies every physical need by which we sustain this bodily life. Of course: food and water and air. But it is more than a sterile "place," even as the trees of the garden were more than merely "good for food." It was meant to satisfy *all* of the needs of a rich human life. The trees were also "pleasant to the sight!" Lovely to look at. Creation was meant to be a "home" for us.

Nature exercises and fulfills our senses. It satisfies our longing for sweetness, for color and sound, for graceful proportion and music and beauty. It comforts us, like a home indeed, and causes in us love for it.

Creation is for us: when our seeing is obedient and accurate, we orient ourselves within the world. In relationship with nature, we may take our own measure in the order of things: not so large that we are gods, not so small that we are meaningless, neither too proud nor too mortified, a little lower than the angels, and yet the crown and the glory of God's creation. Sky is up and earth is down and we are in between. How consoling it is to recognize a rightful *place* for us. We are, yes, finite creatures. But nature defines the wonderful shape of our finitude: the keeper and inhabitant of so splendid a "home" must be something splendid too. And lo: I am.

But we are for creation: God put humanity "in the Garden of Eden to till it and to keep it." Every element of creation should find in the hand of humanity the labor that loves and admires it, that helps it to accomplish God's command for fruitfulness and multiplication. Our *work* is meant to be nature's blessing. And nature's blessing should bless us back. I tell you the truth: so long as we would serve the world in righteousness (the righteousness of God), the world would continue to be our Paradise, and there would be no need of another heaven. Once, when the Natural Relationship was healthy and "Good," this world *was* Heaven for us. God met us not in tents or temples, but in the Garden, where he walked with us in the cool of the day—

And here is the highest and the tightest element of mutuality between ourselves and nature: that our "work" on earth—our actual service to and within creation—approves for each of us our individual value. It is in the Natural Relationship that our lives are proven important. While we are workers at any good labor, we are not meaningless ciphers!

Whatever the present attitude may be, "work" itself was never a curse. Our various jobs, our "work" declares our purpose on earth; it is our conscious, personal participation in the webbing of the universe; it is my relevance. More than that, within the Communal Relationship it becomes our repute and thereby—in the best sense of the term—our glory.

The farmer is, in virtuous farming, important. His is not merely a material relationship to the ground: it is spiritual and existential. The wheat he harvests is the crown on his sunburned brow, and his rest thereafter is an honor well deserved. He is whole and healthy—because of his work.

In exactly the same way, the teacher is important and glorious. Likewise, the electrician, the athlete, the physician, the tailor, the baker, the candlestick maker, and that extraordinary amalgam of all of these, the housewife. Dear laborers, in the obedient discharge of our labors we are servants of God to God's creation, exercising the Image of God in us.

And this is the sweet return: "that the Lord your God may bless you in all the work of your hands that you do." That particular blessing does not promise some sort of financial prosperity; rather, it promises joy. That you will *like* to work, and that the work itself will be your own supreme self-satisfaction. That by it you shall be assured: you are accounted worthy in the universe. Lo, ye are of more value than many sparrows!

THE INTERNAL RELATIONSHIP: "I AM—BLACK!"

"For thou didst form my inward parts, thou didst knit me together in my mother's womb."

How lovely the image, and how homely: the maternal God bowed over the yarn of a human body, murmuring, "Knit one, purl two . . ."

The psalmist is picturing here the Internal Relationship (the individual's relationship to self) at its most basic level, the body that grew in its mother's womb. Our biological life is maintained by the healthy interaction of all its physiological systems: the cardiovascular with the pulmonary with the nervous systems, and so forth. As these keep balanced relationships among themselves, we (individually and physically) are healthy. In the right relationship of tissue and blood and bone, we live. When that relationship is troubled, we sicken. When the knitted yarn is sheared, when bodily relationships break altogether, so do we. We die. This is the same for every discrete organism in the world.

But for human creatures, there are other levels of Internal Relationship. Even Talitha, after her rising, could, like Adam, know herself—know not only *that* she is, but *what* she is and *who* she is with a conscious, devastating accuracy.

She might, moreover, like what she sees.

Could she—should she—also love it?

❦

In the summer of my daughter's fourth year of life, the six of us—two parents and four children—drove across the country to the mountains of Colorado to participate in my family's reunion there.

Talitha peered at the world with an irritating enthusiasm. Her phrase for the trip was, "Don-cha *love* it?"—flopping her tongue out on the word *love* so that it left little dribbles on her chin. She drove her brothers (then seven and eight) to gloom and to bloody expressions. Every morning, every sandwich, every stream and tree in the landscape received from her the same obnoxious approval: "Don-cha *loooove* it?"

"No, Talitha! No! We hate it."

Joseph and Matthew, thereby, declared a deathless hatred for several states, two mountain ranges, countless sunsets, and finally for their Grandpa Wangerin.

Well, my father rose up before all his children and his grandchildren and one Sunday morning began to preach, standing high on a crag, his white hair blown wild by the Colorado wind, his voice a roar of the prophets. Talitha was impressed.

Ere Grandfather Wangerin had finished the oracle, she jumped up, threw out her arms to embrace all things, and cried at the top of her lungs: "DON-CHA LOVE IT?"

"Siddown!" hissed Matthew. "Siddown, shuddup, and be *sad*. This is *church*."

On the journey back home we stopped in Hays, Kansas, for lunch. Hays on the prairie is nothing like the inner city where we lived. Hays struck my sons as foreign territory, spacious, unpretentious, drawling, polite—and white.

We took a booth in a comfortable restaurant, six of us crowding around one table.

A waitress approached, digging a pencil from her apron, preparing to write our orders on a small pad. She glanced up at us, then froze a moment, frowning. One by one she gazed at the children. The children did what they figured you do in Hays: gazed back.

The waitress began to tap the pencil against her nose.

"Field trip?" she asked.

Suddenly I saw us as she must have seen us.

"No," I said. "No, family reunion."

"These ain't your students," she said.

"No," I said.

"Your *kids*?" she said.

"Yes," I said.

"All of 'em?"

"Yes."

That slowed her a moment. She pondered the information, tapping the pencil against her nose.

Then her face brightened.

"Adopted!" she announced.

"Yes," I said.

She grinned. She leveled the pencil carefully first at Matthew and then at Talitha. "That one and that one. Right?"

"Yes," I said. "Right."

Well, then—having solved the riddle, the woman wrote our orders on her pad, turned on her heel, and marched toward the kitchen door.

But before she had left the dining room, Talitha, beaming, declared, "I know how she knew I was adopted."

"How?" I said.

The child stood up and threw out her arms and shouted louder than grandpa on the mountain: "BECAUSE I'M . . . BLACK!"

The waitress was halted in the kitchen doorway. Hays, Kansas, turned in its chairs to stare at us, its many mouths agape. And then Talitha caused her brothers a mortal anxiety by asking the diners, one and all, their opinion on this particular issue.

"Don-cha," she said with angelic joy, "just *love* it?"

❦

This is the Internal Relationship (and very life for my child), that Talitha does more than merely "know" herself; she also has feelings about the self she knows. Her life takes its mood, its manner, and (in every sense) its "humor" from the quality of this relationship to her self: whether, for example, she scorns or else esteems the self. Out of this interior nexus arises something of her peculiar personality, the general cast of her *life,* coloring all her relationships.

When the child announced her racial characteristic, it was like the announcement of a birth. Knowing oneself grants a certain existential independence; therefore, daughter Talitha had *become.* But discovering oneself to be "Black" in this society is to touch an issue of ancient complexity. What shall Talitha think *about* her race hereafter?— which is as much as to say: how shall she view her self? As racists do? Shall she hate this self? Divorce her self from self? Or grow bitterly proud, damning the despisers by elevating Black above all other races?

Or what about this:

We had a neighbor once who stared at Matthew and Talitha with a dog-eyed, teary, trembling pity. "Poor babies," this neighbor pronounced her sorry sentence upon their lives. "Poor, poor babies. Oh, you are such saints to have adopted them! Poor lost, lonely, little pickanninies—"

The woman clearly considered herself benign, a friend at the deepest level to us and to our children. In fact, her attitude was corrosive and her racism merely tenderized. What? Shall Talitha *pity* herself for her color? Should she perceive it a handicap and her *self* a cripple?

Yet color is only one characteristic. The baby was born with an overbite. What about that?

This is the inescapable point: that the *quality of one's Internal Relationship shall qualify one's life entirely. All else may be well, but if one despises one's self, nothing satisfies. Life itself is dreary. If there is felt to be no worth within, then there's no point to living. The quality of the Internal Relationship must, as in the previous three, be healthy. And good.*

And righteous!

But for each of the other relationships, the healthiness was love: obedient love for God, self-sacrificing love for others, the dutiful love of creation by the work of our hands. Does that pattern continue? Is it right—is it righteous—for one to love one's *self?*

This question is so crucial that it becomes, in the end, a matter of life or death, good or evil, wholeness or brokenness: should my daughter Talitha love herself?

Well, yes!—if she loves herself in the terms and within the order that God has ordained. Such loving shall make her life the rich abundance God intended, and she shall exult in the loveliness that she is.

But, no!—not if she loves herself in the terms and by the perversions of this sinful world, whose concept of love begins with the self. Such loving ruins relationships. It will isolate her in the end. That is, it will kill her, grieving those who had loved her on the way.

The sinful world is simply wrong about life and death and loving.

A self-absorbed society thinks "life" is bounded by the skin of an individual. It pictures "life" as "self," considering the self the essential element, the "living" thing. It pictures "life" as contained, particularly, within the physical body. If living is something the body does, then dying is the decease of this mortal flesh. Simple definitions. But deceptive. And dangerous.

This sort of life-and-death ignores relationship altogether. It absolutely rejects the intimate connection between one's healthy living and one's righteousness. Health is physical only; happiness is self-satisfaction; love must therefore be some gratification of this self's desires. What does *righteousness* have to do with any of this? Nothing. In the world's eyes, righteousness is a deadly *binding* of the self and an imprisonment, therefore, of that self's freer, fuller life. There is no room here for obedience.

Thus, the sinful world celebrates self above all other things (since self is the final judge of goodness, the recipient of every "good" thing). Likewise, it puts the love of the self above all other loves. It reverses the necessary order of creation and holiness by saying: "*First* I must love my self before I can love anyone else." It acts like God, living and loving in a solitude. Other kinds of loving become the choices of the self, only so long as the self considers itself served by them; for no other loving, no other relationship is seen as necessary for life. The only code this self obeys is that which proceeds from and preserves its self, that which fulfills and enlarges the self. A perfect independence, a complete self-sufficiency—*I need no one but me*—is considered the highest sort of freedom.

And there is the wretched deception: one so "free" is merely one alone. Beginning and ending with the self isn't life at all, but isolation. Which is death.

And here is the danger: such "freedom" hurts others by sundering dear relationships, killing them little by little.

No, I do not desire my daughter to love herself in these terms. She would displace the Lord God, taking upon herself the authority only God can handle.

Moreover, she would be dying and grieving like any other, but she would not understand her trouble. The self-centered definition of life-and-death does not see that the breaking of relationship is death. Therefore, though relationships surely break for the selfish soul, and though it grieves the loss, the selfish soul is baffled, unable to name the source of its sorrow. It knows not *why* it is sad all the time. So it hardens into bitterness, or rages against the world, or picks on innocent people, or else sinks down in the slough of despond.

No! I beg heaven to preserve my daughter from so horrible a love of self.

Rather, I pray that she would come to love herself in the proper sequence—as a *result* of the other three relationships that God extends to her. For the righteous love of one's self is not the first love, nor even the motivating love. In God's design it is the last love, the final benediction, the *finishing* of our wholeness. It comes unexpectedly. It comes as a stunning gift.

Talitha, in order to end in love with your self, start with God. Love

God with all your heart, and with all your soul, and with all your mind. Trust him completely. Obey him.

And then, in perfect trust, know this: that whatever God makes is beautiful. Whatever God loves is lovely, just because he loves it. And whoever lives within his will is full of grace and favor. Daughter, perfect hands have fashioned you. And God loves you, Talitha, so much that he sent his Son to save you.

Well then, kid, what does that make you?

That makes you a knock-out! You are that beautiful thing, the handiwork of God. You, by his love, have been knitted lovely. The colors God chose for the yarn—they make me cry. You are God's! It is not wrong to love what is God's. Girl, you may with a boisterous joy gaze upon your face. With pleasure consider the marvelous parts of your self—and in pride, in royal pride, like the Princess of Heaven cry out to the world at the top of your lungs, *I am . . .* BLACK! Oh, boast of the business of God. Then come to me and whisper in my ear the question I want with all my love to answer.

Whisper, *Don-cha love it?*

Yes. I love you, Black, my baby girl. I love your brass, my bold, outrageous child.

I love you.

You.

> **T** *ell me, girl: how is it you can rust*
> **A** *t four? The talk scrapes in your throat*
> **L** *ike hinges like to bust;*
> **I** *dle joints lock and loose on a corrosive note;*
> **T** *iny flecks of oxide make your glances bold—*
> **H** *ow is it, girl, that rust on you is just*
> **A** *nother brown more beautiful than gold?*

Ah, Talitha, the soft sorrow in my poem means that loving you also scares me. It's an exquisite experience, a surprising life for me, that I love you and that you love me back.

But life is vulnerable. Relationships break. And there comes to any dance that we might dance the one we can't control, breathing a while on the backs of our necks, waiting a while before she touches us, and separates us.

Such separation is dying.

And her name, therefore, must be Death.

It is time to attend to Death.

6   Death Is Suffered
in Separation

B efore there was dying, when life fulfilled the will and the word of the Creator, in that deep past, the primeval nostalgia of humankind, in Eden, I might have been Adam.

And then I might righteously have spoken thus with myself:

What do I think of me? Why, I love my life. And, having read in the love of others what that life is, I also know who I am. Walt, if you please. The genuine Walt. And since the image is accurate, I know what may and may not be for me; this Walt need never disappoint me.

I know that I am created. That's an important admission. I am not God. I'm limited. I can't do all I might imagine nor accomplish my every desire. Not only finite by nature, I also choose to restrain myself, both in obedience to God and in kindness to others. Love constrains me. I sacrifice much of myself for my wife and children.

I am content with limitation. That is to say: 'twixt me and myself there's a happy, satisfied harmony. I know me well, and I wish to be no more nor other than I am.

How can I (a serpent asks) be content with finitude?

Well (I answer), for three reasons.

First, by my loving obedience to God I am kin to Infinity Itself! The holy relationship to the Creator is life for me; it outstrips the limits of the creature. Why should I bewail my natural weakness if God's power is made perfect in it? In God this stripling is very strong. Omnipotent.

Second, by my loving relationship to other people I am made whole. No talent I lack, but someone has it. No insight, but someone will give it to me. Look, when my son flies on a vertical jump ten feet high and seven feet forward to slam-dunk the basketball, I myself, his father, soar. That we love each other gives me wings.

And third, I have a job that serves the universe and validates my presence here. I needn't be embittered by what I cannot do, if what I can do is necessary to the function of all the world. I scrub the kitchen floor—which, in the intimacy of God's cosmos, brightens the galaxies. It is all one, the floor of my house and the vault of heaven, since love combines it all.

So what do I think of my life? Small Walt, thou Name among a trillion names, lie down. Rest. Rise joyful in the morning light. Fear nothing. Live forever: thou art graven on the hand of God, and that hand turns the wheel—

But Eden is over.

Death intruded, once and twice and three times. And now it threatens a final, fourth intrusion.

Death was no accident. Nor was it a mystery when it began. God had explained its causes to our greater grandparents and had placed into their hands the power to choose between life and death. Life would last as long as love did, and love to God is obedience. Death would begin the instant disobedience did, and disobedience is sin.

Sin caused death, and Eden was over. And this was the nature of death from the start, that they had to get out of the Garden. A flaming sword divided them.

As life is experienced in relationship, death is separation. That first death and then the second and the third—all deaths are the same in the sundering of relationship. The real difference from one to another is the *sort* of relationship sundered.

Well, and there's a difference in sequence too. The first death caused all the following deaths. All of them.

APOLLUMI

It is a word of the Lord—in the Greek, at least—that defines dying as the breaking of relationship.

The disciples themselves used the word in terror when they thought that they were "perishing." They were crossing the sea of Galilee in an open boat when a storm rose up. A black wind ripped the seas and sent waves athwart the sides, filling the boat with water. But Jesus was sleeping undisturbed. "Master!" they screamed. "Master, don't you care that we are perishing?"

Perishing: *Apollumetha*. This is dying in its most familiar form.

But for Jesus, death is more than drowning, more than the simple decease of the body. In Luke 15, he uses the same word in three parables to draw a stark picture of what dying *means*. Then, at the end of the parables, he joins his picture-word to the Greek word *nekros*, which is the common mortal "death," so there need be no doubt that Jesus applies the word *apollumi* to all dying.

"Which of you," he asks, "having a hundred sheep, if he has *lost* one of them, does not leave the ninety-nine in the wilderness, and go after the one which is *lost* till he finds it?"

"Lost" is Jesus' word *apollumi*. There is no physical death here, not like the drowning the disciples feared. Yet death is here.

Shepherd and sheep have enjoyed a mutual relationship. The one (like God) gave love and leadership, protection and provender, while the other gave love by following, by trust, good will and good wool. But now the sheep is "lost." Shepherd and sheep are so effectively separated that one can neither know nor experience the other— except in memory, except in yearning. But memory and desire make the present separation painful. And the more the shepherd loves the sheep (or the sheep its shepherd) the greater the pain. Pain? Call it grief.

Death is one's being "lost" to another. Cut off. Sundered. And the grief can be so deep that we rush to passionate, impractical action, leaving ninety and nine in the wilderness for the sake of one we loved.

I'm saying "we," as if we were the shepherd. But Jesus has a specific death in mind—the first of all, the cause of all other deaths. More than merely earthly, this separation is cosmic and spiritual. He is the shepherd. We are the sheep. He's speaking of the horrible divorce between God and humanity, which he came to heal. In the very scope of the parable, then, we realize that it doesn't matter how lowly the relationship (to livestock) or how high (to the Life-Source): in all cases death is separation.

Jesus repeats the same pattern in the second parable, wherein a woman seeks her "lost" coin.

But the third parable is the most revealing. Here Jesus touches on the various kinds of relationships that may be sundered; and because he tells it step by step as an experiential event, he puts the dyings in their sequence, one and two and three.

1. *Primal.* "There was a man who had two sons," says Jesus, "and the younger said to his father, 'Give me the share of property that falls to me.'" But inheritance should not fall to a child until a parent dies. In the eyes of his son, then, the father is dead. That spiritual separation becomes dramatically physical when the son exchanges the property for cash and leaves, journeys to a far country. Note that all this was initiated by the son himself.

And then what? Why, one separation leads to another.

Apart from his parent, the source of his goods, his "living" is limited. It can't last forever. By squandering (the behavior that demanded his share in the first place), the son is separated from the property his father gave him.

2. Now occurs a series of similar separations, altogether (like the cracking of many bones) a second sort of dying for the son, at the end of which he fears yet a third sort of dying.

The Natural Relationship: By a famine, nature breaks relationship with the boy, no longer nourishing him equal to his need, "and he began to be in want."

The Communal: Society likewise divides from him, since no one "gave him anything," and he who offers the boy a job either scorns him or is utterly ignorant of the young man's identity as a Jew.

The Internal: As a result of increasing isolation, he ends in a pigpen wherein he is treated worse than swine. This is a religious solitude, since Jews considered the pig unclean and the place most foul: he is separated, now, from his heritage, his character, his identity, his *self*.

And then this most personal of the three lesser separations, these little deaths, finds expression in what the boy says of himself: "I am," he says, "no longer worthy—" thus severing the self from value, worth. This is the nature of his dying: he is a nothing now. But he goes still farther and frames his Internal separation in the context of the first separation, the primal dying: "I am not worthy," he says, "to be called your son; treat me as one of your hired servants." That relationship by which the boy has been identified from the start, his sonship (without which he is a cipher, a no one) he believes sundered, a most killing loss. *Apollumi.*

3. And in consequence of his many little dyings, he feels the cold encroach of the third sort of death, the death the whole world knows and fears:

"I perish here with hunger."

I am dying.

THE DIVINE DRAMA

Thus, in the prodigal's story, Jesus pictures three different events of separation. And by the father's cry he names them all both "loss" and "death": "This my son was lost (*apolosos*) and is found, dead (*nekros*) and is alive."

Death is suffered in separation.

That is the core of the thing, the essential element. Listen! Listen: that *snap* of the branch of relationship, that *is* death!

Now we, like the Lord, might arrange in their dramatic sequence the various sorts of dying we prodigals still do suffer.

"In their dramatic sequence," I say, because this continues to be a drama between the Father and the children. Jesus told it as a story because it is a story: history, past and present and future. This dying we do, it is not merely a doctrine of the church; for us it is experience. It is the single most significant play now being played on the stage of the universe, God the protagonist, the First Actor, the First Agonizer (the Greek word means "Wrestler"), humankind the antagonist, the other actor and wrestler.

Here, then, in four acts the four separations, the four sorts of dying we may do:

Act I, The Primal Dying: The first death for all humanity (none is exempt, though many may never confess it) occurred when we collectively and individually broke relationship with God our Creator. The children sinned the original sin, demanding an absolute personal control over their lives, their goods, the goodness the Giver would freely have given so long as they loved by obedience.

The children disobeyed.

And the end of righteousness was the beginning of dying, the *nekros* that Paul talks about: "You were dead through the trespasses and sins in which you once walked, following the course of this world, the prince of the power of the air, the spirit now at work in the sons of disobedience." Dead.

Act II, Many Secondary Dyings: The first death, the cause of all deaths (since God remains the source of all life), is then manifested in the host of little dyings we suffer during our conscious lives on earth. These are the breakings of those relationships that are life for us: sunderings from other people; the hurtful divisions between ourselves and the rest of God's creation; the serious severance of self from self, when one in earnest sorrow whispers, "I hate myself," and another, "I'll never, never be what I want to be. . . ."

This act, while still we walk on earth, is the seeming longest; it runs through countless scenes, as many scenes as we have days to live. But the nearer we come to its ending, the shorter the act begins to feel. Here is "the human condition." Here we suffer grief with loud cries and conscious particularity.

But here, dear prodigals—if all of our lesser dyings finally persuade us of the death to come ("I perish here with hunger"), if we let the grief do what God intends for grief to do (that is, to begin a healing, renewing, a resurrection)—here, I say, we may by faith arise and return to the Father to confess: "I have sinned against heaven and before you. . . ." And God, says Paul, "who is rich in mercy, out of the great love with which he loved us, even when we were dead through our trespasses, [will make] us alive together with Christ."

Act III, Corporeal Dying: Every little dying in the second act carries in itself the terrible shears of the single death of the third act. They all announce the death to come. And it *shall* come to all.

Act two, however long is seems to have run, stops suddenly at act three—and act three itself is done in an instant. It is, all at once, the sundering of every earthly relationship, Communal, Natural, Internal, all, all. It is the sudden ceasing of the body, its decease. It is the death commonly called "death"—and the secular world assumes it to be the last death, and many, therefore, fear it precisely so, the End of Everything Eternally.

Even we, alive in Christ, do not avoid this death.

But we realize that this is *not* the last death after all; that there is yet a fourth, more horrible, death; and that it is from the fourth that we are saved.

Therefore, though we hate the third death at its approach, we enter its act without despair, because we pass through it to life again.

Act IV, Dying Absolute: If the secular world is unable to admit the Primal Death of the first act, then it lacks the means to know of the fourth death. Both first and fourth stand at the edges of time, the one at the start and the other the shut of this present history. Moreover, the fourth death apart from some divine alternative is too appalling to conceive. The world shudders, if ever it could imagine such a death, and chooses rather to despise or else to dismiss an eternal God rather than to believe in the horror of the fourth act.

Was the second act long and the third act short? This one is timeless. It lasts forever.

But we faithful can conceive it. We can name it, in fact, because this is precisely the death we need not die. Jesus died it in our steads. It is the absolute, eternal annihilation of all relationships; it is a cold, perpetual solitude. It is the logical consequence of the first death.

It is what Paul (using the same word Jesus did, but now in its extremest, most fatal form) calls "perishing," *apollumi*.

It is Hell.

7 The Primal Dying: In Adam's Fall We Sinnéd All

H ere we must speak not only of first causes, but also of patterns repeated. For the source of our dying is not hidden in primeval mists or lost at the beginning of things; it is here in the hearts of us all; it is a persistent, willful, individual denial of the Father of Lights, from whom descends every good and perfect gift.

That I die comes also of this: that I kill.

And we have handed the behavior down from generation to generation since Adam. *We* have. We bequeath what we receive. We do. All of us.

❦

On a particular Sunday morning, Talitha and I were walking the six blocks to church, I to preach and she to worship, father and daughter being also pastor and parishioner.

She wouldn't hold my hand. Independent kid. And she'd rather walk in the street than on the sidewalk. This too, she said, came of independence. Well, what she said was, "I can do what I want."

The irony, of course, was that she wanted what every other kid of our inner-city neighborhood wanted. They all strolled in the street, too confined by sidewalk rules; they all regarded this as an act of independence. They each followed the All, and none therefore was free, but every one of them thought so.

But Talitha walked the sidewalk at my command, reduced to proving her freedom by pouting. Poor child, repressed at seven: she'd never get the chance to grow up!

We were passing a row of shotgun houses on Bayard Park Drive, each exactly like the other, white frame, narrow, the front door provided with a single slab of concrete for a porch.

Talitha stumped ahead of me. Since this was two blocks from church, I let her go.

But suddenly there rose a muffled screaming in one of the houses. Talitha's head snapped up. Her foot froze mid-step. I quickened my pace.

The voice was guttural, distorted, so savage and passionate that I couldn't tell whether it was a terrified man or a woman in fury. But the sound mounted, higher and higher, like the diesel shriek of an engine, and I felt a sort of horror in the realization that this was a woman after all. There was, in her unrestrained cursing, a thrilling, terrible freedom—the triumph of fearless blasphemy. Someone conceived herself equal to God!

I really did want to hold my daughter's hand right now. But I didn't have the chance.

Just as I drew near to her, the screen door at our right exploded and a boy came flying out backward, wheeling his arms, trying to catch himself, but falling and skidding until he stopped almost at our feet, facing the way he had come.

The screaming hadn't ceased.

It entered the morning now as a physical force, the destroyer of Sundays and small boys.

An enormous woman rolled out onto the porch, pointing two fingers like pistols at the boy, roaring a single epithet over and over, a word so foul I shivered for Talitha.

The boy and the woman, both, seemed oblivious of us, though he sat in our path and we had stopped because of him.

"Do me a favor, you little—" the woman screamed that filthy word again. She drew back her arm and threw an imaginary stone at him. "Do me a favor, and die!"

Talitha stiffened.

My own face drained of blood.

The boy—Talitha's age—showed no expression whatsoever, sitting and staring at the thunderhead above him.

Then the woman turned and re-entered her house with a crack-slam of the door.

The world was suddenly terribly silent.

Do me a favor. And die.

We three were frozen a moment. I discovered that I had laid my hands on Talitha's shoulders, her father, her protector, her pastor too, but sorry, sorry that I could not hide from her these evils of our society. Several times already this year I had given my daughter my helpless hug. When she came in the kitchen so stricken with sobs that she couldn't talk, I held her. I knelt before her and held her and stroked her shuddering spine until she said, "Why did Andrea's brother beat her up?" Little Talitha pulled back and begged me, "Why? Andrea didn't do nothing. Why did he make her ears bleed? Daddy, I saw him hit her in the head with two fists! Why—" but she was speechless with sobbing again. And then my love was all my answer, my yearning, my sorrow, and my helpless hug.

Now on the sidewalk I did not kneel to hug her, though I was ready to. I expected her to sob for this boy as she had for Andrea—but pity moved her now to a different response, surprising me. Here were signs of her growing boldness. She pulled her shoulders from my hands and took three steps forward and slowly extended her own hand to the boy as if offering him something, candy or kindness.

She was tentative, but utterly genuine.

"Do you," she said. "Can you—?" She stopped, uncertain. She had an overbite in those days that caused an odd slushiness in her speech. She shrugged. "Wanna shake hands?"

He turned to look at her.

She was so delicate then, a porcelain child.

"Well," she said, "and then d'you wanna come to church with us?"

The boy stood up and raised both hands, aiming them at Talitha as if they were pistols. "Do me a favor," he hissed. Then he drew a breath and screamed so high and sharp, his voice cut like the bloody edge of a knife: "Do me a favor, you little ——, and die."

He ran away.

Talitha stood paralyzed.

That morning my youngest child, seven years old, allowed me to carry her the last two blocks to church. She didn't ask; I offered; but neither did she deny me. I carried her as an infant, my brittle baby. I made a cradle of my arms and a fortress of my chest, and I bent and kissed her brow—and then that was the last time, ever. Never would I have the chance to hug my child this way again; never would I be so completely her superior, because never again would she be so needful a baby.

Now: I wish I could end this episode of the ring-growth of my daughter with a happy peroration about her maturity, how her instinct for sympathy grew better by growing bolder, how a father's heart grew prouder thereby—

But I can't.

One or two years later (how many I don't know because I can't recall the girl's age at the following event; certainly she was old enough to take or else to launch full ground assaults), two or three years later, I say, while I sat working in my study, I heard such savage explosions of shrieking that I raced from the room with the sense of serious danger. The ruinous world had smashed into my household.

Danger, yes. There was danger in the front hall. But strangers? No.

Bold Talitha had attacked her older brother. Actually, Matthew was much the stronger. But in those days she was living under fewer rules. She was the freer, therefore, and the more furious. This child could be an inspiration of rage, like the wolverine confronting enemies thrice her size. Matthew's astonishment and—for just a moment—his basic moral restraint gave her the advantage.

But as I came in the boy's desire for survival was prevailing. He pinned her with his greater weight.

She resorted immediately to the more fiery weapon, her tongue.

"Do me a favor, you ——," she screamed. "Do me a favor and die."

Now hear the significant revelation of this episode. Neither soften nor avoid it: that Talitha, regardless of adoption, was as truly and profoundly my daughter in this cry as in my cradling arms—in *sin* as in my love.

For I am a son of Adam. And she who is a daughter of mine must likewise be a granddaughter of Adam. And though it may not have been from me that she learned the horrible words, it was within the family, after all. If not the words, certainly she received the ability, the tendency to use them, as a bequest. The child is only more bold than I, not different in original sin. No, not different.

Sin came into the world through one man and death through sin, and so death spread to all men because all men sinned. . . .

"All men." Me. Talitha. We. All.

O my daughter, not from violent women and nasty boys would I most protect you, but from the violence in ourselves—and from the death it causes.

❧

THE COMMAND

The instruction that God gave Adam (and Walt and Talitha) was as simple as sunlight. No tricks. Yet it was crucial to the good continuance of life, the blessed relationship between the Creator and the created.

"But of the tree of the knowledge of good and evil you shall not eat, for in the day that you eat of it you shall die."

Obedience was essential to the preservation of life. As simple as sunlight.

But temptation beclouds things, making simplicity seem subtle and suspicious after all. The goodness of God can be drawn in a few strokes. But the sin of the children takes longer to tell since we (like Eve) do more than remove ourselves a world away from God; we must also excuse the removal and deceive ourselves in the process.

Well, it's too horrible immediately to recognize the consequence of sinning: *Die! You shall die.* Sin begins the tragic descent of the individual and of the race—yea, of the entire creation—from life to death. Thus the deception. We *think* we've chosen life when in fact we have initiated a cosmic suicide.

But you and I can gaze with an accurate eye. (I'm speaking to my child as well as to the greater family within which she is sister to you all.) This is what the first death, our Primal Dying, looks like, over and over again:

—*One Alone*: What makes us vulnerable to the lies of Temptation? Certainly not our gender. Eve was not deceived because she was female, but rather because she was not taking advantage of the wholeness that God had given her, the fullness of life. She met the Tempter alone. She had only one perspective on the conversation that followed. She lacked the mirror that Adam was; he might have revealed the changes taking place in her. She lacked the talents that Adam had, which, with hers, would have made a whole community against deceit.

So the Tempter meets us one at a time, when we think the "I" is stronger or more important than the "We." So the Tempter encourages within us the elevation of the Self. ("I'm worth it"; and "I deserve a break—") So sin begins with the individual who is questioning the value of her relationships. . . .

—*Doubt*: Trust is the soul of every healthy relationship. But in this case, where God requires complete obedience from those who don't have complete knowledge, trust is an utter necessity. We trust in his word. We *believe* that God alone should possess "the knowledge of good and evil," that he will choose the good for us and by his command protect us from evil.

—*Trust*: we are content in ignorance. We are at peace with the limitation.

Temptation, therefore, seeks first to crack trust with doubt. Specifically, it goes after the *Word of God*: "Did God *say*," says Temptation, asking analysis of the words themselves since such objectification exchanges the life of warm relationship for cold, intellectual scrutiny. "Did God (really?) say, 'You shall not eat of any tree of the garden'?"

Clearly, God did not say that.

Is it wrong for Eve to stick up for God, then? Is it wrong for any of us to confront temptation with the facts? Isn't it *right* thus to argue on God's behalf?

Tell you what: it's dangerous! It accepts the premise that God's Word ought to be scrutinized for truth. It gives as much authority in this matter to our intelligence as to God's simple and holy authority.

—*A Personal Equality*: When the Tempter confronted Jesus with exactly the same strategy, trying to make the Son of God argue on behalf of the Word of God, Jesus did not argue. Jesus did not stick up for his Father. He didn't take even the first step toward doubt.

Here was the Word: God the Father had said, "This is my beloved Son, with whom I am well pleased." Straightway Jesus was led into the wilderness to be tempted by the devil. When he was hungry the devil said to him: "*If you are the Son of God* [prove it], turn stones to loaves." Now, if Jesus had responded even to "prove" the Word of the Father, then he would have made his own ability equal to that Word, a necessary piece of physical evidence with which to back it up. Trust is weakened.

But Jesus *does* nothing. Instead, Jesus shows marvelous trust in the Word of God by actually quoting from God's words in Scripture, and by choosing a passage that focuses on the Word: No one lives (lives, he says, touching upon the significance of this primary relationship and the soul of it) "by bread alone, but by every word that proceeds from the mouth of God."

There. That is the response of faith and the gesture of a genuine trust.

But Eve was not (and we are not) always content by such inactivity, by being such a seeming non-entity in the God/us relationship. It would have been enough to do nothing.

But we don't do nothing.

We act as though God *needs* our support. The instant we answer Temptation with words *of our own* to strengthen the Word of God ("We may eat of the fruit of the trees") we have elevated ourselves to a level of some equality with God. And although this is not yet in itself a sin, it is dangerous.

Even as it increases our importance in this Primal Relationship, it focuses our attention a little less on God, a little more on our Self.

—*Self-pity*: And the more important we are, the more confining seem the rules imposed upon us. The equaler *we* are to God, the more equal we wish our circumstances to be.

And the evidence of this new discomfort within God's restrictions is that we exaggerate them. We ourselves (like the Temptor) lie a little about the laws, as though they chafed a little much. We say (piously), "We may eat of the fruit of the trees of the garden. But God said, 'You shall not eat of the fruit of the tree which is in the midst of the garden, neither shall you touch it, lest you die.'" Woops! That new phrase is not God's, but purely our own, *Neither shall you touch it*. This is the whine of the child who says unto her father, "You never let me have anything." Never? Well, not never. It just feels like never because self-pity is increasing.

Thus, the sign that (1) Temptation is working, that (2) we are decreasing God's importance as we increase the Self, and that (3) God's commands are becoming irritants that we might one day have cause to ignore, is this exaggeration of the effect of the law upon us and the implied suspicion regarding the motives of God.

Self-pity reveals in us the question whether God's decisions really are good, whether his Word really is true and altogether loving.

That's doubt.

We haven't yet actually sinned. But the attitude that might justify a sin is taking root.

The difference between the Creator and the created is beginning to receive serious attention and to trouble us, so that we no longer feel exalted by the love of One So Great but rather reduced and restrained by that very Greatness. Greatness, now, is not our goodness, but God's alone, precisely because the Greatness seems to be his alone, withheld from us.

And that is the other side of doubt: suspicion. Even so are we prepared to believe the shining lie.

—*Flat Deception*: "You will not die."

How can we possibly accept a direct contradiction of the Word of God as the truth? Well, the argument offered next speaks to our suspicions and flatters the changes that have taken place within us: "For God knows that when you eat of it your eyes will be opened, and you will be like God, knowing good and evil."

Ah, we want to hear that the Self can receive the authority of the Deity, possessing the knowledge of Good and Evil, deciding apart from God what is good and what is evil—good *for us* and evil *for us*. We want to believe that life is thus in the Self alone. We want to believe the lie. We, therefore, empower the word of the Liar: "You shall not die."

And: "You will be like God."

No longer satisfied merely to be in the image of God, we want to be *like* him. This is exactly the station we imagine for our mighty selves; it accords with our new self-esteem. Freedom! This is perfect freedom, to be complete in the Self, an infinitude like God's. Limitlessness.

—*One Love Exchanged for the Other*: So the attitude becomes an act. So disobedience destroys righteousness, and sin begins and by sin cometh—

"When she saw that the tree was good for food, and that it was a delight to the eyes [though every other tree was, by God, *pleasant to the sight*], and that the tree was to be desired to make one wise, she took of its fruit and ate."

Her wisdom was of greater value to her than God's. The love for our Selves, thus, exceeds our love for God. It becomes the supreme, defining love, the source of our significance, the reason of our existence, the fullness of our being: self-sufficiency.

What then? Why, then we have, by choosing this marvelous autonomy for ourselves, severed ourselves from the Source of Life?

With opened eyes, now choosing the Good and the Evil according to our own desires, we have set ourselves against God and against his choices. We divorce ourself from God, and with good reason—for his "good" feels to our flesh like an "evil"; but our "good" of personal independence is condemned by God as his and everyone's "evil." So hostility must arise. We severed ourselves from God as from an enemy. This is war, God against gods.

"See," cried Moses, "I have set before you this day life and good, death and evil." He was not using figures of speech. "Life" and "death" are not metaphors but matters of fact. And Moses begged the children: "Choose life!"

But we, by choosing autonomy—we have chosen death.

—*Death*: All we have gone astray: we have turned every one to his own way.

When the child decided that freedoms from parental restraint (like walking the street instead of the sidewalk) were a delight to the eyes; when the youth saw that certain words were to be desired for showing one to be cunning and wise; when, therefore, they took and ate, then God was no longer their God. They were each their own gods.

Whenever a human cried, for his sole sake, "I deserve this thing! I have a right to it!" and therefore took it by fraud or by force; whenever a human acted purely from personal desire, according to her notion of the "good," mindless of others and of the will of God; whenever the self thus takes dominance; whenever the attitude is pride and the motive self-centered, then we are Eve. We are severed from God. And we are monstrously deceived, for we are even more limited than we had been before, being bounded now by mortality itself, the sternest of limitations.

—*The Continuing Self-Deception*: But that which began by a lie still needs a lie to support it among us.

Severed from the Source of Life, we were "dead," writes Paul, "in trespasses and sin." This remains our mortal condition, but this, precisely, we spend extraordinary funds of energy trying to deny.

"You will not die," says a tempting Society. You are free! You (it declares in commercials, in pop-psychology, in schoolyards and

movies and furious fights for "rights" in this land), you are in charge
of your fate, free of restraints in this free country. You can do
whatever you want, so long as you hurt no one else. Believe whatever
you want. *Be* whatever you want to be. Anyone who argues otherwise
is regressive, repressive, and boorish; no one has the right to impose
his morality upon you.

Hey, man, do your own thing!

Feel good about yourself.

"What the mind can conceive and the heart can believe," preaches
the wisdom of the world with religious fervor, "the hand can
achieve." Anything. You can accomplish anything, if only you put
your mind to it.

And you will live forever. At least, you needn't think of death till
death is here, and it shan't be *here* till the last flick of your physical
existence. Therefore, act as if you'll live forever and, while you live,
you will!

Lies, one and two and three. Lies: because no one is unlimited,
either (1) morally or (2) conceptually. No one can "do" whatever
he wants. And (3) death is here right now. Death is daily present.
Daily death crashes our dances and breathes on the backs of our
necks—for none is not dying, no, not one.

But to the degree that we crave life, even to that same degree we
hunger for the lies; we do ourselves empower them and so deny our
death. For if we are the center of the world, then our personal death
is the obliteration of the whole world. Who can imagine so hideous
an enormity, that things generally should cease to be?

—*Good Grief*: What, then, could undeceive a world so dependent
upon deception?

Finally, the *experience* of the truth in spite of all lies. The actual
experience of dying persuades the little god that he is finite after all.

But when, before his Corporeal Death (which is the one the world
admits as death), does the little god die enough to lose his lie?

When one by one his resources (here, in the "far country" of this
world) prove finite and he (like the prodigal severed from the father)
runs out of them. In other words, when those relationships that once
were gifts from the Great and Good Giver, those relationships
necessary for his life one by one break—*then* the poor man wakes to
his dying. Each severed relationship is a little death. And it hurts
with an existential ache; for, though the deceived may not yet admit

it, each broken relationship is proof of the Primal Dying and prophecy of the Corporeal Dying to be. Lo, we who thought we controlled our personal fates discover that we are powerless in the mills of the universe.

Now comes a choice: No, or yes.

The defiant "No!" Either ego resists this truth with all its might; it can suffer the hurt and fight its message, both at once. That is to say, on account of every Secondary Dying we grieve a little, but we may choose to ignore that the ache is "grief."

We are able: we can be sad without seriously seeking the cause in ourselves. Blame others for the sorrow. Sentimentalize the sadness, enjoy it, wallow in self-pity. Or cover the pain by any means: chemical substances, hectic happiness, a hedonistic satisfaction of the physical, vague philosophies, working so hard we cannot think, loving some idol that promises deathlessness.

The deadly "Yes." Or else we can allow the ego its dying. Recognize and admit the experience. Confess the cause of it. We can, thus, choose to lose our lives—in order to find them again.

Every Secondary Dying, precisely by the grief that it causes us, is a call to the deeper truth and a means by which we might return to the Lord. That is the goodness of grief—even the goodness of a painful grief: to teach us our need again, and to turn us again to trusting.

8 Secondary Dyings: In the Day That We Ate of It

O riginal sin is exactly that, the "origin" of all the dyings we suffer thereafter, the primary cause of them all, though lesser and more immediate causes might be found for every secondary death.

For God said, "Don't," regarding the tree, and then he declared consequences: "In the day that thou eatest thereof thou shalt surely die."

In that very day? Immediately?

Yes. By disobedience the rupture between God and humanity started immediately. Yes.

But there was another day, wasn't there? Adam and Eve continued to move and breathe and have babies—to live. And we are those babies. The world has continued. Isn't "day," then, a figure of speech? Doesn't it mean "time"?—that in the day they disobeyed, death entered time, and in time they would die?

No. In *that* day, in the common events of their daily and common lives, and in the particular day of their sinning, they did die.

Death is the breaking of those relationships in which we experience life; for when the relationship breaks, I myself am diminished. I am no longer the person I had been before the break. And as I am conscious thereafter, so I suffer not only the loss of something vital to myself, but also the loss of that previous *self*—because that vital thing had defined me. It is gone; the self is changed; the person I used to be is likewise gone. This is the Secondary Dying. And in the day we sinned, in *that* day, all the good and vital relationships, gifts of the Giver, weakened: disobedience troubled Communal Relationships, and Natural Relationships, and Internal Relationships, all three, which straightaway sickened and started to separate.

Watch:

—1. *They sewed fig leaves together*: God had intended humanity to be both "naked and not ashamed," completely open to one another, completely available, each the very completion of the other. Our wholeness, personally and communally, was in trust, maintained by the law of harmonious love.

But when we chose each to become our own autonomous gods, our "eyes were opened and we knew that we were naked." Nakedness, suddenly, was a problem. Complete openness to one another (when any other might be an opposing god) became vulnerability. Complete disclosure seemed rash and dangerous. So we covered the nakedness. We put on clothes. That is, sin persuaded us to hide the truth of ourselves—to conceal ourselves from one another!

The self-centeredness of sin made us fear the differences between us, for one might use his strength to rule another, or one felt threatened by her natural need. Differences became weapons or occasions of scorn; differences, among people striving for private advantages, became divisions. The survival of the fittest required those unfit to fake it, to lie, to pretend and scheme and manipulate. And the best of the people, those who did not seek to elevate themselves, did nevertheless cover themselves: merely to exist, they kept secrets, locked their doors, maintained a healthy suspicion regarding strangers.

The point of the fig leaves is this: in the day we disobeyed our God, *in that day* we began to separate ourselves, at very deep levels, from one another. There began in that day a desperate inability to know our neighbor (or our spouse or our teenager) fully and completely. There began in that day a series of Secondary Dyings: divorces, betrayals, gossip, abandonment. Ah, people—there began in that day as many kinds of communal breaks as there are Communal Relationships. Death: she has a hundred forms, and no two dancing partners are now inviolable, for even if they love each other very well, yet one might collapse and leave the other to suffer a Secondary Dying in that she is alone on earth a widow.

—2. *Cursed is the ground because of you:* The whole created world was meant to be our home. Natural Relationships not only supported the body's life, but were also the arena in which we worked out the good purpose of our existences. Work ennobled us. Work was good. So intimate was the relationship between humanity and nature that the Hebrew words for "Adam" and the tillable "earth" are almost the same word. A happy pun: 'twixt him and the ground was life!

But in the day we ceased to obey the Creator, creation itself suffered the curse, and we suffered the separation.

Earth now begrudges our work and distresses our labor, bringing forth "thorns and thistles" as easily as wheat and abundance. Now, under the terrible convulsions of nature—or else under the vast indifference of the stars—we can feel alien in this place, scarcely at home. Such feelings are cold death to us, a Secondary Dying—and we grieve the recognition.

"In the sweat of your face you shall eat bread." The work that should have contented our existence now is as likely to drain us, exhaust us, frustrate us. Day by day we are diminished by the sweat, the sheer difficulty of self-support, toiling in places that neither love us nor wish to see the whole of us: "You're not paid to think!" The sweat, the drudge, the aching of body and heart—these teach us our finitude in the universe.

"Till you return to the ground, for out of it you were taken. You are dust." Dust: it is the only certain relationship between ourselves and the earth, that in the end it will claim our bodies. Ah, what a futility! *This* is now the curse (not the work itself), that if dust we are, then dust is all we do, and the best of it must rot in the end. In flashes of insight, the laborer is overwhelmed by the knowledge: "Nothing lasts." Immediately he is downcast—because these insights are not ephemeral musings; they are experiences of the sundering between himself and God's creation; they are real and individual deaths. He is grieving. He has died a Secondary Death.

—3. *And to dust you shall return:* And so the Internal Relationship also, in the day we denied our God, began to disintegrate. The breath (which the Creator had breathed into clay) and the body (the clay itself) would not be united forever.

With every significant physical trauma, the body is taught

mortality—and we suffer separation from the future we had planned for and desired: it is no longer sure. In physical sickness we feel the dust we are and suffer the knowledge that we do not control even the *corpus* in which we "live." We suffer a separation from self. A Secondary Death. We grieve.

And when the Lord God sent forth from Eden the man and the woman, they suffered separation from the best "image" of themselves—the "image" that had been the picture of God in themselves, his signature on creation. Still and still, we might *dream*; we might imagine a sweet self-image, like unto a god; we might strut and display a wondrous self-esteem. But again and again these things break against the hard fact of our finitude. We are limited, fleshy beings. When the dream and the fact are torn asunder within us, then *we* are torn asunder. We suffer an internal separation as though the cherubim had cut us in twain with the flaming sword. We die a Secondary Death. We grieve truly.

Or, in the words of Jesus' terrible parable, the prodigal "comes to himself," meets his real self indeed, and all that was wonderful in radical independence, even the deity of that self, dies.

WHY ART THOU CAST DOWN, O MY SOUL?

Two blocks from church on a Sunday morning, when she was but seven years old, my daughter felt pity for a child her age, whose self had just been whipped by the murderous tongue of his mother. Talitha put out her hand to help him—and, like a hideous changeling, that child rose up in the form of the mother, cursing as he'd been cursed. Talitha was stunned to silence. And once more before she took independence truly unto herself, I carried my baby in my arms.

But what had Talitha met on the sidewalk? The society that shatters love, that rips apart its own most vital relationships? Yes.

And what else? A woman whose despair, whose dismal loss of any personal purpose on earth, had caused her such sorrow that she would lash out even at her son? The consequence, then, of separation between a good earth and one of its keepers? A laborer lost in futility? Yes, that too.

But whom did Talitha meet on the sidewalk, finally? Whose face did she look into when it cursed her? Her own. Yes. Herself. She met the she that she would be a few years later.

And in all three, with speechless sorrow, I saw me.

Do you see you?

And does it cause you sadness too, this quick picture of the separations in a sudden and single incident?—this tiny story of the dyings?

If so, please forgive me for troubling your day. But at the same time, realize: you are leagues ahead of many in the world who simply do not *know* why they are sad. "Why," they ask with no hope of an answer, "why art thou cast down, O my soul?"

Knowledge, even the difficult knowledge of the sources of sorrow, is always an advantage. Always. Knowledge itself may not *change* things. To know what has truly caused your sadness may not abolish the sadness. But it is the beginning of comfort: you have named the thing. You have sought the cause and found it; it is no longer hidden. The real thing is before you. Now, knowing its name and its character—both the general character all such causes display and the specific nature of *your particular sorrow—now you may yourself begin to participate in its healing.*

Why art thou cast down, O my soul?

Because the soul has suffered a sundering, a little death. Lo, there is no need to be embarrassed because of sadness. Death is a very good reason; and sadness has, now, a name. It has as well a clearly discernible pattern and an excellent purpose.

Its name is grief.

And as we shall see later in this book, its purpose is to heal you of the immediate dying and of the source of all dyings.

But first, dear soul, attend to the Secondary Dyings in order to recognize them all.

Why are you sad? Come, let me be your pastor a while. Your counselor. As carefully as I may—but with a detail that can teach you to recognize them for yourself—let me sketch the causes of sadness. I'll name them and tell a story or two along the way, and perhaps you'll find your own experience therein. Surely you will see that not all causes are "unnatural." Many are the passages of living, despite the sadness they engender; and if such natural events cause you to cry, well, you won't be embarrassed by your sorrow anymore. I'll show you.

Come.

9 What Actually Happens: The Experience of Secondary Dying

Again, we will classify our secondary dyings according to the three kinds of relationships in which we live and that, at breaking, kill us by bits—whose pain is the seizure of grief.

Please keep in mind that this is a necessary diagnosis, preparation for learning how that same grief heals. Grief is a grace of God! Grief is the gift he slipped into our error, a hook to return us to him after all.

LITTLE DEATHS 1: COMMUNAL RELATIONSHIPS

What we're about to describe is more than "loss," though that's the term most often applied to these causes of sorrow. Losing possessions need not change a possessor. But the breaking of relationship alters me. In others I have discovered my self. With others my self finds its most articulate expression. Among others I know that I *am*. So the separation, even from one other person, changes me, reduces *me*. I die a little.

Moreover, each such death must prove me mortal; it reminds me of the ineluctable limitation of my being; it carries the weight of the Primal Death and foreshadows my physical death to come.

Yes. For these that I am about to discuss, I have a right to be sad.

Passages

Now, then: it was three years ago, in the autumn of the year, at ten o'clock of a Friday night, that I drove to the high school stadium to gather my child and bring her home again.

My youngest child. A freshman now. "A woman," she said, "of parts and notions. I know what I know." Lo, how the girl was changing! She knew what she knew, and she went to football games without me—alone, in those days. Bold and alone. But I was her father and wouldn't allow her to walk the streets without an adult: "Because it's dangerous," I said. "I know what I know."

She was lovely still. That wasn't changing. The lashes of God and the raven brows with which we first discussed the world—these were beautiful still, so black as to break my heart. And her complexion in autumn always lost the darkness of summer and melted into caramel. My daughter was caramel still.

But it was what she chose to *do* with the loveliness that confounded me.

This teenager ruined beauty with alien clothing, the issue of some foreign mind, I thought, or of madness. T-shirts under T-shirts wore Talitha, all of them XX-large; black pants as tight as torture on her father's heart; plastic earrings the size of small rock bands—and everything draped with a drop-dead insolence: "Chill, Dad." The child could pop her hip so hard it tipped tables over. I guessed that her clothes had become her language now, a sort of slang I couldn't interpret. Maybe that was the point.

Maybe I was just getting old.

That Friday it had drizzled all day. The trees were shedding their leaves in a sort of remorse. I parked the car on a side street and walked through mist to the stadium, my collar turned up, my hands in my pockets.

There were two minutes left in the game: a seismic thunder rushed at me as I ascended steps to the stands. Hundreds, hundreds of hooting, bellowing, glittering, healthy, heroic youth. Adonis! Diana! Hercules! Grey-eyed Athena—oh, my! All the young gods, strong and thoughtless. No daughter among them that I could see. No matter. I would find her in time.

The field had been gashed by the game, and every player was covered with mud. They skidded through muck, cannonading each other under the bright lights, roaring their furious pleasure.

And I recalled the glory of my own autumn games, the deliberate thump of our bodies, the grand insouciance we displayed before our screaming peers, as though nothing could make us smile since everything had been anticipated and nothing was new, no, nothing under the sun. I remembered the slouch with which we arrived at parties thereafter, rather allowing the praise than begging for it. We were stone blocks of bravery then. Couldn't dance fast, but Lord, how we killed the girls from the corners with our *savoir faire!*

Suddenly the present game was over. The stands began to drain of people. But something of my memory lingered, and with a perceptible slouch—really feeling at one with the river of teenagers—I flowed from the stadium, down the steps and out. At the main gate I turned to face the oncoming crowd, since Talitha would have to pass me here.

I felt happy in the autumn mist. I nodded to classmates as though they were my own. "Good game, hey?"

"Hey."

"I suppose y'all be goin' to a party now."

"Hey."

I leaned back against a tree exactly as, in my day, heroes leaned back against their lockers in the corridor: arms folded across the chest, knuckles beneath their biceps, one foot up at the butt so the knee projected, a confident, idling power.

"Good game, hey?"

"Hey."

There poured forth an eddy of five kids especially boisterous. One lean fellow was carrying a girl on his back and shouting mindless jokes. He had a ratchet voice and a lisp. He dumped the girl and roared with laughter, knocked silly, it seemed, by his marvelous sense of humor.

Immediately behind these five, solitary in her T-shirts, walked Talitha.

She didn't seem to see me. She made a sharp left turn and trudged along the stadium wall.

I flung myself forward, jogged a little to catch up, then fell in step. "Good game, hey, girl?"

She didn't answer.

"I couldn't wait in the car because it's three blocks away. You'd never find it."

Silence.

"Well," I said. "So. Did you sit with friends? Did a bunch of you sit close to keep warm?"

Talitha quickened her pace, moving ahead of me, her head bent down against the cold moist air.

I let her have the lead and the privacy. Maybe she had sat with no one at all. She seemed sad. I trailed behind.

Then two youths dashed past me. They slowed and closed on my daughter, one on either side of her, both with the rolling tread of leopards, twitching their tails. They cast sidelong glances at her. She still had her overbite in those days.

"Yo!" they said, as though calling across the street.

Talitha, trudging forward, said, "Yo."

"So! Babe! You gotta ride?" That voice—rusting, ratchet, adolescent—a really irritating voice. "You desperate," it said, "for a silver Buick and a pretty driver." It lisped. Pimples on its vocal cords. A pointless stack of hair on top of its head. Audacity!

I hurried my pace until I drew alongside this skinny youth.

He didn't acknowledge me.

Hunkered down from a willowy height in order to peer at my daughter, he said, "You wanna move wif *me*, girl?"

He said "Wif." What a catch this fish would be!

All at once Talitha stopped cold, halting us all, causing a moment of confusion. For us. Not for her. She hooked her thumb in my direction, rolled her eyes, and verily growled, "I *got* a ride."

And so it came to pass that I was noticed.

The two youths froze me with unembarrassed scrutiny, while I tried to freeze them back.

"Ooooo," said the lean one, the ratchet-voiced. "Who's this?"— evidently not talking to me.

Talitha, her head bent, mumbled, "My father."

"Adopted, hey?"

News. It took a moment to compute the contradiction of colors.

"Adopted, hey?" Then: "Sorry, babe!" The leopards stretched and vanished all in a single, liquid motion.

But then my daughter began to run as fast as she could down the street, and I had to race to catch up with her.

"Talitha! Talitha, we've got to turn here!"

At the car she chose the back seat.

I, of course, had to drive. The windshield wipers said, *Skrit, skrit.*

I said, "Didn't you enjoy the game?"

Silence again from my youngest daughter. I glanced at her face in the mirror. Sullen. On account of the overbite, she found it difficult to close her mouth.

"Talitha," I said in a tone that required response, "what is the matter?"

"Nothin'."

T-shirts under T-shirts can hide whole human beings. I felt sad. Talitha can ruin her beauty with grim expressions too. I drove creepingly in the rain.

Skrit, skrit, skrit—

I said, "Did you think that boy was worth the effort?"

"He's going to a party," she blurted. "I'm not."

"You will. We'll loosen your curfew when—"

"When I'm old! You couldn't care less!"

"You know there are good reasons—"

"When I'm old like you!" she cried. "Old! And the only good reason is that you don't trust me!"

"Talitha! It's a matter of maturity, not trust."

"What's that supposed to mean?"

"Well, you're still too young—"

"See? *You* say I'm young. You just don't trust me."

"I trust you exactly equal to your age—"

"It's embarrassing!"

"What? Your age?"

"No, Dad. You!"

"What?"

"Embarrassing. My father hangs out in public places! Puts himself where everyone can see him, grinning, waving like he thinks he's a celebrity, old man with his knee stuck out. Old man!"

Skrit, skrit, skrit—

I began to drive the normal speed again. We entered separate meditations, my daughter and I. And then at home Talitha took herself directly to her bedroom, my poor and partyless youngest child—while I withdrew to consider the changes.

Forty-five years old. Only in nostalgia would I ever be the conquering hero again. Only in the quiet vault of private memory. That was gone. But that was the least of my sorrows.

My daughter was gone.

Talitha of the T-shirts was cutting ties. Her shears were very sharp. She was gathering all that she had and, by degrees, taking her leave of me—journeying into the far country of adolescence.

I declare, it is natural and right, and I knew so even then. Ever and ever I remained my daughter's most enthusiastic fan. But she couldn't know my applause; she refused my tenderness, and therefore tenderness abided in silence inside of me. She objectified her father in order to distance herself, in order, in some ways, to *be*. I was forced to become more warden than lover, an imposer of rules "for her own good."

Necessary and right: I do declare it. But I suffered it. Because I was dying. Our relationship was breaking. That life—which in me was fatherhood of a particular order (the one who bore his baby in arms, who protected her from hurts and all horrors, who told her stories until she fell into her moistly snoring sleeps at night—that one, *that* father) was passing away. I had every right to my sadness.

But (given such knowledge!) I had no more right to blame her for leaving me than for developing breasts. A father scorned may *want* to yell: "You never listen anymore! You're breaking my heart!" A mother in death throes may *want* to lash out: "Obstinate! Pig-headed! Impertinent! I don't know what's come over you! You make me sick. You'll be the death of me yet!" And their cries are half right: sickness and death are here indeed. But parents should hold their peace and grieve in private—for there is no fault here. No, not fault. Passages happen as they must happen. The child doesn't *choose* teenagerhood; it chooses her; and she herself is involved in grief equal to her parents'; for she too is dying in order to be born; and she is bewildered both by her action and by the pain it causes; she doesn't know the word "grief"; and those who might have taught it to her are precisely those from whom she is separating: her parents.

Who can know her loneliness?

No fault, then. Bereavement, rather.

There was a boy in her eighth-grade room who called my daughter "nigger" once too often. She had complained to the school officials. But, except for three students, Talitha among them, the entire school was white. Nothing came of her complaint.

The boy persisted.

So Talitha hit him—*bip!*—on the nose.

It bled wonderfully. Thus was he punished.

She was punished too—though mildly, since the teacher now saw the extent of her difficulty through several years of elementary education.

I myself didn't learn of the incident until she was a freshman in high school and the teacher, with an open admiration for my brazen daughter, told it to me.

"Why didn't you let me know what was happening?" I asked.

And she said, "You're white. I took care of it myself."

O my daughter, I do feel sad at your growing independence, even as I marvel and thank the Lord that it should be—for how would you survive without such strength? But you, like adolescents everywhere and every-when, use the differences between us as if they were knives to cut us apart. And you get one more knife than most teens do: color. "You don't understand, Dad," you say. "It's a Black thing." It's a Black *thang*, you say, insisting on the Blacker vowel.

But my love leaps over the differences, girl, applauding in you what is *not* like me. My love embraces our differences, genders, colors, ages. It is my love, therefore, that suffers the separation you force in these places.

This is what I think: if I weren't hurting to lose you, neither would I love you. It is a sign: my grief reveals my love, dear daughter. The one is equal to the other.

Yes. Yes, and still: I love you now, Talitha. And I always will.

❦

Regarding all "passages," then: people develop. For good or ill, they "pass through" stages in their earthly existence. And this natural evolution absolutely requires others in relationship with them to suffer a sundering.

It's a most subtle form of separation, though, since it is the *role* one plays that changes. A certain relationship remains; I will always, in some sense, be Talitha's father; but the sort of father that I had been I now am not. Because of these normal passages, the identities of the people in relationship change and are lost. Their old selves die with the old role, and presently they suffer grief.

—There is, then, no mystery nor any blame for the mother who cries when her "baby" gets married. Motherhood is dying in her. The child is "leaving" in order to be "cleaving" to her spouse, and the marital relationship both shall and must supersede the parental one.

Why does the mother of the bride cry? For happiness? Well, yes. But for sorrow too. Do not demean her dignity—nor dishonor her deeper sense of mortal passages with platitudes about "gaining a son." There is a death here, and these are the tears of grief.

—Likewise, the children of aging parents grieve.

When elders slip toward senility and children must assume the role of parent to their parents, no one should be shocked by feelings of a sudden and tremendous sorrow. Nor by feelings (oddly) of anger, or depression thereafter. Even though the elder is physically present to be honored and nursed, the old relationship (that of adult to respected adult) has cracked and can't be mended. This is, though without corpses, a death. Sorrow, anger, depression are grief, right and natural and good.

—Or when anyone important to us has been disabled, whose lifestyle is altered thereby forever, we will be affected in two ways:

1. We will suffer a sympathetic sorrow with the individual who is severed from the previous self, who has suffered a death.

2. And since our own relationship must therefore be altered, we will grieve on our own account, for we have changed.

The first response is human compassion. The second is our private dying. The first we suffer in common—as a gift to the one we love. The second we suffer alone. It is critical to recognize the difference between these two, since the former must be kind, while the latter might take the form of anger. Now, anger can rightly be directed at the change we both must undergo—that is, at the impersonal circumstance, the cause of our friend's crippling. But anger must never be directed at the invalid! If our anger should be misdirected, death multiplies, and a new relationship might never develop again.

—Or when a colleague at work enjoys a significant promotion that puts her several removes above us, we may be affected in several ways:

1. We may rejoice with her for her good fortune.

2. But since the relationship has been fundamentally revised, we might confuse ourselves with feelings of grief, as though someone had died.

As time goes on, our friend (with whom we had shared genial secrets and equality) may assert a commanding authority over us; so we meet the end of a relationship we thought would continue. Rightly, then, we grieve. But it would be wrong to aim this grief at our friend. Such blame might block any new relationship, an evolution of friendship from one plane to the next.

—Or when a dear friend discovers some radical difference in himself, some characteristic hitherto hidden; when, for example, he feels convinced that he is homosexual; or when he comes a cropper, poorer than anyone thought and in desperate need—what do we feel then? In the midst of every other emotion, *both* the friend and we ourselves will suffer the radical revision of an old relationship. So what will we feel? Grief. Name that rightly, or anger may turn into accusation, rendering new relationship impossible.

Grief, in such circumstances, is right and righteous. Tears and sadness have their place. But a flat, angry rejection of the other is the doubling of death. He who already has died unto his old self is now cut off by his friend as well. Count: two for him, one single death for you—but your death caused his second death, and that latter was not necessary, if only you had perceived your grief *as* grief.

Thus the "passages" of friends and relatives break the familiar patterns of our lives. "Everything flows," saith the philosopher truly. For good or ill, people change, breaking the relationships we had enjoyed with them, causing us daily to die. Do you begin now to know why thy soul is cast down and sad?

Displacement

And people move.

I mean, they uproot themselves; they break or strain or stretch the countless filaments of relationships in which they had lived all the years they dwelt in this neighborhood, this city or state.

We are woven into communities, though we may be unconscious of the webbing that supports us—the shopkeepers, neighbors, church families—until we move to another town. And then we become terribly conscious, because of the breaking. A thousand tiny *snaps*!

Should anyone wonder, then, why even the happy move that one had planned for can cause such mortal grief? *As if someone had died,* we whisper, bewildered, believing that all the old friendships will last. *We'll write and visit each other still. And there are good people here to receive us. Yet—* Well, now you know: someone did die. You, at displacement. And the period of distress, the overwhelming sense of vulnerability and loneliness and even the heavy lethargy that follows, are natural after all.

—Here is one reason why an elderly mother now living alone might refuse to leave her home (her neighborhood) to live with her daughter's family.

There may be obvious and abundant advantages to such a move; she might, in fact, live longer because of the care at hand; but *for* those few years of life she'd have to die countless tiny deaths. And so she says, with genuine wisdom, "I do not need the grief." She means grief.

Think: now she experiences a living relationship with a particular slant of sunlight through her kitchen window; with a scent in the weather that she doesn't even think about, but which she needs because it signals to her soul the shifting of the seasons, the sliding times of the day; now she hears the tread of the postman, the cry of the child next door, the tone of a particular pastor's voice (maybe the cadences more than the meaning of that pastor's words—does it matter?); now her memories have a thousand cubbies around the house where they sleep like pets, to awaken and to accompany her through the deeper and the harder nights. To leave is to sunder all this. It would be to die before the severer death for which she's preparing herself—for which preparation she *needs* the postman's step.

—And of course, this is the sorrow one suffers when it becomes necessary to place him in a nursing home after all. He is bereaved of the whole environment by which he calculated his existence. And these many Secondary Dyings coming all at once do prefigure with intensity the third death, the decease of the body.

Therefore, when Grandma—though seeming quite healthy to you—pats your knee and murmurs with solemn expressions, "I'm dying, honey. Dying," you needn't contradict her nor think her especially morbid nor scorn her for self-pity or exaggeration. "I'm wasting away," she says, and she is. The isolation of the nursing home echoes ahead the isolation of the casket. Imagine, then, what a wheel-chair communicates. Imagine what "confinement" must speak to her soul.

These are extreme examples of displacement.

But even the lesser experience is not unlike them, and the grieving it causes is no shame on us.

—The child starts a new school with fear. Homesickness *is* sickness, not to be belittled or wheedled away.

—The family decides to transfer membership from the church it had attended for years: let it be ready to suffer some moodiness, maybe some nasty bits of bickering among themselves, maybe just dull sadness.

—"Seller's Remorse" is a condition I've just encountered. After accepting our bid on her house, the woman who owned it grew sorry to leave it, though she was moving no farther than over the lane. She became incommunicative. She withdrew into herself, avoiding agents and buyers alike. And we, awaiting her departure, felt grimmer than Simon Legree.

The Betrayal of Trust

Every Communal Relationship—to some degree modeled on the Primary Relationship—has a covenant, a code of behavior that gives form to the relationship and to which each partner is committed. This code is mostly unspoken, but both partners know it; and as long as both obey it, the relationship is protected and nourished as a living thing. Likewise, it serves each partner, who can drop defenses and trust the other, who can enjoy the stability, strength, and fulfillment of mutual exchange—who live therein and thereby.

Trust permits life to flow among people in relationship.

Trust is as precious as the arteries of a physical body: they carry the blood.

The rupture of such trust, then, causes life itself to hemorrhage. When one member of a relationship sins against the relationship by breaking trust, all of its people suffer mortal shock. Without forgiveness, without stanching the flow and healing the wound, something dies. And the more significant the relationship had been, the more grievous shall be the feelings of those bereaved.

Denial is not strange in one bereaved; and if anger appears only to disappear in compulsive efforts to understand or to redefine what happened—if the one betrayed swings back and forth from vengeance to conciliation—neither is that unnatural behavior. Nor would plain depression be inexplicable. These are the pattern of grief. To be sinned against is to suffer significant death and therefore to grieve.

Here is the clear connection between our Primal Dying and a particular Secondary Death. Really, it should be unthinkable for one to betray the trust of another—unless the traitor could justify his act. And he does. We do. In a sublime self-centeredness, as the gods whom this relationship was meant to serve, we find it possible to blame the other for our treachery, believing she deserved it or started it or was ungrateful or . . .

There are myriad justifications, for we have minds of a weedy fertility and spirits affixed on ourselves. Even so has it been since first we decided to open our eyes and see for ourselves what is "good" and what is "evil."

And with sadness I note that this particular Secondary Dying, the killing of people by people in covenant with them, is likely more common than any other. Those who love us most are also most vulnerable to us. Daily we kill and are being killed. As Moses did not use mere figures of speech for "life and good, death and evil," neither do I. We kill. Death and grief do always companion transgressors.

—When the government that had been trusted by its citizens betrays that trust, a whole nation can grieve, hugely and dramatically. And then it might protect itself from grieving thereafter by ceasing to trust at all. I have a friend, once a politician and Republican, who experienced such mute rage after Watergate that he repudiated the party. Rage became an exhausted sorrow. In his eyes I saw the same expression as that in some vets of Viet Nam. Betrayal murders love.

—When management breaks faith with an employee, especially if the relationship had been more than merely economic, it is not weakness on the employee's part that then debilitates him. If he sits down in his living room as a man diminished, unable to speak, unable to find words for his feelings, it is because he grieves. Some years ago that grief, as anger, formed labor unions. Now what shape shall grieving take? And what must it do to a nation?

—Professionals can break the hearts of those who depend upon them, can leave clients "broken" indeed, especially when their skill is prized and required by society.

Doctors are dear people; but just as dear as they are, they may be deadly. Those that breach the code of public and private trust kill, if not the body, something—and then grief is a monstrous confusion thereafter, for the patient swings between guilt and vengeance. It is the *grief* of a society that has found expression in litigation.

Like doctors, so bankers—all who advise and control the public's money. Those that abuse the trust are not cynical only, but criminal: killers.

Likewise attorneys, in whose hands lies the future of a client and his trust.

Likewise all who counsel people in weakened conditions, of whom they might take advantage—sexually, mentally, mortally. It is always mortal, and the consequence is always some form of grief.

Likewise, at every level mentioned above, pastors. Their position receives relationships of such complete need and tenderness—the bodies *and* souls of communicants—that a sin in this place is tantamount to blasphemy. Yet pastors do abuse the vulnerability of those in covenant with them. Ah, it is murderous. Moreover, even a pastor's private sin (seeming to involve no one but himself and perhaps one other) can destroy a people's credence. Can kill. And then an entire parish grieves. I have seen churches spiritually silenced by the act of a pastor, complete congregations withdrawing into sadness and depression, or else falling apart in recriminations—and no one knew that this was the manifestation of grief because something dear had died.

Such grieving among a people, once the cause is recognized and the consequence named as "grief," is *natural*!

—And when the anonymous thief breaks into my house and steals from me (even if I am not home, even if the theft is a TV only), I shouldn't be astonished by the depth of my reaction. We trust (we *must* trust) the goodness of the community around us. The thief destroyed that general trust and with the TV stole security away. Suddenly this isn't *my* house, under my control. It's been invaded, and I suffer my helplessness to guard good things. I suffer the mortality of society. Of course the feelings will go deep. I am grieving.

—And what does the wife experience when she discovers the

adulteries of her husband? Something has been slaughtered. She grieves.

—And yesterday you had a friend, both necessary and near to you. This was one person with whom you experienced the fullness of your own individual life, because you revealed the whole of your soul to her: naked and unashamed, because she loved you and she honored you. You saved for her alone your secrets, your dreams (however silly they might sound in any other ear), your memories of sweetness past, your hundred fears, your thousand weaknesses. With this friend there were no fig leaves, no clothing to cover the uttermost You.

How comforting it was to know that there was one someone with whom to cry or laugh or sit in silence, unexplaining. Yesterday you had a friend, the completion of your being.

But last night, while you sat in a restaurant overhearing the conversation at a table beside you, you discovered with mounting horror that others were discussing your secrets, not in kindness but in gossip. Your personal business had become the news of the neighborhood, snatched out of your hands, strewn abroad, impossible to recall again.

Your friend! She was a busybody!

She had talked.

She had leaked your life away.

And today you sit in your apartment, crying. Naked and very ashamed. Today there's no friend and no friendship. You can't stop crying. You're furious with yourself for having lost self-control.

I put my arm around you, though we are hardly friends yet and I don't know you well. I tell you the sad news: that you may not be able to sleep tonight; that tomorrow the whole world might seem alien and strange to you; that in the weeks to come you might not be able to concentrate on the simplest tasks of your job, and you might let your apartment get messy, and you may sink into a mindless depression. But immediately I tell you the kinder news: this is all normal. Don't think something like a poor diet or crummy weather caused your sorrow. Dear, you've suffered a significant death. The very arteries of your communal life were cut asunder. Trust was destroyed by her that was your friend, and lifeblood ran from the wound. You have a right to grieve.

But even grief has its good purpose. Let me become your friend now, and be patient. Soon I will explain the serious therapy of grief to you.

Divorce

Less frequent than the betrayal of a trust, but more intense a death, is the overt annihilation of the covenant that had shaped the relationship: the public divorce of two parties, the dissolving of vows, marital or otherwise.

Wrong is always at the source of divorce.

Whose wrong may be an impossibly painful debate; but that *some* wrong slaughtered relationship is not for debate. Where there is divorce, there has been sin. And the grief of the divorcée can be worse than the grief of a widow—deeper and darker and harder when the spouse departs by divorce than by decease—because sin sits in the breach and leers. Evil makes an anguish that fate alone could not: this death was not inevitable; someone did it to us; hate, then, complicates the grief.

What sort of divorces occur among us?

—When close communities ostracize a member (churches excommunicating one, neighborhoods scorning one, nations exiling one) more people than that individual member may suffer the break; but his pain is the more terrible. The one "cut off" from the others is *apolosos*: lost. Jesus' language continues here the image with which we began our definition of death. A person torn from the body of his community suffers as wrenching a death as if someone should "cut off" his right hand and "throw it away." The hand of Jesus' parable and the experience of the exile are the same: each is *apoletai*, "lost," severed, dead.

Even so may an employee suffer when suddenly fired from her job, cut from the company.

Likewise the child whom, for some reason, the family collectively rejects: *apoletai*, perishing.

And the teenager who genuinely believes that she is ugly and laughed at by all of her peers, this newly pimpled adolescent, angry and sullen at once, both arrogant and timid: the change in her should be no mystery. She feels clean cut off. Whether it's true or not, she suffers the death of segregation; she *perceives* a divorce between herself and her most necessary community. The isolated child is grieving.

—When the judicial system of society finds one citizen guilty of crimes and thereby abrogates the social contract that had existed between itself and him—no matter how hardened the criminal, no matter how righteous or wrong the verdict—the citizen enters a period of profound personal grief. The "sentence" shall kill him to one degree or another. Surely, imprisonment increases the grief by multiplying the varieties of death one dies (displacement, etc.); but even he whose reputation has been ruined by public opprobrium suffers the loss as death.

—Cain cried out to the Lord: "My punishment is greater than I can bear. Behold, thou hast driven me from the ground [from *Nature* as well as from the *self*, since Cain was a tiller of the ground], and from thy face I shall be hidden [from his *Creator*]; I shall be a fugitive wanderer on the earth." He is severed from *community*, and so the separations are complete: in the cry of Cain is the lamentation of one completely cut off. It's a death-wail. Even though the Lord would spare his *body* by a signifying mark, Cain has died the death.

He stands for us all: the primal divorce, our own annihilation of the covenant between God and ourselves, begins the thousand divorces that finally must send us, like Cain, into utter exile, crying: "It's greater than I can bear!"

Every divorce reflects the first divorce.

Every divorce predicts the terminus.

Every divorce: even yours, though you had no guilt in the matter, my sister. No, you did not!

I knew you were innocent. I affirmed it to any who asked me. I had known you and your husband so long and so well that I could see he was the sinner. He was Cain to your Abel. And yet you prowled around like a criminal crying, *More than I can bear!*

In fact, you felt a furious sense of guilt, didn't you? I'm so sorry. That's the original sin in any of us. Every divorce ignites the primal sin of humanity whole, and all who participate are burned by it, burned on the outside by the fires of others, on the inside by thine own. Oh, my dear! I tried so hard to ease you, to assure you of your personal purity in this bloody death. But I failed.

I remember you. I remember the nearly violent extremity of your grief.

You came into my office one afternoon looking thin, nervous, like a terrified fawn about to bolt. Your hair was unkempt, your face severe. I thought you were angry. You weren't. You were fighting for composure in front of me, and it made your features wooden.

You pulled from your purse a legal document.

"Pastor," you said, "I . . ." But that's all you said.

You handed me the papers and sat on the edge of the chair before me. You crouched more than sat. You crossed your arms at the abdomen. I thought you were in pain.

I glanced at the papers. Your husband had taken legal steps to break the covenant of your marriage. He was divorcing you.

Had you expected this, I asked.

Eyes down, you shook your head, and I believed you.

Then you lifted your gaze to me and nodded.

No, you had not expected this. Yes, you had. Both.

I believed both.

Are you going to contest this divorce, I asked.

You gaped at me as if I were a stranger.

I said, "Do you have an attorney?"

Your gape grew more and more aghast.

"Something has begun here," I said. "It doesn't matter if you agree or if you think he has the right to do this; it's started. You will have to act," I said. "You can't do nothing. Have the two of you talked? Why is he doing this? Can we all talk together? I really need to know whether there's some chance of reconciliation between you two. What? Is there another woman? What?"

There was a long period in which you simply didn't speak. I asked soft questions, none of which you answered. But you had come to me. And I needed some information in order to proceed. The date on the papers suggested that you had held them a while before coming.

"Has he moved out? Where is he?"

Suddenly you rose up from the chair. With an animal howl you pressed both hands to your temples and bent at the waist. I saw your teeth. I went to the door to close it. You turned and ran toward a wall, turned again and rushed to the opposite wall, wailing and wailing a high, horrible note: *Eeeeeee!*

Oh, I wanted to hold you. I could only watch and wait.

"What did I do to him? What did I do?" you cried. "He's killing me! I can't stand this. Oh, God!—what did I do to deserve this? Ahhh!"

Back and forth you ran in my office, actually wringing your hands.

Melodramatic—except that you meant it. "He's killing meeeeeeee!" you wailed, bending down as if tell the earth your sorrow. "He's killing—"

Abruptly you stopped. The room fell silent. Slowly you raised your wet face to me, and then you smiled. Cock-eyed, stupid smile! And then you began to giggle. You shrugged and burst into laughter and sat down again, helpless. "Oh, Pastor, I'm sorry!" It was an inane, harsh, barking laughter. Mirthless, wide open, and fierce. "I'm sorry," you said as it subsided. "I'm sorry. I really think I'm going crazy. I cry and I scream and I laugh and I can't control it, I can't help it, I just can't. . . ."

Again, you were silent, and then the tears rolled from your eyes without sound or apology. You gazed straight at me and wept.

I went to you, then, and knelt beside you.

"This is not your fault," I said.

You whispered, "It has to be. I love him. What else? I must have done something."

"This is not your fault."

"Oh, Pastor, I know how emotional I get. I must have missed something important. I must have done something wrong. He isn't a bad man."

"No. It's not your fault."

"Almost exactly three years ago," you said, "we stood at the edge of the river. We walked in the evening. The sky gave down a crimson light, and his complexion glowed. He was so solemn and so beautiful, and I could hardly stand it because I loved him so much. I took his hand and pressed it against my face and told him he was beautiful, but he didn't say anything. He took his hand away. Now he's killing me."

"Is there another woman?"

"I don't know. I don't think so."

"Will he speak with me?"

"No."

"I'll call him."

"Thank you. He says that he doesn't hate me. He doesn't love me. He's finished. He's just finished."

"Do you have a lawyer?"

"No."

"Get one."

You gaped at me again. Your chin trembled. Suddenly you drew a shuddering breath and, looking directly into my eyes, emitted a shriek of bereavement so wild that I grabbed your shoulders and drew you to myself and held you hard, that you might feel the form of some relationship around you. My arms, at least. I kept you from exploding in your grief.

Grief.

No, he did not reconcile, despite my counseling. You experienced a long descent through grief. Grief!—and worse than had your husband died the physical death. The man still walked about. There was, then, no funeral, no casket, no closure. And at times you hated him, and at times you begged him not to hate you—for the corpse continued to live and to stink, to affect you. His physical death would at least have left your memories intact. But this death murders the entire past that once had been good. Even a crimson sunset is corrupted.

Divorce is murder.

The grief that attends divorce is exceedingly complex, because the life of a marital relationship is of the highest order among humans. Moreover, it sends cracks and fissures through many another relationship: the children of divorce are aggrieved (whether it was "amicable" or not); so are parents of the couple and siblings and friends and any who had honored or benefitted by this marriage.

But those that are thus sundered do themselves suffer the extremes of grief, desperation and guilt and rage and pity and despair.

I remember you. Your bereavement revealed a more dramatic passion than that of the wives of the men who died at war. Yours lacked honor. Yours had no communal ritual for conclusion.

Marital divorce is the naked thing itself: self-centered pride. The first sin—and the worst of all.*

The Decease of the Beloved

The widow knows.

The motherless child, likewise, knows.

---

*So similar in behavior and intensity to the grief of a widow/widower is the grief of a divorcée, that I urge those who have suffered either—or who wish to help those that are suffering either—to read carefully Part II of this book. In this chapter we are concentrating on causes of grief, and therefore only touch grief's beginning. In Part II we'll attend to grief's whole drama, even to a good conclusion.

The father who buried his son, the mother who miscarried (whose baby, in loving relationship, had been a living being), the friend bereaved of a friend, neighbors whose neighbor has died, and fans whose hero is gone too soon—all of these know that no dying is so devastating as this by which the relationship, more than ravaged, is abolished altogether.

But whose death *is* it when the beloved's body ceases to be? His death, surely. His third death, in fact: Corporeal Dying.

Yet it is his widow's death too. His third death is her most difficult of secondary deaths. The loss of relationship is the loss of life for her. She says, "I don't live any more." She says, "I only exist." She says the truth.

Here, then, is the plainest cause of human grief. The widow's experience defines all Secondary Dyings. Her grief is the paradigm of grieving, whatever the causes might be—and so we will give much attention to her in the second part of the book, always aware that we speak for all who have suffered any sort of death. Grief is the same, despite the differences in its intensities; grief is always our pulley back to God.

LITTLE DEATHS 2: NATURAL RELATIONSHIPS

Perhaps because we spend so much of our lives in the artificial environments that coddle our bodies (lo, how like gods we are, creating times and seasons to our taste, light and dark, warm and cold, the dry and the wet as we please), perhaps because we seem to control the weather itself, we are mostly unaware that we've become strangers in the universe. The moment we broke from the Creator, creation itself began to groan and ceased to be our home.

We *think* we are Lords, possessors of the earth.

We *think* our work ennobles us, that we are not nothing beneath the stars.

We *think* the elements and creatures of the earth ought to serve us, support us forever and ever. . . .

But events prove otherwise. And every event that stuns us with news of our natural finitude is, for us, a dying.

Natural Disasters

Floods; terrible, wandering *Hurakan,* the hurricane; exploding mountains that darken the skies with soot while pouring forth rivers of fire below; the grinding and popping of tectonic plates along old faultlines, tremors, earthquakes; drought; *Sirocco*, the blistering wind from Arabia and with it locusts, frogs and gnats and flies in swarms, plagues on beasts and plagues on humans—what are all these things?

In legal terms: "Acts of God."

What are the convulsions of nature over which we have no control, but that we must honor and study, obey and escape if we can?

"Signs and wonders," once, against one who exalted himself above the God of the Hebrews; elemental gestures by which to humble Pharaoh: "that thou mayest know that there is none like me in all the earth." Acts of the Creator God, indeed.

Surely, every such event is perfectly right in the balance of natural laws. Nature never ceased to obey the Creator! Hurricanes, for example, are not evil; they redistribute heat from the torrid zones of the globe to temperate regions. But when they strike our dwellings, our plans, our children—our *selves*—they affect us in the same way the plagues of the Exodus affected Pharaoh. They humble us severely. We wake to our weakness. Over and over we admit the might of God, confessing sins of ignorance and arrogance. "Over and over," I say, because we keep forgetting. Our hearts harden. We rise from our rubble in pride again—until the east wind blows again.

What, then, are these events we name "disasters"?

Experiences of human fragility, the extreme finitude of our persons. The breaking of that relationship with creation whereby we exalted ourselves as owners of earth, and Pharaohs of the land.

They are the sudden discovery that earth is *not* our home, that the universe is vastly indifferent to us: thus, they are our exile (again and again) from Eden.

Such separation is a dying.

Such dying produces grief.

Terra Johnson's house burned down. Neither she nor her family were hurt, but all that they owned was destroyed.

For weeks thereafter, Terra exhibited an efficient serenity: "At least," she said to many people, "we have our lives." She said so to her husband while they lay awake at night, and he took her hand and agreed: "We have each other."

All the people who knew her marveled, saying, "How brave, how faithful Terra is."

The church prayed a public prayer of thanksgiving: "At least," said the pastor, "thou didst spare their lives."

Then, six weeks later, when friends had begun to forget the crisis and the Johnsons happened to be grocery shopping, Terra started to cry and could not stop.

Her skirt had caught the corner of a high display of oranges. She turned to free herself, but she turned too fast. The pyramid slipped, the oranges came tumbling down, she knelt to retrieve them, she spread her arms as wide as she could, but she only managed to scatter them farther away—and so it was that on hands and knees in a public place, Terra, helplessly, started to cry. She burned with embarrassment, but she could neither rise up nor quiet her crying. She wept with angry, shuddering sobs.

Almost immediately her husband was at her side. "It's all right, it's all right," he begged. "Come. Leave the oranges alone. Let's go."

But Terra wailed, "It is *not* all right! Nothing is all right."

Her husband knelt beside her and tried to put his arm around her shoulders. His face, too, was trembling toward tears. With great earnestness, intending to comfort her, he said, "At least we have our lives—"

But she shouted through a clenched fury, "No, we don't! We do not have our lives! That's what we don't have! I couldn't hold it together. I couldn't keep things together. Everything's flying apart—"

And so the truth was spoken.

Terra's outburst isn't strange: grief had finally caught up with her. A tiny frustration had triggered a deep regret, terrible convictions of personal impotence. Until that moment she'd maintained serenity by maintaining denial. Now she saw and felt and was forced to acknowledge the dying.

Not only had the fire separated Terra from familiar things, it had also destroyed her sense of control. Their house had been her "world" within the world, heat in winter, dry in rain, security against all dangers—a fortress. It had been human-sized, the good order of her family, a place of "dominion . . . over every living thing that moves upon the earth." The fire had severed her from such necessary strength. The fire had announced that nature does not love her or those whom she loves and would as soon swallow her children as swallow a stick.

"I'm scared all the time," she said to her husband. "I'm scared for the children. I'm scared when you're traveling. I'm just always, always afraid—and I hate it."

She felt a tremendous dread that the people—her own people and all humanity—might be alone in the universe, an accident in space and time. Terra was suffering a painful estrangement from the cosmos. She had a right to her outpouring of sorrow—even over oranges she could not retrieve.

Famines are not punishments. Floods are not a retribution. If they were, we might feel better, arguing that *some* relationship exists and we possess *some* significance among the stars. Objects of the hurricane's wrath must be equal to a hurricane's greatness, yes? It's better to be hated than not to be noticed at all, right? But the hurricane has no wrath. The fire that ruined Terra's life—it had no heart.

So Terra grieves the separation from a "good" creation, wherein we used to see the mercy of the Maker. But sin dimmed that vision until creation seems rather to hide the face of God than to reveal it. God has absconded. He who once strolled the garden in the cool of the day has become the *mysterium tremendum,* an awe-ful thing, veiled by the measureless dark, altogether unapproachable.

"I'm scared," said Terra. "Anything could happen at any time. What's to protect us? I can't protect us. I am always, always afraid."

The Futility of Labor

"It happens," writes Albert Camus, "that the stage sets collapse":

> There come moments when our work—that activity by which we discover our worth in the world, by which we compact a reputation and exercise a personal value—there come moments, I say, when our profession, our daily labor, suddenly looks like the painted set in a theater, and that set collapses. All our valuable work collapses, and with horror we stare to the other side of material things, the spiritual deeps where we always believed meaning to be, but we see nothing. Bare nothing. In the assizes of the universe, all our labor appears as the absurd and witless effort of ants.
>
> It happens that the stage sets collapse. Rising, streetcar, four hours of work, meal, sleep, and Monday Tuesday Wednesday Thursday Friday and Saturday according to the same rhythm—this path is easily followed most of the time. But one day the "why" arises and everything

begins in that weariness tinged with amazement. . . . Weariness comes
at the end of the acts of a mechanical life.*

"At the same time," says Camus, the end of a mechanical life
"inaugurates the impulse of consciousness." We begin to *think* about
what we've been doing, what we've assumed to be our good. And
thinking starts with the serious question of meaning: *Why?*

*Why do I do what I do? Is it worth the time and effort? Does it mean
anything? That's what I wonder. My salary feeds us. My work keeps us
alive. But beyond the immediate necessity, what does my work accomplish?
What is it in the universe? My mark! My signature. "Kilroy was here."
My work identifies me. Is it of some glory? Goodness? Even just a grain of
lasting value? Am I? Am I?*

Which is to say: *Why am I?*

And then if such questioning occurs with urgency and passion, but
without an answer equal to it—then one experiences "that odd state of
soul," says Camus again, "in which the void becomes eloquent, in
which the chain of daily gestures is broken, in which the heart vainly
seeks the link that will connect it again."

The work of our hands no longer delights us, having been separated
from the handiwork of the Creator, whose Being *is* meaning in the
universe.

In such moments of strange "awakening," we discover ourselves to
be strutting, sweating ciphers. For dust you are (whispers the endless
emptiness), so all you do adds up to nothing but a dusty death.

"It happens that the stage sets collapse." What causes the cold
awakening and the personal drama of existential dread? "It happens."
Strangely, it just happens.

That is to say, it needs no crisis nor trauma to trigger it; this
Secondary Dying, unlike that of the "natural disasters," begins *within*
the individual and is therefore the harder for others to understand, to
have patience with, to console. Suddenly, for no apparent reason, the
laborer is sad—and it has something to do with her labor. Friends and
co-workers get exasperated. "What, you're bored? We all get bored,
but we work anyway." Or, "This day-dreaming is plain laziness! Get
to work." Or, "Do you know how selfish your gloominess is? Snap out
of it!"

---

*Albert Camus, *The Myth of Sisyphus* (New York, Vintage, 1955), 10.

And so forth. The one for whom *Why* has no answer is even further isolated by those for whom *Why* has no interest.

Dying

But this death began one night when the physician couldn't get to sleep for thinking about the number of patients who had died in spite of his best skills. His mind took a spectacular leap, seeing at once the entire congregation of all his patients finally as corpses. By morning he was haggard. Every time he touched a human face thereafter, he felt the skull beneath the skin, and it made him shudder.

A college student came to me near the semester's end. He was not prepared for exams; but that wasn't his worst plight; that wasn't the sickness in his soul. His eyes were stunned, as if suddenly slapped. He sat down opposite me and lifted his hands in a gesture of helplessness. He opened his mouth and said, "Wha—?" Something between *why* and *what* and the inability even to distinguish his words. The question embraced absolutely everything in his world, which was the world. "Wha—?" He lowered his hands. Then he lowered his face. Then he began quietly to cry.

Why am I doing what I'm doing? Where's the worth of it?

I do often see the grief of human futility occur during the period between adolescence and a settled adulthood.

Likewise, it occurs at mid-life, when one is forced to take the long view, at the end of which is dust. That future, now seemingly nearer and certainly coming, curses our present. So the banker begins in misery to wonder whether all her figuring (and all her accumulated wealth) mean anything "in the end, mean anything *really.*"

A grey hair.

The clear admission that younger people are doing a better job.

All of the children have left. The house is hollow—and so, it seems, is the soul of the parent who stares past all the old stage-sets of her significance (the furniture her children used, the pictures, awards, memorabilia) toward a present uselessness, and sighs.

The sudden, sincere conviction that this twist, right now, of my radial drill press (in a metal piece whose final purpose I will never see) means nothing; that this telephone call, right now, to one more buyer before I go home for supper means nothing; that this class, right now (that I've taught the same way for decades), counts nothing since the students don't really "give a damn"; that this ticket that I am right now issuing to one more obnoxious driver will accomplish nothing; that no one cares, and nothing changes, and I'm wasting my breath and my time and my effort—the sudden and sincere conviction of futility is the beginning of this Secondary Death, nearly invisible to others but devastating to one's Self, for it causes a long and melancholy grief.

Albert Camus again:

> During every day of an unillustrious life, time carries us. But a moment always comes when we have to carry it. We live on the future: "tomorrow," "later on," "when you have made your way." . . . Such irrelevancies are wonderful for, after all, it's a matter of dying. Yet a day comes when a man notices or says that he is thirty. Thus he asserts his youth. But simultaneously he situates himself in relation to time. . . . He admits that he stands at a certain point on a curve that he acknowledges having to travel to its end. He belongs to time, and by the horror that seizes him, he recognizes his worst enemy. Tomorrow, he was longing for tomorrow, whereas everything in him ought to reject it.*

Mid-life is no small mountain for many of us. "I'm fifty. I don't want to think about it. I don't want to celebrate this birthday. Why do I feel so sad?" Why, indeed. The sadness is grief.

But the greater grief may be no mountain at all, but the valley of the shadow . . . of death.

The third time when we are most vulnerable to this Secondary Dying, the sense of futility at the end of things, comes when we enter what society calls "retirement." Worker after worker, however he might have looked forward to the freedom, is astonished by the sorrow that seizes his soul. Sorrow? Why, gloom and a bitterness too, which seem to have no cause.

Grandpa sits in his chair and stares at the wall. He's healthy. He's sharp. He's able. He's free! And yet he is so sad. Worse, when we try to help him he scolds us, as though we did something wrong. But we love him! He's sad, and he's mad when he should be happy. We do not understand the man.

Well, but his hands are empty. And so is the self. And so is the

---

*Camus, Myth of Sisyphus.

world, therefore. All at once the man is not *doing* anything he considers genuinely important.

That which used to authenticate his being, and his being *here*, has been torn from him. He has been sundered from his reason to be, his worth, his purpose, his name, his repute, his glory. Can we stress enough the separation that is death to him? He is like "Adam," whose name means "soil," who was sundered from the *soil*, the stuff of his work and his identity.

Grandpa is not suddenly peculiar. It doesn't have to be Alzheimer's Disease. Don't dismiss him as senile and cantankerous. First seek causes not in his mind but in his spirit: he has died. He is grieving.

Then I considered all that my hands had done and the toil I had spent in doing it, and behold, all was vanity and a striving after wind, and there was nothing to be gained under the sun.

When that thought—the "Why" without an answer—seizes us, it doesn't matter what disturbance had caused it: we taste the dust in any motivating purpose and all our goals seem fatuous.

The curse upon our willful estrangement from God is a lonely estrangement from his fields and all their fruitfulness. That which we dress and till, the weeds will steal as soon as we cease. That which we do, it dies with us.

LITTLE DEATHS 3: INTERNAL RELATIONSHIPS

The various separations that the individual can experience within the "self"—self severed from self—we will list under four categories. We are complex creatures: *physical bodies*; dreamers scheming our futures; *minds*, consciously maintaining images of the self; and *spiritual beings*, aware of morality after all.

The Broken Body

Thanne left a message for me in my Chicago hotel room: *Call home immediately.*

My wife is not given to melodramatics. I am. She's much the realist between us. If she uses the word "immediately," something is urgent, something is not well.

"Thanne?" I said into the telephone.

She said, "When are your lectures done?"

"Tonight."

"Can you catch a flight home tonight?"

"If someone drives me to O'Hare by nine."

"Wally, get to O'Hare by nine."

"Why?"

I thought of some danger to her or the children, though her tone was calm and kind and efficient.

She said, "Your X-rays show some spots. Some large shadows. The doctor wants to do an immediate bronchoscopy. Tomorrow, if possible. Fly home tonight."

"What's this bronch-thing? What does he want to do to me?"

"He puts a tube down your throat to look at your lungs. He wants to know what's causing the shadows."

"Thanne?"

"What?"

"What did he say to you? What does he think?—about the shadows, I mean?"

"He said, 'Does your husband smoke.'"

"So?"

"I told him the truth."

"So?"

"Wally?"

"What."

"I love you."

I said nothing for a moment. I stared at the carpet between my feet. I had two lectures yet to deliver, one that afternoon and one that evening. The X-rays were in Evansville, but my lungs were in me, and I was in Chicago.

Thanne said softly, "Please come home tonight. We've reserved a room for you at Deaconess tomorrow."

For all our haste, the bronchoscopy proved a failure. The wall of my right lung was so fragile that the point of the tube broke through, causing the lung to flood with blood. It seemed to me that I was drowning. I couldn't cough: the instrument kept my throat open. I made a strident huffing sound, trying to expel the liquid from my lungs. No good. I rolled my eyes up and felt afraid, unable to cry out or to say anything.

They withdrew the tube.

Later, the doctor came to my room and said, "I'm sorry. We couldn't see the obstructions. We can't explain them." He spent time gathering his thoughts—perhaps easing me with his calm voice and his very slow pacing.

Then, "Best to be safe," he said. "I suggest that we perform a thoracotomy. This is a surgical incision through the chest wall in order to remove the bottom lobe of your right lung. It's best," he said, "to be safe."

"How long will this take?"

"Well, the surgery itself is several hours. Recovery will be six weeks. I mean, you'll be here about ten days, but you won't be ready for activity again for a month and a half. We'll pry apart your ribs, and you'll feel as if a horse had kicked you on the right side. Twice."

Thanne and I told the children that I had to go to the hospital and that I would be sick for a while.

Of the four, Talitha said nothing.

Mary hugged me and cried a bit. Joseph and Matthew stood back, as if waiting the word that would draw them forward to me. They presented solemn faces. Matthew said, "It makes my stomach hurt."

Talitha went to her room.

I spent a night sitting in my study, staring at books and bookshelves all around the walls, thinking how little I had appreciated the room that God had given me, and my children, and my dear wife. My wife. Thanne.

The word was "Cancer." They were concerned that my lung contained tumors.

Sometimes I wish I could define myself as soul alone. When this body gives me trouble, I want to say, "It's detachable. Ignore it. The real me is purely spirit, caught in the cage of this corpus." But I can't. My self is (as Adam's self was) as much the clay of the earth as the spirit/breath of God. My visible and evident *self* is shaped by this (square-jawed, blue-eyed) face, this frame (six-foot-one), this particular slouch, this brain, these physiologic capacities. My body is more than the "cage" in which my soul lives. It is in fact my material substance and much my *self*: both how I live and who I am.

My body is that part of me that Thanne embraces, however much she likes my mind. It's my body that lies abed with her at night.

Of course, then: when this body begins to suffer internal separations (even of the physical kind, radical changes now and forever), so do I!

When pieces are cut from the body, when the body itself diminishes, I do too.

I die a little.

Sitting in my study the night before the surgery, then, I began to suffer a sadness of separations. For when the things of one's deepest affections seem suddenly more beautiful because they are suddenly more remote and possibly untouchable, that is grief.

I climbed the stairs to the hallway outside the children's bedrooms. I listened to their breathing. I bowed my head in darkness and loved them unspeakably and wished I had loved them better all their lives.

Talitha always made moist snorings when she slept. Her overbite made it impossible to close her mouth properly. I heard the distinctive noise of my daughter. I crept into her bedroom and knelt by her bed and pressed my father's cheek against her forehead, that marvelous brow by which we once had spoken together. Now, as I knelt, she rebuked me—the first, in fact, of two rebukes and the easier because it was unconscious. She put her hand against my chest and pushed with surprising strength. I didn't resist; I sat back on my heels. She yanked covers and turned toward the wall. *Girl,* I thought, *so strong and beautiful, whatever you think of yourself, I am your father. I know what I know. And I love you.*

The surgery itself was more my wife's pain than my own, since I slept as deeply as Adam when God caused Eve to be. After the procedure seemed complete, my side was sewed up and my body was wheeled to intensive care. But then it was noticed that I was bleeding internally. The staff reacted with urgency. The surgeon returned to the hospital, briefed Thanne on the problem, and rushed to O.R. for a second procedure. Thanne saw how strained his eyes were; and all her friends had already gone home; it was very late; now, then, began her most difficult waiting.

Two things eased her. Her sister came and prayed with her. That first, and that for a good long while. And then I, in the middle of the night, demanded—*demanded*—to see her. A nurse came out of intensive care to give her the message.

What, Thanne asked, did I want?

The nurse told her to find out for herself.

Good and patient, weary Thanne went to my side, and I, in a fog of anaesthesia, bellowed: "You tell them, Thanne, you tell them right now, and you tell them for sure that *I am not their honey!* Tell them! Tell them!"

I think I thought my dignity was involved.

Thanne thought I had none of that left. She sat down and howled with laughter.

And so things began to heal. Tubes maintained the life in me. The scars in my lung were found benign. There was no cancer. I was not dying.

Nevertheless, I had died.

My body, cut from its wholeness, was less than it had been. And my daughter signaled the rupture with a second rebuke. Talitha: for me an honest, spontaneous mirror of changes.

After several days of recovery, Thanne asked the children to come with her to the hospital to visit me. They crept into the room, smiling and uncertain.

"Hey, Dad. How's it going?"

"Fine," I croaked, unable to draw a good breath, let alone to release it. "Fine."

"You feeling better?"

"Yes."

"Dad?" said Matthew.

"What?"

"Are you going to die?"

"No. No."

"Good." He grinned. It had been a small boy's question, but even a young man was glad for the reassurance.

But Talitha, when she came into the room with the others, had immediately turned and left. She had to do homework, she told her mother. And no, she said, she was too busy to come back.

Before the family departed, leaning very much on Thanne and wheeling the catheter stand beside me, I wobbled out to see my daughter myself.

She sat with her head bowed over a book.

"Talitha?"

She glanced up. "What?"

"Do I get a hug?"

She dropped her eyes to the book again. She was silent a very long time. She was frowning, as if angry.

"What's the matter?" Thanne said. "You've got a problem here?"

Talitha muttered, "No."

"So, what's the matter?"

She said, "He's strange." She got up from the table and moved away with a beauty in her tread, a strength in all she did. The girl had health and youth and all her parts. She said to her mother, "He's . . . different. Changed. He's strange."

She left the waiting room.

He was *me*. In Talitha's sight I saw myself. A gaunt figure, wild-eyed and old and slow. and broken—asking for hugs: I was different. I was not the same man who had flipped eyebrows with her, who had argued after the football game. Pieces had been removed, more pieces than merely the right lung's lobe; and for Talitha my countenance announced the change, the ravaged expression of a body revised: here came one in whom time and age had just collided, one who knew in the painful shuffle of his present movement how desperately short his life is.

Talitha reflected no less than the truth.

In the instant, of course, I felt sorry for her rebuke. But we had survived worse breaks than this, and I would not always be stinking and gaunt. I'd wheedle another hug from her.

Finally, it wasn't my daughter that grieved me, but what she reflected; she saw first and truly what I didn't truly begin to suffer till five months later: the very specific severance of my body, the loss of its old virtue forever.

The latissimus dorsi are those good-lookin' muscles that curve from beneath one's shoulder down the sides of the rib cage. Weak men like me admire the latissimus dorsi on strong men: they give triangular shape to a strong man's back; these muscles flare like the hood of a cobra; and they flex to withdraw the arms like pistons.

I always liked my latissimus dorsi—even if I never gave much thought to them. I know I liked them, because (this may seem a small thing; it surely is lesser than other disfigurements; I seek no pity; I merely record the cause of grief) because I surprised myself how sad I felt, how truly sorry I was, to learn that I had lost that muscle on the right side.

Surgery—twice the slicing of all flesh on my right side to pry the ribs apart—had traumatized the poor muscle too much to grow together again. Vestigial tissue gathered in a sort of pouch under my armpit, muscle going nowhere, muscle doing nothing. For five months I thought it just took time to heal. But in July we went canoeing, and I could not draw the paddle back on my right side. Forever and ever, I had lost that cobra beauty, that strength, that particular function of my right arm.

It's like baldness. One can live without hair. But one who *had* hair for a while, whose self-image still combs a head of glossy hair, grieves the separation from the body he used to have, the self he once had been. And though the world may not be terribly sympathetic to changes it judges minor, the loss of one's self is always significant. It is suffered as a death.

I suffered my small grief privately, counting all the ribs on the right side, since nothing sheathed them any more: the skeleton stands out; the bones bespeak my deaths, my many deaths. I felt ashamed of myself that I should grow so sad for so small a revision. But I did, through a season of austerities when my daughter refused my touch, suffer.

Different. Changed. He's strange—

❧

When the body breaks and separates, so does the person.

—It is the grief of bereavement that an amputee of any sort experiences, sad for the lack of a leg or a larynx.

—The pain of a paraplegic is more than physical torment, as great as that is, and more than the mighty frustrations of incapacity; it is grief in the extreme, and it is likely to present all the stages of grief, and it will require the consolation we give the bereaved—because this one has died a terrible death, a severe internal separation.

—Clearly, a mastectomy is more than removal of cancerous tissue. With her breast has gone a significant part of the woman's self, though just how significant only she can determine. She will measure it by the depth of the grief that follows, sorrow and anger and a thumping gloom. She will measure it by the feelings the hugs of her children cause in her, the touch of a beloved man.

One dear friend of mine told me how fearful she was of her grown children's touch—not that they might hurt her delicate balance, but that they would sense the radical change in her even through their fingers' tips.

She expressed this fear curiously, by "hagging," she said, "the children," making herself so cantankerous and difficult they wouldn't *want* to touch her.

Then she would weep in secret because no one touched her. She pitied herself and infuriated herself, both at once, thinking that she herself was the cause of all her woes.

And then one morning the visiting nurse neglected to visit.

But Kathy's bandage absolutely required changing.

Her son happened to drop by.

Necessity overcame her reluctance. "Would you—?" she whispered to her son, embarrassed to be asking such a thing.

"Would you, um—?"

Kathy tells to me now that his response raised her to life again; the gentle touch of her son as he cut the old bandage, the unchanging expression of kindness in his face as he washed the wound where her breast had been, the slow bindings with clean cloth her whole upper torso—all this proved that though she had changed, his love had not; and though she had died indeed, yet she could live again.

Amen!

—The inability to bear children can initiate, both for a woman alone and for a couple together, the process of grief.

It may come as a sudden discovery by a physician's diagnosis: the self-image of fertility, all the dreams this entails, the plans both private and marital, these things are clean cut off and gone.

It may occur as a hysterectomy—that must therefore be recognized as more than merely a surgical procedure. Depending upon one's expectations and character, a hysterectomy can trigger serious sorrow, for which no one need ever apologize.

Menopause, likewise (though we know it is coming), causes various levels of grief. A woman is cut from the self that had been. Whether she bore many children or none; whether she ever wanted children; whether a youthful appearance is important to her or not, she can no longer do things she could have *chosen* to do before. Choice is canceled. She dies a little. So her emotional vicissitudes are more than hormonal; they are also funereal: she is taking leave of the self she met in adolescence.

—Impotence for men in this present society is often a loss grim enough to cause mute grief.

—And why do the hearing-impaired sometimes deny their increasing deafness? And why does baldness anger and obsess a balding man? And fatness make moody the soul of one who hates the fat? Any time the body disappoints us, severing us from the hope we had placed in it, we are bereaved.

—And deep, deep, deeper than speech is the grief of a woman robbed of her body altogether. This is the unspeakable effect of sexual rape: that her body is suddenly not her own. It was *plundered* (the Latin meaning of "rape"), carried violently away, ripped from her control, torn from her personal self. For a while her physical self is vile in the eyes of her spiritual self. One can scarcely conceive of a sundering more mortal than this; but multiply this death by the many deaths the victim must die: for she is sinned against. Society exchanges the face of kindness for the face of the Beast from the Abyss. Whom shall she trust hereafter? Moreover, the genders have been sundered for her, since it must be a *man* raping when a *woman* is raped.

Grief, both naturally and dramatically, must follow such a rending of flesh from spirit, breath from clay. This victim is killed and then killed again.

The Death of Dreams

In the city where I live and in this very neighborhood—influencing my second son so strongly that he does not see himself at all except he sees himself this way—are hundreds of boys for whom the *Imago Dei* is the *imago NBA.* Each boy dreams of a future on basketball courts, from high school through college, to be drafted by a professional team. Their visions may be of a future time, but the vision exists now, and now these boys believe in it. Motivation. The glory of self, all self-esteem. They are healthy and proud because of what they will be. The dream empowers their present existence.

How many of these hundreds will realize the dream? Will my son? No, not my son. He is too short.

Of a hundred, ninety-and-nine will not. One might.

And how shall they survive then, when reality destroys their pride and their purpose?

I yearn for your safety and health and life, my son!

Only God is omnipotent, Matthew! That is to say: only God can dream and make his every dream come true. For God, the dreaming *is* the deed. But we are finite, always dreaming beyond our capacity, always reaching beyond our grasp. When we shunned the omnipotent God, we severed ourselves from the reality of our righteous dreams. We retained the power to dream, all right; but we began to dream impossible dreams.

Matthew, the world lies, exactly as the Serpent lied to Eve. The world says, "You can have it all." You simply can't.

The world lies, my son. Its commercials promise delights it can never deliver. They pretend to care for you. They don't. They care for your money.

Matthew, the world tells dangerous lies! "What the mind can conceive, and the heart can believe," say motivational tapes, the hype of the world, "the hand can achieve." No! "You can all be basketball players, if you wish. You can do anything you wish, if you just put your mind to it." No! "Nothing limits you but your own imagination."

No! No!

We are not gods—*that* limits us. We are creatures of a measurable size. Matthew, you are five feet, ten inches; that's what and who you are. You cannot, by taking thought, add one cubit to your stature.

Ah, but when the young run hard against the reality that kills their dreams, they die. They lose the future that had honored their present selves; they lose the selves that they had loved; they begin a process of grieving, and no one names the sorrow. No one notices. The world that lied will scarcely return to comfort those bereaved of dreams.

Yet, kids hanging out on street corners may be suffering more than laziness, the Devil's workshop. Self-hatred is a pernicious mortification.

—And poverty generally is a pit for such grieving, since so many of the poor truly believed the blandishments of a consumer society. The world lies. The world, therefore, has brought down upon itself the warfare of the underclass!

God creates us with limited talents, ten or five or one. As long as we live in him, these talents fit the design of the universe, and we are something glorious. But divorced from God our talents are merely one or five or ten. Dreams and pride will always multiply the figure; reality will always divide it. And when the dreams die, so do we. The poor are the grievers in this culture. Almost nothing rips families apart as violently as the lack of money, the destruction of dreams.

—A missed promotion at work can suddenly reveal to the laborer that he has reached his top, a level much lower than he had hoped for. He suffers more than others think he should.

—Not everyone who thinks he's a writer is; or an artist; or a hero within her community.

—And in every marriage there comes a moment when spouses realize that romance is seldom as sweet as dream-machines had alleged. Most of marriage is humdrum and wholly practical; and when they are forced to admit as much, spouses suffer grief at the loss—silently, perhaps, and severed from one another in the awakening.

—The self-image need not be exaggerated by greed or foolishness in order to shatter. It may be a *good* self-image; it need only be exaggerated past our capacities.

I yearned to be (I believed I was) a good father.

Wise and creative in my care, I hoped that Talitha might have received no better father than me. But one evening when I went into her bedroom to reprove her for some sin, she screamed: "I don't appreciate you coming in with your beady little eyes and red face, yelling at me." Yep. Beady they are, and red I get. My self-image as the calm father was stung to death. I withdrew; I went down to my study; and I grieved.

—Why do you think the self-righteous find it so hard truly to know themselves as sinners? Because that knowledge kills the compatible image; such knowledge is killing, and grief is painful.

Truth-tellers, then, and prophets and the Scriptures themselves seem dangerous. Avoid them. Hate them, in fact.

Failure

If self-image is what we think we are, self-esteem is the value we place upon it. We like to like ourselves.

If the self scores well according to standards one admires, then one can admire himself. The relationship is good; he is content. But if the self should fail some significant test, the relationship breaks. He falls out of favor with himself. Can there be a more ruinous break than this, that one should despise his *self*? It is worse than if the eye said to the hand, "I have no need of you." Worse, I say, because this rejection can be total and passionate: the eye saying to the *eye*, the man to the man, "I have no need of you." This is death.

"Standards." One wishes that we would accept the absolute

standards of God for a righteous self-evaluation, even the law that is written upon our hearts. Instead, the world sets standards we feign would follow: our peers announce what's fashionable; the media persuade us of style; the expectations of a culture or a community or a corporation become the Law for us, a *nomos* by which we live and prove ourselves, by which we "save" ourselves; and the deep teaching of our parents, right or wrong, has established standards that linger long in our lives as the picture of "good girls and boys," "honey, be a success," "make me proud," and "what would people say?"

Standards come from those whom we have allowed to be authorities over us, whose approval we yearn, whether society or business or families or even our own whims and desires.

These, when we feel driven to obey them, become gods in place of the true God, whose standards were established in perfect wisdom and holy love for us. False gods may or may not love us—that doesn't matter. False gods cannot save us—that's what matters, because even from false gods we seek salvation, we seek esteem for ourselves, *we seek to prove ourselves worthy*, by striving to keep the laws they set.

And since the law of any god, whether true or false, requires a perfect obedience, we will fail these laws.

When we fail the laws of the True God, we may receive forgiveness, by Christ's achievement.

But when we fail the laws of false gods, there is no holy option since there is no holy God around: we simply fail. We are severed from standards we honor, from all who honor the same standards, from reputation, from self-esteem, from worth.

To fail is to die.

—So the adolescent is pitched into a real and terrible grief when he fails to make the football cut, when she becomes convinced that her ugliness has stopped the mouths of possible dates and started the mouths of jabbering gossip. Grief!

—To fail any examination by which one meant to validate himself (whether in school or in some skill or under his mother's eye or his spouse's) is severance and can precipitate a lasting sorrow. "Oh, I don't like myself any more!"

How often, even in the tiny failure, doesn't the child rise up and cry, "I hate myself!"

—If one is convinced that goodness is thinness, then fatness will hate itself. The standards of worldly beauty are always treacherous. It is a loveless jury that sits in judgment here below the stars.

—And what of those who never experienced praise in their childhood? The standards established by such parental coldness are altogether too severe ever to be met. Even as adults these people think ill of themselves, dying with every effort since no effort is good enough. They live in a quiet, continual, cringing grief, their souls cast down forever. Heavenly Father, save them from the "selves" their parents had demanded, for every little failure seems to confirm the chasm between the self that ought to be and the self that is: "See? I'm useless. I'm no good to anyone. I might as well die."

Guilt: the Dying and the Goodness

The law of God *is* written upon our hearts, even after our separation from his declaration of the Good and the Evil. It isn't only upon the hearts of the faithful, but of all people.

We know the good.

But we do the evil.

And that particular division within ourselves—in this case the *righteous* self-despising called "guilt"—is also a separation of death, a Secondary Dying. Guilt causes grief: the suffering of the self's being torn into two parts, the part that does wrong, and the part that knows better.

—So when a man's conscience begins to accuse him for the adultery he committed, guilt will take the pattern of grief.

—So another man genuinely despairs when a minor theft is found out and disclosed.

I name two sins. But any sin has the same effect when the conscience sincerely rebukes it.

"I do not do the good I want," says Paul, "but the evil I do not want is what I do. Now if I do what I do not want, it is no longer I that do it, but sin which dwells in me." *I am*, Paul says in effect, *no longer I.* Oh, it is a mortal thing, to wake unto one's sin! The relationship between holy desire and real action rips him apart, killing him. "I see in my members another law at war with the law of my mind, making me captive to the law of sin which dwells in my members." The pain is grief: "Wretched man that I am!" And the cause is death: "Who will deliver me from this body of death?"

False gods cannot raise us from such death—not the corporation nor the culture that has run my life, not the parents who may truly adore me, not the public who judges my writing (who judges me, therefore). At best, a false god can commiserate as together we perish. Or else this hungry idol, having swallowed all my virtue, will simply seek others to devour.

To die under the laws of a false god is simply to die.

But God *is* God.

Our God is both merciful and able to save.

And the guilt—which by the stages of grief returns us to him—is a terribly, terribly good thing after all.

Here is the outrageous irony of our Gospel: that to die under the laws of the one true God is the beginning of rebirth for us.

Relationship is life. Our pride and our desire for pure independence had sundered us from God: death. But dying *again,* dying to *self,* dying into Jesus Christ, remakes the lost relationship.

Behold: to die is to live.

God has changed the bad thing into a good thing. The Lord has taken the horrible consequences of our original rebellion—all the Secondary Dyings that began on the day we ate of the tree—and made them the means of our salvation!

Here, then, is the central theme of this book: that the real and dramatic means by which we may be turned back to God again is the grief we experience in all these Secondary Dyings.

We must not deceive ourselves about dying nor avoid the suffering of its grief. Pain is part of our healing. It is by the pain and through the grief that we go, step by step, away from *self* and closer to Christ and back to the Father again.

"Wretched man that I am!" cries Paul, and so must we. We must more than admit it by the mouth; we must *suffer* in fact our essential impotence, in order next to cry: "Who will deliver me from this body of death?"

All else has failed in death. Everything of *self* was proven useless through grief. One name alone endures. It is now not merely a doctrine; it is experience; it is with genuine joy that I shout out loud:

"Thanks be to God through Jesus Christ our Lord! For the law of the Spirit of life in Christ Jesus has set me free from the law of sin and death!"

Talitha's a senior in high school now. This is her last year before the gamier steps toward adulthood: she plans to go to Costa Rica before college as a foreign exchange student. And we have just this week received the news that she has been granted a full academic scholarship to a state university.

She has a passport. Scarcely eighteen, this kid is ready for international travel. She knows Spanish. Oh, yes—and she single-handedly organized the Martin Luther King Day at her high school, after demanding of her principal that the day be devoted to Black history.

What do you think: would she let me hold her hand any more? Do you think my daughter thinks she needs parental support right now?

Caramel.

Last winter, during a week of lecturing in the Twin Cities, I returned to my motel and switched on *CNN Headline News*. The television fills the void of the lonely traveler. Wherever I go, there is a pastel print screwed to the wall, and there is *CNN Headline News*.

I kicked off my shoes and sank on the bed, sighing. I brought several pillows up behind my head. Comfort. I expected to doze a bit. *CNN Headline News* always allows me some repose.

I had just begun to drift off when a familiar voice smote my ear, saying, "President Bush! President Bush!"

I sat up, tingling all down my spine.

No! How did Talitha get to Minneapolis?

"President Bush!"

But she wasn't in Minneapolis. She was on *CNN Headline News*! In fact, she was in Atlanta, on the street, wearing African National colors, an aggressive expression, a pill-box hat, a loose coat against the cold, finger-rings and earrings and necklaces all yellow and red and green. The girl was stepping forward from a group of students in order to be interviewed by a reporter for *CNN Headline News*. The question was, *What do you think of the Gulf war?*

My daughter put her face directly into the camera.

And I saw that face in the cold climate of Minnesota, and I trembled because she was about to speak to the nation. I lifted my hand to caution her, but she would not be cautioned.

"President Bush!" she cried, "what about South Africa? You talk about a new world order. So when do folks in South Africa get a piece of it? You gonna do there what y'all doin' in the Persian Gulf?"

What do you think? Does this child need my hand any more? Should I still offer her safety and strength? Would she accept it?

In recent years her overbite has been corrected. Talitha spent several days in the hospital, recovering from a strenuous procedure in which wedge-sections of her upper jaw were sawn out, allowing the front teeth to be retracted and brought downward. But this is the independence of the child that she absolutely refused to urinate any other way (by tubes or by pans) than with dignity upon her own toilet. She refused pain killers. She demanded to be released (despite a wired jaw and baby food) in time to make a trip with her concert band to Florida.

And this is her independence, that after surgery she began to see herself as beautiful. She dressed so, she met others so, she began to laugh and to date and to study so. She took care of an acne problem. I mean, she took *care* of it. It's gone.

The girl, it seems, can handle everything.

Does she need my hand anymore?

One poor fellow whom she was dating made the mistake of pushing her too far—in front of our house, yea, even on the sidewalk. She flipped him. He landed on his yesterday's lunch. He landed astonished.

This is Talitha, my daughter, adopted ("Doncha *love* it?"), American, African, Black, and Bold. What? Can I hold her hand again? Would she let me? ("I can handle it, Dad.") Does she need me?

Years ago, on the Saturday before Christmas, she and I were walking Main Street, staring into windows. She was barely a girl-child then, delighted to have found her legs and yearning independence. She was charmed by every bright thing in the world. And she was mad at me.

The weather was hard and clear and cold. It had rained the day before, then had frozen at night to create by morning a glinting, crystal universe—a winter's dream, and dangerous. The tree limbs rattled with ice; the telephone wires sagged; our breath went out in plumes; our cheeks were pinched; and the streets were sheets of ice.

To Talitha, everything was lovely. "Daddy! Let go!"

To me, everything was treacherous. "No, girl. I have to hold on to you."

She wanted to run. She wanted to chase her own white breath, to race past shops, to make the trees tinkle like chandeliers. "Daddy, let go!"

But I kept holding her mitten-hand in my stronger glove, and that's why she was mad at me. She stumped beside me, pouting.

Christmas is a killer. The children simply can't contain themselves. The excitement drives them to silliness—and Talitha, caramel daughter, was canny as well.

She grew quiet beside me, sweet, obedient. She allowed her hand to soften in mine, as if malleable—then all at once she dashed forward and I was holding the mitten. "Daddy! Daddy, I tricked you!"

She whooped. She kicked her heels and laughed, and I might have joined in her coltish happiness, running free on a very cold day—except that I loved her. I feared for her.

"You can't catch me!" she cried, turning to run away. "I won't let you."

Well: but I didn't have to run; and no, I couldn't catch her.

It's a common story. Every parent knows it. But it's always painful nonetheless: I loved Talitha. I wanted no harm to come unto her. But how can I help the kid that runs away from me?

Her next step struck ice. This precisely was my fear. She flew up in an astonished loop, then dropped to the hard, cold ground: *crack!*—the back of her skull, her eyes wide open, waiting for pain or understanding.

Oh, my stupid daughter! I rushed to her. There gathered in her face a wildness not of freedom, but of fright. Then she saw me coming. She drew a tremendous breath and became a baby again and burst into tears.

She hurt, my daughter hurt—and in that moment she changed. She stopped resisting me. She hurt, and she needed me—my barely-a-girl-child.

And I hurt too.

I cradled her in my arms. I molded her to my neck and heart, and I rocked her. "Cry, Talitha," I whispered. "It's all right. Cry." The more she confessed her pain with tears, the more she clung to me—who loved her more than life itself.

So I carried her that day. She didn't mind the restriction. I didn't mind the burden. I loved her. And this was the raising of my daughter the Saturday before Christmas: that I carried her.

But that little tale took place before the girl became a challenger of Presidents, a flipper of boyfriends, a thrower of surprise parties for her-own-self, a woman of parts and proclamations, an activist, "I know what I know!" Do you think she'd let me hold her hand the same way now? Ask *her* if she needs the support anymore.

No. She's independent now.

Besides, she's on her way to Costa Rica. I simply can't follow the kid across the continents.

But then who will catch her when she falls—for she will surely fall. And who can raise her up again? Not this earthly father, the loving but limited one.

Rather, her Heavenly Father, Loving and Unlimited!

O Lord, I beseech thee now as at the first, lay thy hands on my daughter that she may live. When she faileth and falleth, then take her by the hand and say unto her, Talitha cumi: *which is, being interpreted, Damsel, I say unto thee, Arise! All the way to Costa Rica, to life, to death and to life again, dear Father, never let her go. Amen.*

—Which things are a parable for all of our fallings, a promise for all of our risings again. It's the fall that teaches us trust. It is trust that allows the Resurrection.

Amen. Amen.

10 The Third Death, the Fourth, and the Difference

E ver since childhood, when I picture my father he's thinking. And when he thinks, it's important, of course, so I am quiet and he does not know that I'm there.

His head is bowed, his brown eyes lost behind the golden frames of his glasses; his lips are pursed—thin lips, severely pursed. A muscle is working at the back of his jaw, as if he's chewing, but he isn't. He's thinking.

If he's sitting at a desk, he sets his elbows on the wood and twists long eyebrow hairs between thumb and forefinger. They curl up like little flames. He has square, strong hands. He could crush mine in a handshake. He could, but he never does.

I am very quiet.

Dad is finding words in his mind. He is good at words. He will preach them or type them on an Underwood upright, using two fingers swiftly. When he preaches, his flaming eyebrows look fierce but his voice is kind, and the words are easy, even for children.

When he writes, the language matches its subject.

His words once laughed at me when I was a student in prep school: "We've noticed," the letter said, "that you have a sophomoric tendency to use large, latinate phrases."

Or else his words will be grave and formal when the matter is very serious.

Recently I received from my father a letter grave, rhetorical, terribly formal. And not only I but all seven of his children, scattered around the globe, received the same communication at the same time.

When I unfolded the letter and read it, I pictured him bowed at the typewriter, brow frowning, the soft eye seeking a better word, square fingers twisting a few white eyebrow hairs, the muscle in his right jaw pulsing, pulsing.

❦

CORPOREAL DYING

My father's third death will be one of the heaviest Secondary Dyings I will have to suffer. Our immediate love is much of my life; our past is my heritage; his mind is my treasure, his approval my dignity, his name is my own.

He is "Walter," as was his father before him, as am I, the eldest of his children. And I sign myself always a "junior" in order to honor the common name. "There are two of us," I say with my signature. "When you see me, you see evidence of him; and I shall—however long he lives, however long I live thereafter—*be* his junior."

My father's third death, the decease of his body, will grieve me elementally for two distinct reasons: so much of me will die when he does; that first and certainly. But more than that, the death of his body must prophesy with stark clarity the death of mine to come. In Walter Senior's third death Walter Junior will gaze at his own.

On this particular journey, we all must follow our parents, who followed their parents, who followed father Adam and mother Eve, with whom we rebelled, with whom we began to die.

Finally, after a lifetime of individual Secondary Dyings, all the little dyings happen all at once and nothing remains. The physiological systems of the body shall cease to support each other; tissue, flesh, and nerve shall crack and decompose; and the seat of our self-conscious selves will dissolve.

Death is always the sundering of living relationships. But this third death is the complete annihilation of *all* the relationships enjoyed on earth.

Then nature shall be nothing to us, and we shall be nothing to nature but a small deposit of dust, something so similar to earth itself that all identity shall have passed from it.

Then people will be nothing to us. The whole human weave that completed our persons shall be altogether sheared. Others will remember us a while; but since relationship requires the mutual interaction of two, there won't be life in the remembering—not *our* life, anyway. The son may feel the loss of a father; but for the father the loss must be so total that he cannot say, "I have lost this or that." He can only say, *I am lost: apollumai*—if, that is, he could speak at all.

But then, too, self may be nothing to self. The internal division must be so complete that the mouth is stopped. Who knows what one might say or know or even *be* beyond the bourne from whence there's no return? Between us *now*, compacted in time, and us *then*, shot forth from time and space and all creation, there is such a gulf fixed that we cannot see past it. Outside of creation, can we even be creatures? And if not creatures—if severed from *this* essential identity—then what? Dead.

Not-relating is not-being.

Dead.

🍎

My father's age has passed its biblical fullness, threescore years and ten.

When he was a young man he was straight and handsome. He used to brush his hair into a peculiar swirl at the peak of his forehead, a dashing loop like the headlamp (I thought) of an iron steam engine— or like the screw of hair drawn on the cow of the Borden's Dairy Products. This curl was ever a comfort to me, because it assured me of my father's presence after a painful absence.

He used to disappear, sometimes briefly, sometimes for weeks, and then I was like a boy holding his breath (except it was tears I was holding), which a person can do for only so long before he breaks his lungs. Then he lets go and howls.

For example, he took me shopping in the department stores of

Chicago, huge rooms with secret bell-sounds ringing *bong-bong-bong,* meaning something to the salespeople, nothing to me but mystery; everything was murmurous, soft, smelling of leather and perfume and cotton sheets. I paused at toys. I squatted and lost myself among the toys.

But suddenly I felt a cold wind of Absence.

I looked up. My father was gone. I looked around, left and right. The entire store was soft and frightening. "Daddy?"

There began in my breast a tiny run of gasps, and rawness cut my throat, and my face felt hot. "Daddy?"

I tried hard to control myself—exactly like holding your breath. I looked down this aisle, then ran to the next, and the—

It was no use. My father was gone. He was lost. I was lost! Bloody panic spouted from my mouth:

"Daddeeeeee!"

It was the sudden sight of the curl on his forehead, turning a corner and coming toward me, which relieved me so much that I'd start to tremble in all my joints and lift my helpless hands and stumble-run in his direction. That swirl of hair, you know—and his thin lips pursed—consoled me and made the world familiar again.

Or here is another example: Dad would abscond whole weeks at a time. And then one evening my mother would tuck us all in the car and drive us to the train station downtown, cavernous, vaulted spaces, echoing heel-clicks on the marble floor. Dim light in that place. High black windows. You couldn't read, if you wanted to. We sat on brown wooden pews. Then voices arose like whispers, all indistinct; but Mom knew. She'd get up and go forward, courageous woman, because people were coming our way, striding very fast, very earnest, not seeing us.

"There," she'd say. "There's Dad."

And above the heads of a hundred thousand strangers, absolutely clear to my sight, different from every other kind of hair in the world, my father's handsome curl!

I threw myself in the paths of travelers, running as hard as I could. My dad had a suitcase in one hand and a briefcase in the other, and I didn't care—I bent my head and ran for his stomach and buried myself, and I didn't have to howl. He was home. I seemed to smell winter on his clothes, as if he came down from the north. No matter. Where his beautiful loop of hair was, there was he. He was home.

"Daddy, don't do that anymore."

"Do what?"

"Don't leave me."

"Oh, Ah-vee—" This was his nickname for me. He'd lift me up and put his whiskery chin against the soft part of my cheek and scraped me so that I hurt and tickled at once. I didn't want to laugh when I was upset, so it raised tears in my eyes. I rubbed my cheek.

"Ah-vee?" he said. He looked solemnly at me. "Wally?"

"What?"

"I never left you in the first place. Where did you think I could go? How could I ever forget you?"

So then he would lower me and hug Mom and wink at me over her shoulder. "How could I ever forget your mother?"

Well, and I was glad to sit next to him on the front seat of the car when we drove home from the train station.

But he left me. I don't care what he said. He went away many times.

And as I grew, I learned to hold my breath pretty well. I don't really mean holding my breath, of course. I mean that mostly I controlled the urge to cry. I schooled myself in not thinking about Dad not being home.

I played. I absorbed myself in private activities, finding hiding places under the living room furniture, crouching in small fortresses and dreaming stories.

Several times, though, when we were living in Grand Forks, North Dakota, I panicked at his absence. In spite of all my efforts, I broke down and cried.

It was like a trick of the air. In the middle of the day, hiding under a dining room table, as clearly as if someone had switched on a radio, all at once I would hear my father call my name: *Ah-vee!* The tone said, *Come here, I need you.*

So I would sing out, "Here I come," and without a thought, I pop out from the table and run through the living room into his study—

But his desk was clean. His chair was empty. The drapes were drawn. He was gone. He had been gone a long time. It was just a trick, this calling of my name. He hadn't called my name, and suddenly I was thinking of him, and I was missing him, and I started to cry.

Well, it was business, of course. He went here and there to preach or to study or to write things. He was an important man. He worked for God.

Sometimes I heard Mom crying in her bedroom. What kid doesn't lie down and die when his mother cries in private?

But on the mornings when my mother announced, "Your father is coming home today," I knew exactly what to do. I was so happy, then. I had a ritual by which to hurry him home. I had a sober and important job.

Right after breakfast I ran to the street in front of our house; I picked a spot on the curb where I could see a good distance both left and right; then I sat down, tucking my feet in the gutter, bringing my knees together. Ready!

My job was to watch for my dad. I had to catch sight of him the instant he turned the corner onto our street—*the very instant,* you see—and to wave him home with loving joy. He drove a green Chevy.

Well, all morning long I waved at the neighbors and strangers driving by. Even if they weren't driving green Chevies, I grinned and waved. Almost all of them waved back. We were great friends. I figured that everyone knew that my dad was coming home, or else why were they all so happy?

It was a wonderful job.

"Good afternoon!" "Hello, how are you doing?" "If you see my dad, tell him I'm waiting."

So the whole day passed, until those whom I saw in the morning paused on their way back from work.

"Your dad's not home yet?"

"He's coming! I'm on the job!"

There!

Far up the road at the turning on my right—there! The dusty green nose of a slow Chevy coming round!

I jumped up and pressed my hands together, speechless with the possibility that it was my dad. The car slid forward, the reflection of tree-leaves sliding up its windshield. I stood on tiptoe, peering—

There it is! There it is! I covered my mouth. There, behind the windshield, was that dashing swirl of wonderful hair! Dad's curl. *The man inside that car is my dad!* And he had such white teeth in those days. Thin lips, white teeth, and he was grinning at me.

So then I let loose wild laughings and hilarious pointings at my father, and I followed the car right up the driveway, and I threw his door open and bolted inside and put my cheek against his whiskers, which tickled and hurt and smelled of winter, and I cried. I couldn't stop crying.

That was the day when it was all right to cry.

Dad and I are older now, both of us. His children are scattered around the world. Mine—all but one—are in college; the baby's bound for Costa Rica.

Shortly after my father's retirement from the ministry, the whole Wangerin family gathered in the Colorado Rockies for a reunion. Talitha was four. This was the trip when she drove her brothers crazy by her happiness, loving everything under the sun.

On Sunday the family worshiped outside, under a scrubbed sky, a light wind whistling the pine boughs. Dad climbed a crag in order to see and be seen—in order to preach. I imagine that he had bowed his head a long, long time, searching the words to give us. Precious words. I remember them exactly.

The man on his mountain, as oracular as the prophets, lifted his voice and called loudly: "I have thought of the best legacy that I could leave my family."

There was, of course, no money. Dad had spent his energies as a parish pastor, a college president, an editor of Christian educational materials, a foreign missionary. Who pays dearly for such dear labors? Mom probably made more money than he. Well, and there was little property: a house in Colorado, books, an excellent desk; I already had his Underwood typewriter. What sort of legacy, then?

The wind blew his hair into a morning halo, a sunlit cloud around the old man's skull.

"This I know," my father shouted, "and this I beg you to receive. Please! I can bequeath you with nothing richer or nobler than the Lord Jesus Christ and faith in him."

Little Talitha leaped to her feet, threw open her arms, and yelled as loud as her grandpa: "Doncha *love* it?"

Her grandpa loved it. He grinned then and hitched his jeans and finished his sermon with joy.

But that was years ago. And now he has written us all a letter, formal and grave:

The Day of Sts. Philip and James, 1 May.
BELOVED FAMILY—

This is the picture I have of my father as he writes the letter I am reading: his head is bowed, his brown eyes lost in thought; his lips are pursed—thin lips. There is a muscle pulsing at the corner of his jaw. But that swirl of hair by which I spied him in crowds of strangers—that's gone. He has developed a high, frowning forehead, and the few hairs left he combs straight back. They are white. The moustache that covers his pursing lip, and the eyebrows he twists, they are white. And the sides of his old head, they are snowy white, like mountains.

The Lord interrupted my Lenten ministries, [he writes—he still preaches in the small towns of Colorado—] *by allowing a kidney stone to move inside of me. Early Wednesday morning Dr. Potter met me at the hospital. I was committed after submitting to X-ray pictures.*

Dr. Potter, suspicious about my prostate, ordered a biopsy. I submitted to that without anesthetic, and he assured me he got a good sample. (He should have. It felt like a shovel in my rectum!)

Today he spent a lot of time discussing the analysis of my sample. There is malignant growth—

My father has cancer.

❧

For my father's circumstance I think of the somber words of the Preacher: "Man goeth to his long home, and the mourners go about the streets." Suddenly a son is intensely conscious that death must be: "The silver cord be loosed, the golden bowl be broken, the pitcher broken at the fountain, and the wheel at the cistern shattered."

"Vanity of vanities, saith the Preacher. All is vanity."

But for myself, staring at the certainty of my own third death, thoughts run rather to Job—a language more lovely, more anguished: "My days are swifter than a weaver's shuttle, and come to their end without hope."

Cancer. Closing one's eyes forever. *That* dying, that end seems so clean a cutting off from everyone and everything that even the Deity who sees all will not see Job: "Remember that my life is a breath; my eye will never again see good. The eye of him who sees me will behold me no more; while thy eyes are upon me, I shall be gone."

And if God himself should go in search of Job after death, well, death will render the searching futile. Job grieves the cut that must annihilate himself altogether: "For now I lie in the earth; thou wilt seek me, but I shall not be."

I don't want to think about it!

Anyone's death can trigger in me the unwelcome meditations of my own! I'd rather go dancing! I'd rather laugh in a frantic ignorance—

"Let me alone that I may find a little comfort before I go and shall not return, to the land of gloom and deep darkness, the land of gloom *as* darkness, deep darkness and chaos, where light is as darkness."

So Job pleads.

So do we.

For whatever we *don't* know about the far shore, this we know so well it stands our hairs on end: that the third death is an isolating event. There is no such solitude as this death is. People do not die together, holding hands and singing songs; they *live* together that way, even to the end. But at the end, one takes the extreme step all alone; that single step is what distinguishes the dead from the living; at the last, the last *is* one's aloneness.

What shall I say, then, to my father? Is this all there is to say with unvarnished honesty? Is everything else that I might say a cunning piety, words by which to *seem* at peace but words by which I deny his dying and my fear, words therefore that sever us even now?—*he is dying and I am not.* Not yet at any rate.

How shall I approach my father when his condition reminds me so bluntly of mine?

What?—shall I mutter platitudes? Smile? Pat his shoulder?

Or what?—get mad at him?

Or what?—grow morose and silent, having nothing of comfort to say to him I love most dearly, whom I want never to die, no, not ever?

What?

Even while reading his letter I want to argue with my father. I'm whispering, "No," distinctly; and then I am putting words to it: "No. You will not die."

. . . *There is malignant growth,* he writes. The man has a steady and accurate sight. But the message irritates me. *If it is localized, I can either opt for a prostatectomy or radiation treatment. The doctor said it depended upon how long I expected to live—*

No! It's a minor cancer, right? How many men recover from this sort of surgery? Almost all of them. You won't die.

People *in general* die. I have preached—and do myself admit—this irrefutable truth.

> *And we all must*
> *Go down to dust.*

Yes, generally and in due time. But not you. And not now. You are my father!

I am writing you an immediate letter in my mind. You must listen to me: Take vitamins. Rest from preaching. Quit work, Dad. You've earned it. What sort of retirement is it when you drive to tiny towns every Sunday to preach to tiny congregations? Do they even realize their good fortune in having a man like you? Stop it! Don't kill yourself! Think of Mom! Think of us!

I see that muscle pulsing. Daddy, don't bow your head. Don't purse your lips. Don't think! Listen to me: you're too young to die. Too *good* to die. Eyes as brown as yours, as soft with sympathy and understanding, lips this thin, and the chin with white whiskers that can scratch and tickle a cheek at once—Father, these things are too real. They can't die.

There cannot be a world without you in it somewhere.

Or I will again become a watcher on the curb, a waver in the neighborhood, waiting for you to drive around the corner in a green Chevy. I will peer through car windows, looking for a beautiful brown loop of hair, and a smile of white teeth—

Dad! How long would I sit and wait for you? All my life long.

Mom will never say, "He's coming home today." Mom will not drive us to the railroad station and stare on tiptoe and suddenly cry, "There he is!" I will not see your curl in the midst of a thousand strangers. No, I will never see the comforting curl of hair again: *Wally, I never left you in the first place.*

Don't lie, Dad! Don't lie! Don't do it to me again. This Absence is forever!

If you die, I may return to my common affairs, shutting you from my mind, attending to the people and the needs that are nearest me, those that love and depend on me. I'll do this and that quite calmly. I'll keep my calendar, flip its pages, finish its duties, be happy—

But suddenly, distinctly, I will hear your voice calling my name: *Ah-vee*. And the tone will seem to say, *Come here, I need you*. And without a thought I'll get up and go to find out what you want. But the desk will be clean, the chair empty. And then, in spite of all my striving, it will strike me like an open hand: you're not here. It was a trick of the air or of my yearning. You didn't call my name. You are gone. Dead. And then I won't be able to hold back my sorrow anymore, and I will cry. I will cry for you. I will miss you so much that I won't be able to stop crying, no, not in my secret soul, until my tears are dried in dust—

> *Dear Dad,*
> *Please don't die.*
> *Your son,*
> *Wally.*

But now this, in the same letter that announced his cancer, is what my father wrote:

My immediate thought while I awaited the performance of the biopsy was from the singing heart of King David: "But I trust in Thee, O Lord. I say, Thou art my God. My times are in Thy hand." I told the physician that I live by the grace of God and am eternally grateful for all His blessings for my nearly three-score years and ten.

His legacy. His gift. His bequest. My inheritance: his faith! Oh, how unspeakably pragmatic, how richer than money and endlessly spendable is the faith of the beloved who dies before our eyes!

And then, my father, surely pursing his lips, surely bowing his head above the typewriter, surely trusting the thing that he sent me, wrote:

And then I thought of St. Paul's sage comment: "We walk by faith, not by sight." And I don't have to generate or acquire that faith. It is a spectacular gift of God. This is the genuine life-death-life principle.

Even still the old man is preaching! But now his pulpit is grander than Colorado's mountain. It is the foundations of existence; his word is real in the universe, and absolutely necessary to me.

For there is a distinction between the final deaths. One only seems final, but it seems so because the other one *is*. Nevertheless, Jesus has died that fourth death in our stead. This is the life-death-life principle my father writes about, that there may be life after one of these deaths.

I will grieve when my father dies. I do not exaggerate the sorrow to come. But I will not "grieve as others do who have no hope"— because Dad will not die, as Job had feared, without hope. Dad will not die forever! This is but the third death; from this death the faithful, who know of the fourth, more horrible death, will surely rise again!

Listen to me: that Chevy *will* come round the corner again, and this boy *will* leap to his feet at the sight of a marvelous sweep of fatherly hair, handsome and smiling and waiting to hug me!

Anticipating with great joy our family gathering early in July. May God bring us all together safely and happily. Keep the faith.
Lots of love, also from Mom.
           Dad.

❦

It is precisely because of the faith of my father than I can consider the death of my father with clarity and completeness, as well as deaths in all their differences and all their extremities. The legacy of his faith, as it is also my faith, has a thousand returns. It offers a freedom the poor world, imprisoned in ignorance, desperately needs.

The death of our bodies is only the most visible and evident episode in the long drama of dying that began when first we severed ourselves from the Lord of Life. The third death is a gathering of all Secondary Dyings in one final convulsion; therefore it is the climax of the drama—but not the conclusion!

DEATH ABSOLUTE

The fourth death is the only death that deserves our deepest dread. It is to be distinguished from the third. And the Apostle Paul helps us, both to distinguish and not to fear.

In 1 Corinthians 15 he argues for the necessity of believing that Christ was raised from the dead. Whether we do or do not believe this, he says, has eternal consequences, for it shall affect the sort of death we die when the body dies. Throughout the passage, Paul uses the functional word *nekros* to refer to *all* who die, believers and nonbelievers alike. In this we are the same.

But when he begins to drive home the transfiguring truth of Christ's resurrection, and when he writes "in Christ shall all be made alive," suddenly he's using two different terms for "death." If there is a resurrection, then those who have died are merely *fallen asleep*. They shall wake again. But if there were no resurrection, then the dead have *perished*—and the Greek word he chooses for this worst of death, from which there is no waking, is *apollumi*, the same that Jesus used for the various kinds of perishing sin consigned us to.

It is the word of Jesus when he announced in clearest terms the purpose of his work on earth: "The Son of man," he said, "came to seek and to save the lost." The lost: the *apololos*. Jesus makes the difference. The cross of Christ divides the deaths for us, so that the third is a sleep from which we might be raised, since the fourth is a death from which we might be saved. "For the cross of Christ," writes Paul again, "is folly to those who are *perishing*—the word is again *apollumenois*—"but to us who are being saved it is the power of God."

Hear, then, of the death those who trust in Jesus shall not die. Hear and tremble and give thanks to God.

It is the Dying Absolute. It is the sundering of every relationship for good, forever, and for all. It is more than the cutting of earthly relationships, for it is the experience of eternal, irrevocable solitude. It is perpetual exile from God. From love. It is, perhaps (though I do not understand this) the death that knows it is dead. Now, finally, one knows what love is, though one is severed forever from loving and being loved. Now one knows God both in goodness and in glory, and fears him, and honors him, and would even believe in him, but cannot, for God has departed from that one eternally. This is the death of every holy alternative: what is, must be the same forever.

It is a divine and solemn irony, for God hath finally granted the sinner, now in his fourth death, what he took from God in the first: complete independence, a perfect autonomy, a singularity like unto nothing in all possiblities—except the singularity of God before he began to create. But he who has died the fourth death is not God; he never could create, and now he can accomplish nothing. He is the god of a little realm that admits one god only, his impotent self. He can only know and despair. He is lost, and "lost" is all he may say of himself forever, no attribute, no other characteristic, no past nor future, that single thing. "I perish." *Apollumai.*

The utter state of solitude is the Dying Absolute. Outer darkness, where there is weeping and gnashing of teeth.

Throughout the generations, it's common name has been Hell.

THE DIFFERENCE

But I shall not perish! I, like the prodigal, will rather be coming home again!

No, this is not a wishful denial of the reality nor some incompleteness of the third death. My body will die. Every single relationship in which now I experience life—every relationship!—will break. I will at once lose my place in the created world and friends and family and breathing, my reason, my senses and all my strength, yea, and my *self*—until the darkness is complete, until I am, from earthly perspectives, a nothing in a nowhere. I will die.

But I will not *perish!*

I shall not be lost utterly. I carry to my grave this promise: that "God so loved the world that he gave his only Son, that whoever believes in him should not perish—" *Perish:* now what Greek word do you suppose is used there? Right, *me apoletai,* the familiar "loss" in its extremity, *apollumi.* "Should not perish," says the promise, "but have eternal life."

How can this be? If death is my impotence to maintain any sort of relationship, and if life is lived in relationship, how could I ever be alive again?

Because the God who created once is Creator still. Because God established a new sort of relationship by his Son—a new covenant in which *God does it all,* and we allow the doing. It's a one-sided relationship, wherein the impotent one, the monstrously incapacitated one, receives the benefit—as when a weak child falls, but the father holds her hand and lifts her up again. The lifting is pure gift. The new covenant is Grace.

This relationship can endure even when I am helpless. Especially then. *This* relationship endures though I am nothing in a nowhere—

because I remain a something in the heart of God! *This* relationship endures in spite of the flat reality of the grave and my own dissolution, my crumbling into dust, because my side of the covenant is not fulfilled by *my* flesh and blood but by Christ's—who continues to live, yes, even while they bury me and the worms translate my subtle brains to soil.

"My sheep," says Jesus, "hear my voice, and I know them, and they follow me; and I give them eternal life, and they shall never perish [*me apolontai!*] and no one shall snatch them out of my hand."

I will die. All my resources will exhaust themselves. In myself and on my own, I will not be.

But the Shepherd remembers my name.

The Shepherd will whisper, "Walter"—and though I have no ears to hear, yet the whispering Lord will give me the hearing.

The Savior will cry across the divisions: "Walter Wangerin, Junior!"—and though I have no tongue at all, the calling will give me voice. The Word of God has always contained my own capacity to answer it.

"Walter Wangerin, *come forth!*"

And straightway I will rise up, laughing and loving and leaping, alive: "Here I am! For you have called me."

Alive again, eternally.

Walter Senior, do you see?

I have, as you begged in your letter, "kept the faith." And this is the proof—that I'm writing my own letter back, fully as formal as yours, though much longer by several hundred pages. On behalf of the seven children scattered around the world, on behalf of the grandchildren now taking their places in it, I send you our hearts' thanksgiving. Your legacy outlasts all others.

And I send you our love.

Whenever you must go, dear Father, go in peace. We will surely follow you.

In the comfort of Jesus I write you.

Sincerely,

    Wally

II
THE PERSONAL DRAMA:
THROUGH GRIEF TO
HEALING

Gloria's Story

11 The Goodness of Grieving

B ut we still dwell in the second act of this Cosmic Drama. That is, we still live our days on the earth, both in joy and in sorrow.

Sorrow and joy are not separate.

Happiness and sadness may be opposites of one another, but not joy and sorrow. In fact, it is *through* sorrow that one discovers a calm, abiding, indestructible joy.

This is a paradox of our faith: joy is forged in sorrow.

And death leads to life.

And grief is the road between them.

It is grieving that drives us from dying to living, from death to life again—from any single Secondary Death that we might suffer, back to the bosom of God, which relationship *is* the fullness of life for us.

Unless, says the Lord, you turn and become like children, you will never enter the kingdom of heaven.

Unless like children we turn to the Father, the third death will be the fourth death for us; we would rightly be terrified of our physical decease, then, because it would be our soul's decease as well, and death eternally.

But the sinner does not turn easily. Neither does he turn willingly. He must, in mercy, *be* turned. Nor does plain preaching often accomplish so total a conversion. He who truly believes he's strong is not prepared to confess an abject weakness, not for verbal persuasions, or reasonable proofs, or even the leadings of those who love him. Rather, something has to *happen*. The sinner must, in mercy, be smacked by the Truth, must run headlong into Truth as one runs into a stone wall, must experience it, *suffer* it after all. If the wall doesn't move, the sinner must.

This is what grief does. This is the effect of the earnest and painful, extended, and personal experience of grieving.

The hit that I take in a serious Secondary Death both undeceives me and defines me. Defines *me*. It awakens me to an essential truth that I had rejected long ago, a truth that my sinful nature hates, *hates*—and utterly repudiates.

Therefore, I (that is, my Old Adam, the sinful self, the major Me of this world) I defy this truth. I fight it. It's a compulsive decision, a gut reaction: I think I've no choice but to fight, because this truth would destroy me!

Battle after battle I struggle to the extreme of my ability; and battle after battle, I lose. Truth triumphs. It is, then, a painful fight, marked by a series of my failures. Truth is Truth, changeless, indifferent to my most mighty effort. Against Truth I spend all my resources. I exhaust myself. I grow hurt and weary and defeated.

This personal, earnest fight—stage by stage descending into the Truth—is a part of the process of grieving. Grief may begin as "passive," "reactive," the pure pain of a sundered relationship; but then there follow these spasms of an "active" grief.

And what is the Truth my sinful self denies? Why, that I am limited. That there's only so much Walt—and the little there is, is helpless, pitiful, and soon to die. I am finite. And when I experience evidence of my finitude, I hate it.

And ironically, my struggle to prove myself strong—to which I commit the whole of my resources—proves me weak, in fact, when my resources are exhausted. If I fight to the end of my ability, then ability is revealed to *have* an end. O Walt! Thou art so tiny! Thou art born to a few days, full of trouble, the flower that must wither, the shadow that fleeth away: thou art dust.

My defeat, then, is altogether in myself and of myself and to myself. Truth need do nothing but *be*. God does not assault us or cause us sorrows in order to draw us back to him. God, rather, waits—waits upon us, waits to show mercy unto us. I, all on my own account, strive against the wall of truth. I sweat and exert my little dust as though it were a deity—and in that very exertion discover . . . dust.

I can't win.

And the pain of my active grieving will be exactly equal to the intensity with which I believed I could win. As strongly as I cling to that Old Lie (*Ye shall not surely die*) even so strong is the pain of losing it, the pain of having it torn from my fingers, my mind, and the core of my heart. To the degree that I gripped the lie, grief will seem a violence; to the degree that I loved it, grief will be deep sorrow. It is my self destroyed in this process.

I simply can't win.

Ah, but I *do* win.

Because what am I now if not a god? Oh, dear Jesus!—I am a child. Helpless, needy, weak, returning to thee, and by thee to the kingdom of heaven! I am the prodigal, come to myself and coming home again. Home again.

This is the purpose of grieving, then:

Within the pale of earthly experience, always to turn the bereaved back to life. The widow cannot remain forever by the grave, nor the divorcé forever before the wreckage of his marriage. They cannot in health continue to exist with the raw, unhealed wound of a vital separation. The goodness of their grieving is that it brings them by stages into the stream of the living again, however slowly, however painfully. It reveals bit by bit the fullness of this death—as each is able to receive it—and when reality is accepted and assimilated, when the wound heals, it urges them into relationships again, which is our earthly life.

And this too is the purpose of grieving:

In the same manner (it is the same experience, but now on a cosmic scale) to turn all those bereaved of the primal, divine relationship back to God, to his love and to that Life that cannot be taken away from them, forever.

This is joy most serene. And lo: it cometh out of sorrow.

12 The Pattern of Grief

D eep inside the church the telephone's ringing. I can hear it
even as I unlock the front doors.

It's a little church. Nobody's home in the morning but me. No
one'll answer that phone but me.

So I yank the door open, bound up six steps into the sanctuary,
turn, and rush up the aisle. My office is right of the chancel—a tiny
room just twice the size of my desk.

"Hello?" I shout into the receiver. I puff for breath. "Hello?"

A woman gasps, "Oh!" she murmurs, then falls silent.

It's September. It's Wednesday, the middle of the week. There's
nothing penciled on my calendar. I plan to do paper work in my
office.

"This is Grace Church," I say. "Can I help you? Hello?"

"I'm sorry," the woman says. "Pastor, I'm terribly sorry."

"Mary, is that you?"

"I let it ring," she says, "but I don't mean to interrupt something.
But it's important. But you sound—" her voice trails away, abashed
"—busy."

"No, no, don't worry about it. What's the matter?"

"Oh!" she gasps again. "Well—"

Mary Moore is tenderhearted, civil to a fault, meek with regard to

148

herself (though for the sake of her children she can be a warrior), and exceedingly self-conscious. At the moment I suppose her hesitation is due to her character and my sudden gruffness.

"Mary, don't mind me. I just got here. I'm not doing anything. What is it? Why did you call?"

But as she speaks I learn that there are other reasons for the hesitation.

"We're at the hospital, Gloria and I. And Marie too," she says slowly, making up her mind to go on. "And Sonny Boy," she says. "They started surgery maybe fifteen minutes ago. And what it is . . . I think we need you. Pastor, I'm sorry. I'm taking it on myself to call you. Gloria doesn't know. But she's in a bad way. She says she's doing fine, but she isn't. It's what Sonny Boy said to her. So then, that's why I let it ring. Do you think you could come?"

"No one told me there was a surgery this week."

"Well, that's right. I'm sorry."

"Is it an emergency?"

"Well, that too. Yes. And Gloria is so anxious."

"They're operating on Gloria?"

"Oh, no! No, on Sonny Boy."

For just an instant I find myself frowning, trying to remember. "Sonny Boy?" I say.

"Well, see, that's part of the problem. It's Sonny Boy. He's proud, you know. He didn't want people to know."

"Mary, who *is* Sonny Boy?"

"Well, and that's the other reason too, you know. He's not a member of Grace. So we didn't want to burden you—"

"Mary."

"Yes?"

"Truly and truly, you don't have to be sorry, and this is no burden. Please tell me who Sonny Boy is."

There is an almost stricken pause. I love Mary Moore. I have loved her since I came to this congregation and became the beneficiary of her extreme gentleness. I wish she would accept my love as perfect freedom, vast freedom and honor, and never be ill at ease with me.

Now she speaks the entire message. "Leroy James Hopson. They call him Sonny Boy," she whispers. "He's our uncle, Gloria's and mine—but he's all the daddy she ever had. We're at Deaconess Hospital. It's his heart. We really thought we could manage, but I don't think so, on account of the terrible thing he said to Gloria this morning—just when they carried him into the operating room. I know that Sonny Boy is not a member of the congregation, but," her voice is barely audible, "please come."

❦

Grief begins as soon as some bereavement is perceived to be real; the perception *is* the reality, whether the break has actually happened or not. Even when a break is only imminent, but fiercely imagined because it is as fiercely feared, grief begins. Gloria, we shall see, has already begun to grieve. If Sonny Boy doesn't die, the process will stop. If he does, why, the beginning of grief was at the moment the doors swung shut upon the operating room, cutting her from her daddy. Likewise, a diagnosis of "terminally ill" triggers grief. Even a lie (as gossip carries lies, suggesting to one friend that another friend betrayed her) causes immediate grief.

Grief is a personal, distressed reaction to bereavement.

Grief is pain.

The pain is *caused* by the sundering of one relationship, but it is *registered* in many (if not all) of the remaining relationships, which are strained or abused, troubled or stunned thereby. Internally, our emotions suffer the stress; our bodily functions are affected; our mental agility, our perceptions of reality, our spiritual balance all can become confused. Externally the pain affects our behavior with other people, so that those closest to us not only sense our grief but feel the pain as well. Surely, they may sympathize with us, but more than that, we hurt them. We may ignore them, nag them, abuse them, exhaust them; but then, because we feel our grief-pain within the relationship that we have with them, we may blame our friends for causing our hurt. Thus, we often misdirect our angers.

But the pain of grief is not merely a reactive sensation. It is also (as we said in the previous chapter) the pain of strenuous activity. Spontaneously, we strive to adjust to the straightened circumstance.

Any death must change us. Grief is, first, the raw awareness of that change, but then it becomes a terrific struggle: a violent disputing of the facts, a striving for life again, a revising of the terms by which we know ourselves, a sometime surrender to despair, and finally a conscious acceptance of the change—in which *we* change. This is a labor, burdensome, aching, and painful. But it can accomplish a blessed rebirth in the griever.

Grief, therefore—though it cripple us so completely that it seems endless while we suffer it—grief has an end: both a goal and an ending.

It is a natural, spontaneous *process* of healing. Even as a broken bone, by no thought of our own but by the nature of bones, commences to mend, so the soul broken by death starts step by step to heal. As a process, grieving has an identifiable *pattern*. It's not a mystery. All grieving (no matter the dying that caused it) can be understood according to certain broadly defined stages. And even the *purpose* of each stage can in general be explained.

Of course, each griever's experience will be unique. And she can feel, in the event itself, frightfully lonely and bewildered. And pain may persuade her that this grief is the evil. In fact, death is the evil, not grief. And we, who are her friends, will know this; we, who choose to become her comforters, will learn the general pattern of the process, the purposes of each stage of grief, so that we might name her wounds and companion her sorrows till grief has brought her back to life and wholly to us again.

❦

Ta-tock-a, ta-tock-a: a starched nurse is leading me down the corridor. She walks so fast, turns so sharply, that I follow behind her. The walls are pale green and geometric. The light is fluorescent, bloodless. The sound of this woman's heels on a hard floor is like short gunshots: *ta-tock-a!*

Leroy James Hopson.

Sonny Boy.

I think I met him once. At a wedding. Buddy's wedding, wasn't it? Buddy is Mary Moore's son. That would make Leroy James, let's see, his great uncle.

The nurse corners into another hallway. *Ta-tock-a, ta-tock-a*: past doors perfectly similar, same, same, same. My tread is silent. Sneakers and jeans. Except that I carry a communion set and a Testament, I scarcely look like a pastor. This nurse is not convinced by such signs. *Ta-tock-a!* She imagines pastors to come in suits. But I hadn't planned this visit this morning.

Ta-tock!

She stops at a door, raps once, opens it, and stands aside to admit me.

"The O.R. waiting room," she says. "Family Lounge."

Well, if this is a lounge it makes no concession to comfort. It's a tiny cube, a windowless room lit by one standing lamp. Here are three women, two on a couch that faces the door, and one on a chair in the corner.

"The Hopson family, right?" my nurse demands. I suppose I've been hesitating.

Mary Moore rises from the couch. "Oh, Pastor!" This dear woman takes two steps to me and hugs me in the doorway.

Gloria Ferguson, on the other hand, remains on the couch, glaring at me. Her dark eyes seem wary and accusing. Her mouth is pinched.

To the left of the couch, on a wooden chair, sits tiny Marie Landers, Gloria's mother, Sonny Boy's sister, a mite of a woman looking lost, moving her mouth in a soundless dialogue.

"Pastor, thank you. Oh, thank you," Mary murmurs against my breast.

"Excuse me! The Hopson family, right?" This poor nurse wants closure. We're standing in her doorway.

"Actually," I say, "none of them's named Hopson." It's a mild joke, but no one chuckles. Gloria's eyes drop to the communion set, and she frowns: *Why did you bring that?*

"Excuse me!" The nurse makes her voice go crack like her heel.

"Oh! Oh, dear!" Mary Moore gives a bleat and backs up. I take one step in. The nurse shuts the door and, *ta-tock-a, ta-tock-a,* departs in the bowels of the hospital.

Mary sits down beside her cousin. I extend my hand. "Gloria? How are you?" With her left hand she touches the tip of my finger. She drops her smoky eyes. She says nothing.

What did I do to make her mad? Come too late? I couldn't have come any sooner.

Now I sit on a plastic chair facing the couch.

I say, "This must be hard on you, Gloria."

Suddenly Marie Landers stiffens as if she's been shot. Her face snaps upward. "BY-PASS SURGERY!" she shouts. "BY-PASS SURGERY!" She blinks rapidly at her own declaration.

Neither Mary nor Gloria looks at her. I do. "Hello, Marie."

Almost always this tiny woman is smiling and bobbing and ready for laughter. When "moved by the Spirit," she says, in church, she can raise her arms and holler, "Amen! Alleluia!" But right now there's a startled fear in her eye. "Sonny Boy," she whispers to me, "is having by-pass surgery."

I look at Gloria. "Is that the procedure, then?"

She doesn't answer.

Mary slips an arm around her shoulders. "The doctor found several blockages," she says. Eternally, Mary will ease all ills. "He says it's not unusual, right Gloria? He says Sonny Boy's chances are excellent, right?"

Gloria's lowered eyes are smouldering. Her lips are pinched. She must be furious.

I say, "I'm sorry I'm late."

Mary says, "Oh, Pastor, you're not late."

I say, "I should have been here to pray with you before Sonny Boy went to surgery."

"Gloria prayed."

"Ah, good. Yes, then you surely prayed," I say. Because Gloria prays wonderfully, with passion and rich conviction. She storms heaven, as it were, convinced that heaven cannot refuse her. She is a thunder upward. But there is no prayer in her burning eyes now. And I seem the focus of some offense. What did I do?

Gloria Ferguson has deep black skin and raven hair pulled back from her brow. It's bound in a knot, below which it explodes down her back. The flesh of her forehead is taut.

"And God will answer your prayer," I say, smiling. "Think of the doctors and nurses as angels, ministers who do the will of the Lord. They are healing your uncle right now—"

Gloria lifts her hands and covers her face. She's softening. I pursue the advantage. "When did the operation start?"

Mary answers. "An hour ago."

"Not bad," I murmur. "It's common for surgeries like this to last three hours. We'll wait. I'll stay with you."

Mary squeezes her cousin's shoulders. She says, "Gloria's been here since five this morning." Sweet Mary, full of pity.

Gloria begins to shake her head.

I lean forward. "Listen," I say. "There must be a hundred people praying for Sonny Boy. The church. The surgical team. Us. And

Sonny Boy himself is in there fighting. Think of that! His will to live is so important—"

Mary whispers, "Pastor!" almost pleadingly.

Gloria lowers her head.

"Yes!" I say. "Sonny Boy's will to live is critical. It can make the difference—"

Mary hisses, "Pastor! You don't know what he said to her!"

"I know that he's not an old man," I say. This is my ministry. This sort of comforting is the thing I do. "I know he's young enough to love life. How old is he?"

Mary snatches a quick glance at Gloria. "Sixty?"

"Sixty!" I say. "See? There's long life in a man of sixty. He's strong. Your uncle can stand a little cutting—"

"Pastor *Wangerin!*" Gloria is glaring at me with black fire. "Oh, *Pastor!*" She's furious. "*Not* strong. Not strong at all. So damned *tired.*"

Poor Mary removes her arm, stung to silence. She saw this coming, and I did not.

Gloria draws a trembling breath. "What do you know about his spells," she cries. "Nothin'. You don't know nothin'. Well, his spells weary him to misery. An' you never seen him climb the stairs, how he collapses on the top step, and he grabs his chest, and he wheezes. I'm the one that holds him. Me. And every time he moves too fast, I think he's going to drop and die. Oh, *Pastor!*" Her eyes are filling with angry tears. "He ain't strong. What he is—he's scared. It's the only reason he said Yes to bein' cut. He's scared he's goin' to die at home. Not strong! Tired! He so damn tired he's willin' to be cut with the knife—"

"Gloria," says Mary. "Gloria, Gloria, hush now—"

Mary Moore has begun to cry.

Gloria sneers at me: "Will to live—huh! Fightin' for his life— huh! You don't know his heart. I do. I know what he said at the door—"

"Hush, hush, hush, Gloria—" To me Mary says, "You see, ever since she was little bitty, it was Sonny Boy took care of her. Even when he went to the army, he signed part of his pay to her. I'm telling the truth: Sonny Boy can be stingy, but never with Gloria. He always took care of Gloria. You see, this is her daddy in the operating room."

Mary has a soft brown cheek, not so dark as Gloria's. The cousins are two sorts of tree bark, oak and beech. "I'm sorry, Gloria," I whisper. "I'm sorry. I make so many mistakes."

Mary says, "Have you ever met Sonny Boy?"

"I think so," I say. "Was he at Buddy's wedding?"

Mary blooms with a conciliating smile. "Yes!" she says.

Well, then: I have the memory of a cream-white suit and a dazzling, audacious man.

"Is he short?" I ask.

"Short, whip-thin. Vigorous. Knows his own mind. Ain't no one can tell him otherwise. That right, Gloria? Leastwise, not till now, when everything's turning around. Right, Gloria?"

Mary puts her arm around her cousin again. Gloria releases a long sigh. Her eyes are closed.

"Now the time has come," says Mary, "that he needs her. He's in the hospital—"

"By-pass surgery!" Marie Landers booms from the corner. She raises an arm aloft. "An' I got here before they tuck 'im in!"

"Yes, Mamma," Gloria sighs. "Yes."

"Mary brought me in time!"

"Yes, Mamma."

Gloria lowers her head to Mary's shoulder, so tired, it seems, so unable. Mary rocks her, rocks her, cousins, good friends, sisters.

Gloria begins to speak with a slurring sadness: "Was dark when I got here this morning. Was him an' me. I walked into the room, and he said, 'Baby, pull up a chair.' I pulled up a chair and sat beside his bed and leaned down and looked into his eyes. Tur-able, tur-able eyes. He didn't quit lookin' at me. But neither did I want him to quit. Sonny Boy don't display his feelings. He don't tell his love." She presses her face against the shoulder of her cousin. "But he loves me."

Gloria Ferguson is beautiful. A rich coffee color. A sorrow as dark as Nigeria.

She talks softly now: "Sonny Boy said, 'I'm glad you come, baby,' an' I patted his hand, and he didn't deny me. I said, 'You scared?' He said, 'Yes.' I said, 'You want to back out now?' He thought about that, then he said, 'No, baby. No.' He was lookin' direckly at me with his tur-able eyes. 'Can't a man be livin' this way no more, just half a man,' he said.

"Pastor?"

Suddenly Gloria is looking at me.

"Yes?"

"I'm sorry I yelled. It ain't your fault. I'm jittery."

"Oh, Gloria!" I feel such a tremendous urge to hug this woman. But her eyes slide to the side, and she continues. "So I patted his hand. So the sun come up. So we didn't say no more. Soon Mary came with Mamma, and it was time, and we prayed together. But Sonny Boy—"

Gloria sits erect. She wrings her hands. Mary had to remove her arm.

"Sonny Boy," says Gloria. "He said one more thing to me."

"It's okay," says Mary. "He didn't mean it."

"But you heard him, didn't you?"

"Yes."

"He pulled me down, Mary. He put my ear at his mouth. He meant it."

"Well, maybe he meant it, but there's no way he can know it."

"A person knows."

"No. Only God knows."

Gloria presses the heels of her hands against her forehead and speaks between her wrists. "So they wheeled him down the hallway, and I walked by him. Holding his hand. He didn't deny me that. He looked so little under the sheet. And thin. And scared. And so damn tired—"

"ALL US HOPSONS IS LITTLE!" shouts her mother in the corner.

"And then," says Gloria, still hiding her eyes in her hands, "just before they pushed him through the doors, he pulled me down. He put his face against my cheek. He said, 'Baby—'"

Gloria lifts her face to the ceiling suddenly. Her eyes are glittering, her breath labored. But she will, by heaven, *say* what Sonny Boy said to her. Mary Moore has began to cry again.

"He said to me, 'Baby, I'm goin' on in here to die, now.' Mary?" Gloria looks at her cousin. "Mary? Did you hear him?"

"I heard him," says Mary. She turns to Gloria. They look at each other. "I heard you too," she says. "And you said the perfect thing. You said, 'Be a good boy and do what they tell you to do.' Oh, Gloria, he *knows* how much you love him. It's *medicine*, honey, how much you love him."

"An' I kissed him, Mary," Gloria whispers through her ruined throat. "Just before they took him in, I kissed his pretty cheek. He didn't deny me, Mary. He didn't deny me that."

❦

Gloria—whose struggle to understand is like swimming in wild waters—Gloria is grieving.

She is a single soul, unique. There's nobody like her. Her grief, then, will take its own peculiar turns. On the other hand, she's traveling a path we all have traveled since leaving Eden: her journey isn't altogether unpredictable. Surely, she may skip a stage if it proves unnecessary for her; but we'll be able to recognize the shortcut because we have a map.

Human grieving is a personal development, the private drama in which one moves through specific "acts," actions, intense activities. An act, by its finishing, causes the next. There is reason to the sequence, though the griever may feel bewilderment only; and there *is* motion, though she feels caught in a single emotion. And since this is healing, always and always, there is hope.

THE FIRST ACT OF GRIEF—

—is, seemingly, not to act.

If the relationship broken is not an absolutely essential one, the pain of the break may be immediate and equal to the relationship's perceived significance. When a piece of the person dies, the rest of her hurts, calling sudden attention to the cut: *Can I fix it?* And, panicking, *Can I fix it fast?*

But if the relationship was indeed essential and the break, therefore, traumatic, the sensation of pain may stall a while, numbing the cut and protecting the bereaved: mercifully, she may neither feel nor know the full nature of the injury. She is in shock. She seems, in regard to this pain, inactive.

Actually something inside her may be very busy preparing the griever (even now this is grief) consciously to confront her death. She's marshaling emotional forces, as it were. When they are ready, the pain that had waited will come with all its strength, even long after the event.

Curiously, she may swing back and forth between knowledge and ignorance, between feeling and numbness, sometimes knowing, sometimes not, sometimes anguished, sometimes performing exactly the right responses to her situation, but feeling nothing at all.

But finally she must know. Finally she suffers in fact. And then, by degrees, the passive grieving issues into intense activity.

THE SECOND ACT OF GRIEF

What she learns in this dying is more than one dying. What she learns may seem monstrous to her: that all relationships are as vulnerable as this one was; that things she had depended upon are suddenly not dependable; that the world, unstable, is also unloving, unreasonable, arbitrary, dangerous.

That she has little, if any, authority over the world, little and less power within herself.

That she is not in control.

Death is the evidence, and pain the persuader: she is not (we are not) god.

She who can die is finite. We are all, in every respect, finite.

So the sensation of a particular pain has inaugurated a pain more metaphysical. The destruction of the "self" that one had imaged and believed in is an ache deep, deep in the bone. Gloria Ferguson, waiting for news of her uncle, may see in his trouble the possible collapse of a world and therein the loss of her own effective identity. This is too much to take without a fight.

So the second act of grieving is active indeed. The griever defies the facts—fights against what *Is*.

To what degree do grievers fight? To what degree, therefore, do they anguish? Well, here are differences. Some kick hard against the goads. Some surrender quietly and easily. Each shall fight to the degree that he had truly desired to be, and truly believed he was, his own sufficiency. Each shall anguish to the degree that he clings to the lie, *Ye shall not surely die.* For the fight is to preserve these things still, to snatch them from the hands of what *Is*.

(This is an important word of comfort: if we have denied ourselves to follow Jesus, if we have already died that death, the dying of grief shall be infinitely easier for us!)

But we who choose to fight what *Is*—to fight convictions of our ultimate limitation—are limited. That is what *Is*. Therefore, fighting with all our mights, we will fail. Each battle is marked by its failure.

Nonetheless, we may engage in battle, attacking with each of three parts of our human selves. . . .

With all our strength: Simply, we oppose our *will* to this present Secondary Dying and all it represents. Against reason and evidence, like children, we deny the death. Lo, we are not broken—just because we say we're not.

There's no divorce here. I refuse to consider such a thing.

I have not lost my job.

My son is not in prison; he'll be home any day now.

The strategy of the fight at first is mere denial. But what is *Is*, and in time our strength to say it is *Not* is exhausted. Willfulness fails.

There is an element of the heroic in grief's struggle; we are persistent, and having failed in one attack, we try another. . . .

With all our heart: We oppose next the pure potency of personal *emotion* to the death and all it must force us to accept. As if it changed what *Is*, we rage against the dying. Anger feels like an empowerment (it's a feeling that swallows the feeling of impotence a while). Fury (so strong in the widow it astonishes her) seems almost equal to death.

I hate the futility of all my labor.

I hate you, who betrayed me—who beat me, divorced me, or merely lied to me.

I hate the system that treated me treacherously and remorselessly.

The strategy is the anger itself. But what is *Is*, and we shall spend ourselves against it until we are spent indeed.

But up again, up with a difference, up and attack with our last personal resource. . . .

With all our mind: Finally we oppose that which in us is peculiarly human, our rational faculty, our restless effort to solve problems, our *reason*.

Again, we attack the evidence. We apply conditional arguments to an unconditional situation, actually trying to reconstruct the world: "If," we say "I do such and such a thing, my beloved will not die." Or, after the fact, we seriously declare: "If only she'd stayed home that night—" and in our minds do truly imagine the possibility, living it even as we speak it "—she would be here today."

Intellectually we conceive of a thousand "If-only's" and do dwell a while in their alternatives.

Or like Job we approach the Creator himself to dispute things, mind to Mind. There's a momentary sense of control: "I may be broken, but will find that higher plane at which this world shall seem a dream to me." By elevating the mind we try to leave hard fact behind. We ascend to the consolations of philosophy: "There's another existence, more rational than this."

At its crudest, the strategy has been called bargaining.

At its noblest, human reason seems infinite—but it only *seems* so because it deals in abstractions and musings, things without corners. Against one fact even the mind must fail.

Finally we shall have fought what *Is* with our whole beings, and so it is our being itself that is proven a failure. Finite. That which cannot be explained to us in words alone has enforced itself upon us by experience: has revealed itself *within* us. This *is* us, terminal, dying.

The lie was a lie after all. We have "come to ourselves."

Grief now shows a dismal vista. This defeat may seem to us the end of everything.

THE THIRD ACT OF GRIEF

There is nothing left for the griever but to gaze upon what *Is*, both the immediate sundering and the doom it has revealed in existence itself. Simply, she is sad.

This is the stage of a solemn inertia.

And here is a new level of pain: the confessed conclusion of human effort, her concession to failure. This pain is called despair.

Others label it "depression," but I ask the harder word because the quality that characterizes grieving now is *hopelessness*. There is no hope; and since hope is our touch to the future, there seems no future either. This third act, though it lasts but a while, seems to be the way the world will be—forever.

In this act the griever again appears willfully passive, doing nothing. She gives up: surrender. She gives up: *sheol*, the pit. Now grief has confronted the unvarnished, unpalliated truth, and no illusion. Lo, death attends absolutely every party.

And the griever expects nothing to follow.

But this void is itself a preparation. For when something follows after all, the griever can do nothing but receive it purely as gift—unexpected, you see, unpurchased, undeserved. Grace!

No sermon could have accomplished this thing. Experience only: it is the personal conviction that we've come to an end that makes any new thing astounding to us. It is the deep conviction of our helplessness that makes any new life hereafter a genuine mercy of God.

We needed truly to sorrow, in order truly to rejoice.

THE FOURTH ACT OF GRIEF—

—may have two parts, the first one secular, the second divine.

Acceptance: Slowly (weeks, months, years) the realization dawns that we are still living. And we are viewing life after all—after all our complete convictions of gloom. There was a tomorrow; it is today; and we *are*. We truly had not expected yet to be. This is news!

We've been purged of illusions, to be sure. We recognize the limitations of all our relationships, and so of ourselves. But we do exist today; and our new wisdom is to celebrate what *Is*, even knowing the proper proportion of things. This day (not the "forever" we had hungered) is beautiful simply because this day *Is*, though it didn't *have* to be. This present moment is a gift.

And look: though will and emotion and reason are clearly limited faculties, they are faculties still, working and healthy. They can no longer be rulers, indeed: but they may be effective servants, used with moderation and sanity. They are our self. We live.

We won't be the same after grief. A certain innocence (whether silly or sinful) is gone. And pain has left a scar that must qualify us forever. But perhaps we won't allow the Tempter to lie to us any more either: only the gullible can think he is godlike.

No longer believing the lie, we can return with truer sight to life again. Even so far may every human come, whether one believes in God or not.

But for those who believe, who know of the Primal Dying, there may be one more episode in the fourth act of grieving. . . .

Resurrection: Grief has purged us of the very premise of our pride; and it was pride (remember?) that had severed us first from God.

Grief, the experience of failures (not the hearing of the ear, but the seeing of the eye and the rough discipline of death) has persuaded us that we are creatures after all and that everything will finally defraud us—except God. Only God is God.

That confession gives us the right perspective: we look *up* to God, creatures *up* to their Creator. In the third act of grieving, God may have seemed indifferent to us. Terrifying, even. His righteousness during that act struck us with our guilt.

For those who believe, then, the despair of the third act holds horrors the secular world might consider excessive. But pity the secular world! For we are being prepared not just for *this* life again but for forgiveness and grace at its most glorious.

The highest joy of the fourth act is beyond a secular comprehension.

It is this, that God does not impose the sentence we know we deserve. The seemingly indifferent God is a Father after all, who hugs us, who slips rings on our fingers and shoes on our feet and food in our mouths, who kills the calf and throws a party—the dance to which Death never shall come.

In the days of our personal majesty, we would not have seen a Father. We could see nothing but an enemy and cosmic hostility.

But in the days of our humility, any gesture from God is dear. Any gesture. How stunning is love, then. And how unspeakably glorious is life everlasting, relationship with the Source of Life even beyond our Corporeal Dyings and into eternity.

This drama of grieving, able so to transform us and lay us like children upon the bosom of God again—this grief rightly we call good.

13 Notes to Those Who Would Comfort the Griever

P astor? Pastor?"
    "Yes?"
"Have you ever seen Sonny Boy dance?"
"Dance?"
"Well, I guess not. You two don't move in the same circles."
"I think I did actually see him once, Mary. And he might have danced that night. But no. No, never."
"Oh, Pastor, one day you should see Sonny Boy *dance*."

Mary has a voice that tends toward spirituals and poetry, yet she frequently seems abashed by strong moods or by sentiment.

She has four children; her children have children. She handles babies at Fulton Clinic with calm efficiency. She has to be both stalwart and realistic and tough in a world that loves neither her nor her family much. Nevertheless, there's poetry in her nature. She bends her head to beauty as if she heard the angels rustle. I love her for loving things.

And I pay attention.

From her generous depths the word comes: *"Dance."*

Dark Gloria, whose head is bowed, nods.

And in the corner Gloria's mother murmurs, "Mm-hmm, he's a hom-dinger." All three women are in harmony on this issue.

Paper cups of cold coffee sit at our feet. Coats heap the chair beside me. The room can't be darker than it was because it has no window, but the passage of time makes it seem darker.

Leroy James Hopson has been in surgery for three hours.

Yes I remember! I saw him, yes, at Buddie's wedding. I'm sure of it. I was the pastor presiding. I recall that I turned at the altar and saw, in the midst of the congregation, a man in a cream-white suit.

Coat and vest and pants and a wide-brimmed hat were all richly, audaciously white. The band on his hat and the bud in his lapel were a similar pink. The face of the man was grinning. A dapper little man, straight up in the pew, his head tipped back, presuming himself the focus of public attention, a celebrity. When he saw me see him, his eyebrow lifted a slight degree and his lips parted to reveal the most dazzling, snow-white teeth I'd ever seen. And if there was any doubt whether the smile was meant for me, the man raised a hand and *saluted* me. In church. Without removing the hat.

"Mm-hmm," said Marie. "He's a hom-dinger."

And Mary remembers: "They'd always end at Fly's, you know, him and his friends. And Fly's'd be jammed, and the jukebox music, and the smell of liquor and pomade and Chanel Number Five."

Marie hums her memory: "Mmmmm."

Gloria is silent.

"And there'd come the moment—"

Suddenly Mary sits erect. "Pastor, he's not a big man, but he's well-knit. And there's a flash in him can grab the rowdiest weekend crowd. D'you know what I mean? There'd come a moment when Sonny Boy'ud push back the tiny table and stand up, and someone would say, 'My *man!*' and then all the chairs and tables were snatched aside to make space in the center, and all the faces made a ring around Sonny Boy."

Gloria's head is bowed and her eyes closed. This I know: right now she is a young woman at Fly's on a Friday night, and her uncle is natty and healthy and ready.

Mary whispers, "He'd smile first."

Gloria nods.

Mary says, "He'd kill you with that smile. Oh, he's proud of his pretty teeth. Well, so he'd smile and slouch, you know, through first chords of a juke tune, and maybe slush his feet a little. A low laugh'ud ripple around the room, gettin' ready. Kill them with the smile, kill them with the wait: they couldn't stand it. Sonny Boy knew. Even when he was drunk.

"Gloria, remember? Remember, baby? All at once—ha ha ha! All at once he'd drop his shoulder, Mm! He'd tighten his spine, he'd snap his hands on high, he'd clap, Mm, mm! Remember, honey? Suddenly, like a top, the man was unwinding: smoothest, sweetest, sassiest, click of a tap-dance, Mmmm! Oh, Pastor! Tiny feet as quick as crickets. The music is fast, but Sonny Boy's faster, spinning, chattering with his toes, popping his hip. Oh, he would crouch and drag that heel across the floor, then leap to a whirling motion. He *smoked,* and the people would shout with laughter. They couldn't stand it. They clapped, and he threw back his head and laughed and danced and danced—"

Bang! The door swings open and hits my chair.

Gloria jumps.

"Hopsons?" The nurse has thrust her face into the lounge. "Is this the Hopsons?"

"No," says Mary. "Yes!" she cries.

I rise to let the woman in.

"No, no," she says. "Don't move. Just checking." She departs: *ta-tock-a, ta-tock-a.*

I really do not like that sound.

There follows a silence. We're not in Fly's any more, and Sonny Boy isn't dancing.

But Mary says, "Well, he would lift his arms like a buzzard's wings—"

"Mary!" Gloria's face is up and hard.

"What?"

"That was long ago."

"But you never lose your love for dancing."

"He's tired. Man can't climb the stairs without collapsing."

"They're healing him, Gloria."

"They're cuttin' on him. They're cuttin' his heart."

"But they can't," says Mary, "cut out his love."

Gloria pinches her lips and doesn't answer.

"Not his love for dancing," says Mary, looking directly at her cousin. "Not his love for a person."

Gloria stares at the door behind me.

"Do you remember the Tradesmen's Ball, Gloria?" Mary's language is very precise now. "This year? Not all that long ago?"

Gloria nods once.

"Did Sonny Boy dance then?"

"You know he did," Gloria snaps.

"And did women in long gowns want to dance with him?"

Gloria's mouth tugs toward a pout.

"But who did he choose?" says Mary.

"Well."

"Yes, and didn't he *bow* to his Gloria and smile with his pretty teeth? Wasn't it Gloria and Sonny Boy who swept the floor?"

"Well."

"And what did they play? What did you two dance then?"

"Jitterbug."

"Right! I knew you'd remember! No more'n a year ago. Think of that. And the lights were low, and people watching, and what did the jitterbug turn into then?"

Gloria has allowed a true remembering to soften her face. She smiles. "The two-step," she says. She has so rich a complexion. "And the two-step," she volunteers, "became a waltz."

"Girl, what a memory you got! Is Sonny Boy planning to attend the Tradesmen's again this year?"

"Yes," says Gloria.

And Mary whispers, "You see? They can't cut out his love, not for dancing, not for his daugher, not for his girl, no."

This time when the door opens, no one jumps. Neither does it hit my chair. It swings in cautiously, and after it a tall, cadaverous man steps into the lounge. He's dressed in green, his shoes and his hair in green cloth, the surgical mask at his throat, green. There is a fine spray of blood across his breast. The dots are black. This man glances at my face, my jeans, my face again.

"Oh!" Mary Moore gives a tiny bleat and rises. "This is the doctor," she says to me, and to him, "our pastor. I called him—" Her voice subsides. The reason for speaking at all seems to be fading in her heart.

The surgeon lifts his arm and rubs the back of his neck.

Mary sits again and grabs Gloria's hand.

Marie Landers has begun to rock. She's making a low sound in her nose. A humming—as if she is too busy to listen to others just now.

"Well," says the surgeon, "the operation lasted longer than we expected. I'm sorry. And I'm not sure what to tell you—"

Silence. Not even a breath stirs in the room.

"It is possible," the surgeon says, "that Mr. Hopson suffered an infarction just previous to surgery. Heart attack. Minutes before we opened his chest."

Marie Landers hums louder.

The surgeon continues: "I want you to know that everything went exactly as we'd planned it—" For the first time he seeks someone's eyes; but Gloria's are stuck to the blood on his shirt. Mary gives him attention, and he seems grateful. He says, "We're asking Mr. Hopson's heart to respond, to take over and beat on its own. Do you understand? But the muscle is so . . . damaged. Mrs. Ferguson, we have some options—"

But Gloria is glaring at the blood on his shirt.

Mary Moore says, "Options?"

"Yes. We will try them all," says the lanky surgeon. "Right now the team is doing everything it can, I promise you. And as soon as he responds, I'll come back. Okay?"

Even Mary has dropped her eyes.

This young fellow seems to need an answer. "Okay?" he repeats.

So I say, "Okay," and he gives me a grateful look and backs out of the room.

I really hate this "family lounge." Windowless, bleak, unkind, and unsupplied! There is no Kleenex here for tears.

Mary and Gloria are fixed in postures of confusion. Gloria's mamma is rocking on a straight-legged chair with a wordless fury, humming.

"Mary?" I say.

She turns her eyes to me.

"Gloria? Mary? Do you mind if I pray now?"

Mary says, passionately, "Please do."

Gloria says nothing. She looks as if she's still staring at the blood.

I fold my hands and lower my head. "Jesus, we need you," I whisper. "Don't leave us now. And Sonny Boy needs you. Heal him. Strengthen him. Save his life. Please bring him—"

"Ah!" I hear a strangled sound. Then a shriek: "*Pastor, Pastor, Pastor!*"

Gloria's crying out. She has suddenly snapped to a rigid position, flat from her skull to her toes, but she's staring with terror down toward her feet.

"My *legs!*" she screams. "Pastor, my *legs!*"

Her legs are as hard as ax handles.

"Gloria, what's the matter?"

"Oh, Pastor, they hurt! My legs hurt!"

They are vibrating in a sort of spasm, and Gloria's beginning to slide down from the couch. Her dress hikes up her thighs. The muscle above the knee is solid. The shoes shake off. Gloria's toes are splayed apart, cramping.

I move forward and kneel beside her. I grab her legs under my left arm and lift them and snatch a wastebasket, flip it and place it beneath her heels like a footstool.

"It's all right, Gloria, all right, all right—"

She's hinging at the hips. Now with both arms I drive her back and up, till she is sitting; and with my fingers I begin to massage the wooden muscle.

"They hurt!" she wails. "Pastor, they hurt so bad."

"I know, I know. Close your eyes. Breathe as deeply as you can. *Mary!* Get a nurse. Baby lotion! And tell them for God's sake to find some Kleenex for this room!"

Mary vanishes.

Poor Gloria, so frightened by her own body that she breaks my heart. And she truly tries to breathe deeply. She is shivering.

"Why do they hurt?"

"I don't know."

"Pastor, why do my legs hurt?"

"Maybe because you're scared. Scared to be sad." My forearms ache. "Hush, Gloria." *Hush, my sister. Hush.*

And with all her might she does.

Gloria's coal-black hair is pulled severely back from her forehead. Her eyebrows are up, vulnerable. Her eyes seem incapable of closing, watching me, starting to trust me. She has a small mouth, roundish cheeks. With the heels of my palms I knead her legs up and deep and down and deep, and she does not whimper, and I love her, I love her.

Gloria hushes. So then the only sound in the room is a humming. Oh, pity the tiny Marie! Rocking swiftly on a four-legged chair not built for rocking, forgotten in our haste, she has wrapped her arms around herself and has found a hymn to sing. I stroke my Gloria's terrors in rhythm to this hymn:

Precious Lord, take my hand—

Then Mary returns. And the nurse appears. This woman cocks a professional eye at my massaging. "I can do that," she says.

"No!" I hiss. "You can't." It's my job and my Gloria. "What you can do," I tell her, "is give me the lotion, then go get Kleenex for this heartless room!"

The nurse withdraws.

I pour cool lotion on my sister's legs. She shivers. I rub the swifter to warm it. She closes her eyes. And the knots in her legs begin to loosen.

"Mary?"

"Pastor."

"I'm sorry I yelled at you before."

Mary does not answer me. Instead, she touches me. She lays her hand on my shoulder and keeps it there, forgiving me.

I want to cry.

Marie Landers has not ceased her humming:

Through the storm. Through the night.
Lead me on. To the light—

And so we wait till the surgeon returns to speak another word regarding Sonny Boy, Leroy James Hopson, dapper man, dancer, the smiling celebrity in a cream-white suit.

❦

COMFORTERS: KNOW THE SCRIPT BUT READ THE GRIEVER

Clearly, grievers do not all suffer the same. Some souls stick in the process for years, never coming to any sort of final acceptance. Some souls are healed by the external trappings of mourning more than by the internal transfigurations of failure and ache and renewal. Some glide with a wonderful trust straight past the battles of the second act of grief, arriving quickly at a simple sorrow, the sorrow alone: they bow their heads and are sad. None of these variations, of course, is "wrong."

The script outlined in the previous chapter as the Four Acts of Grieving is not a rule to be followed. Rather, it's a tool for interpretation, so that no one need be baffled by the sometimes outrageous or illogical behaviors of grief, neither friends nor kin nor the griever herself.

But in this chapter I speak especially to those who choose to become care-givers for one on a difficult journey: the griever's comforters. (No matter how close you may be to this person apart from her bereavement, it must be a *choice* to take upon yourself the delicate job of comforting her, a choice made willingly, consciously, with foresight and commitment. Comforting shall require much of the comforter.)

No gesture of grief is isolated. *She* may not know why she does what she does. She may fear that her broken emotions and wild compulsions are evidence of a sort of insanity, sudden, inexplicable, estranged, and isolated. Coming from nowhere. In fact, every gesture and every mood is experienced in the stream of all her grieving, which soon reveals a continuum, a necessary form. The comforter can recognize the form according to general human patterns of behavior. Even if the griever "spirals" through the pattern, repeating certain acts again and again with greater or lesser intensity, yet because the comforter can name the behavior he is himself neither frightened nor useless, but remains a stable element in the midst of chaos.

Comforter, know where she's at in her journey *according to the script*. Though you need teach her nothing right now, you are her knowledge: you yourself have become the "knowing" that assures her of sanity and hope and healing, though she *recognizes* none of these things.

On the other hand, do not impose the script upon her, nor presume to know which act she's in without first reading her behavior. Always take your cues from her. By instinct *she* is leading; in patience you are serving.

And expect anger. Since you will be one most available to her, you'll likely become the target of her moods. (1) Don't demean the mood by disbelieving. *It* is real, even if *you* are not its real cause. But (2) don't take it personally. It is love that offers yourself as the "other" in all her dramas; it is wisdom that knows you are not the "other" at all, but her blessed opportunity, her comforter.

When I met Gloria in the hospital, she wouldn't talk to me. Her eyes had a smoky glaze of rage. I don't think that what I said made any difference. There was no right nor wrong so far as her fury went, because she was angry at Authority Itself, Whoever or Whatever was the cause of this hateful circumstance—and I was the closest thing she had for Authority in the moment. It was my service as her comforter that I should receive the rage without returning it or being wounded by it. (What good is the incapacitated comforter?) It was also my trust that, having exploded, she would change and love me again—especially if the explosion had not offended me and sent me away. My steadfast love must finally prove to her that Love is steadfast, and life continues, and forgiveness heals.

Gloria was struggling in the second act, opposing emotion to an unacceptable possibility, the death of her uncle.

Three hours later she switched the strategy. Now suddenly she set her will against the foe, a dramatic denial of the nearness and imminence of death, because it had just invaded the lounge in the person of the doctor, his surgical "greens," and that spray of Sonny Boy's blood on his shirt.

When Gloria's legs seized up, one might have demanded that she stop acting like a child: "You know there's nothing wrong with your legs." Or one might have panicked at the urgency and weirdness of the crisis. In either case one would have mistaken a good opportunity.

Read the griever: she was, in fact, doing a reasonable thing and at the same time giving her comforters chances to comfort. She was exchanging an impossible pain for a possible one (the mortality of Sonny Boy is overwhelmed, for the moment, by spasms in her legs). She was avoiding the greater horror by finding a lesser, stranger one: "My legs! They hurt!" The comforter does best to accept her perspective (the grimmer facts will reveal themselves soon enough), to be grateful that he now can do something at all (can touch her who so needs touching, but for whom touching can be dangerously ambiguous), to play his role without embarrassment or hesitation (even if it is, in a sense, "role-playing"), and so to love her. To prove himself an ally.

It is in precisely such a moment, when the griever makes the outrageous demand, that the comforter wordlessly declares: *I am here. I will be here. I will companion you, however far we must go together—*

And so, the covenant is established and life engaged in death's despite, by a comforter.

COMFORTERS: PREPARE YOURSELVES

Here is ministry so ancient, so common among us, so eminently human that no one needs post-graduate degrees in counseling or psychology to perform it.

Nevertheless, two preparations are necessary, both for your sake and for the sake of the bereaved. The first is general and ought to be accomplished sometime in your adulthood, whether or not you are ever required to comfort a griever. The second is specific and ought to be accomplished with direct regard to the particular griever you choose to help. Both are your spiritual preparation.

First, make peace with your own death and with Death Itself. Second, purge yourself of any false or selfish motive for consoling this person.

Make peace with death, or the death you confront in comforting may threaten you as much as the griever and trigger in you your own process of grief. You shall be no comforter then, but one in need of comfort—and the blind shall be leading the blind.

I have met the physician who refuses to meet his own death. He's a cold sort. With terminal patients or with families of the deceased, he speaks of professional issues. All is mechanical: it works or it doesn't. It can be fixed or it can't. But between the *can* and the *can't* are percentages only and no human soul. So here is a persistent denial. Seeming so strong as to be unapproachable, this physician in fact is unapproachable because he is weak: fearful he might catch the grin of his own Dying in the face of the bereaved, his limitations, his finitude. Death.

This chilly manner is not, of course, restricted to physicians. There are as well chilly pastors, chilly counselors, parents, spouses, friends.

On the other hand, I've met doctors so overwhelmed by the tragedy of death that they themselves show signs of grief whenever the dying comes near to them. They seem (they are!) most generously human. When the patient weeps, so do they. When the patient hurts, so do they. They offer an ocean of compassion; but it can conceal trouble—like the rage that in a griever is necessary but that in a doctor comes like the shark. These (counselors, pastors, friends, any who would comfort) do not lead. They mimic. They befriend, indeed, but they can't inspire confidence, because they are not confident. They seem to a griever the most sensitive of all who surround her; they feel what she feels; but they know no hope nor serenity nor assurance for the future—and therefore what they do not do is comfort.

The comforter is called to walk a middle ground: to be familiar enough with death (and clear enough regarding his own death) that he can gaze with sincerely compassionate eyes at the grief of the bereaved (they are one on this journey together); and yet, at the same time, to be objective enough about any particular death (to be free *from death*) that he can maintain a leader's distance for the sake of the griever (no, he is not taking the same journey with her; he isn't grieving). In other words, the comforter must (1) already have engaged his own personal war with dying and (2) even now be assured of the victory to come. He knows suffering, but he, in Paul's words, does "not grieve as those who have no hope." The very character of his comfort derives from the experience of these contraries: both death and hope.

And we have a faith that does not shrink from death. The fundamental concern of our faith is *both* to reveal with fearsome accuracy the nature of death, *and* to draw the sting from it by the victory of the resurrected Christ. We, of all people, need to deny nothing true, the bad and the good. Of all people, we are most able to confess the grand proportions of death: so terrible as to defeat us all!—but defeated, rather, in Jesus.

Therefore, let comforting arise from your faith. No: comforting is not the *preaching* of this faith; it is the genuine *living* of it by those not frozen in denial nor lost in perpetual grief. You who once were a standing dust are now the walking Gospel. You are able.

And purge your motives, since anything less than the willingness to make personal sacrifice will not endure this journey through.

The comforter is the servant.

Expect nothing in return for your ministrations. This is both spiritual and realistic. The griever has suffered the rupture of some significant relationship; she will be unable then to give reasonable and mutual attention, to other relationship including the one she has with you. Of course: she is dying, and death puts stress on all her relationships. For a while (as grace will always have it) it becomes your commitment to uphold not only your side of a covenant but hers as well—in order that life continue for her. For the time being, and specifically for this business of comforting the griever, expect nothing. There's nothing to give and nothing to gain. She is leading, indeed; but she ain't payin' for it; you are grace to her now.

You will grow tired. Often there will seem no end to the griever's morbidities, her unaccountable demands, her maudlin pawings, her silences and sadnesses. Perpetual watchfulness will drain you because you *are* her life just now. It is a godly work, to be life for another. But it's exhausting. And if you had expected something in return, you will be deeply disappointed; and disappointment may justify withdrawal; but if you withdraw—if you take life away from her—she dies all over again.

I must be as clear here as possible. Expect *nothing.*

—Not her gratitude nor the praise of the people. For she will often be angry at you, and the praise of people who do not also help will sound like a mule's bray in your ear, aggravating.

—No, nor meek obedience either. She shall not see you as her savior, her hope; she shall sometimes not see you at all; she shall at other times (if you had expected anything) seem most arrogant.

—Nor rational behavior or communication. ("She doesn't even *try!*" may be your desperate complaint.)

—Nor even, in your private midnight soul, should you seek the rewards of self-satisfaction, the pious sense that you're doing good and are a good person, therefore. Such comforting, though overtly sacrificial, is spiritually self-centered: it judges success or failure by the comforter's feelings rather than by the griever's progress. I promise: a selfish contentment must turn into discontent, and by a terrible irony the comforter will blame the griever for it! You'll hold her responsible for the unrewarded disruption of your own life. You'll wonder whether she's troubling you on purpose. "She *likes* to be sad! She just wants the attention!"

Thus, "expect nothing" means, more sharply, "seek nothing for yourself."

If you had sought or expected anything, then it is at this point—battered, tired, feeling no accomplishment, no honor nor inner reward—that you may be inclined to quit. "I've got my own life to live. She's just using me. She's not even trying. It's ruining my family—" and so forth.

The comforter must choose to be a servant, to serve God by serving the least of his children.

The comforter is not a teacher, a moralizer, a quoter of helpful Bible verses, a preacher of timely sermons!—just a servant, serving.

The comforter is not a prophet, pointing out the errors of the bereaved, interpreting sorrow as a visitation of an angry God, but a servant, serving; and grief is the mistress of this house. Grief commands; the comforter obeys.

The comforter is not a professional mourner, matching sad stories with sadder ones in a very sad universe; the comforter cannot be that merchant of misery who takes a dangerous pleasure in having found one soul sadder than himself and who, while seeming so deeply sympathetic, is in fact feeding on others' sorrows. That's a parasite. That one loves the grief, not the griever nor the healing.

It's necessary to know and to name such apparently "Christian" comforters (the platitudinous "preacher," the accusing "prophet," and that most humble of servants, the "parasite") and then to protect the griever from them. They serve themselves; they enjoy a false superiority over one who is vulnerable; their friendship is treacherous.

The comforter is not a professional martyr, making a show of his self-denials, helping those on social ash-heaps whom everyone else neglects.

The comforter is, simply, a servant of God, so healthy in the holy relationship that though he is no lover of grief he will live beside it for love of the griever; so happy in the divine relationship that grief shall not impair him; so empowered by his relationship with Jesus that he expects absolutely nothing from his relationship with the griever: he *is* Jesus come near unto her, and his presence in every sense is Grace.

Comforters, analyze your motives to purge all that is fraudulent or self-serving. This is your second preparation and will permit "a living sacrifice, holy and acceptable to God, which is your spiritual worship."

SOME PRINCIPLES FOR COMFORTING

Though the causes of dying can be explained, death itself has no solutions. Comforter, you're not required to fix the mortal break, but rather to companion the broken.

Certain questions have no answer. Any answer, then, feels cheap or absurd, cheapening the questioner. What the griever most needs is to ask the questions passionately and honestly, and to be heeded when she does. So honor the questions. But though all your being yearns to solve things, do not belittle deep mysteries with piddling answers. That's what Job's comforters did to him.

In other words, the first principle of comforting is that your presence is of more importance to the griever than any solutions you might propose. This is comfort for the comforters: you don't *have* to say the right thing, to see to the depths of the universe, to know doctrine as wisely as do grave clerics. If you don't know what to say to a griever, say nothing. Simply, in an unembarrassed candor, *be*.

The griever, who suffered the sundering of relationship, needs relationship. You are her life. It requires only your proximate bodies, eyes unafraid to gaze at her, arms willing to hug her when she thinks she's about to fly apart, hands to touch her, kindness. Kindness.

Note, please: it doesn't matter which Secondary Dying she has died. The world gathers to comfort a widow. You, however, perceive death in divorce—and so you come to comfort. You see death when a dear dream has finally been destroyed, or where one was fired from a job, or in the radical ripping of a hysterectomy, or in the imprisonment of one's beloved son. You see the death; you know the onset of grief; you come; you comfort. God is with you.

God is with you, and when the griever tests your durability she discovers eternity: you won't leave. God, with you, is with her too. For her, you simply *are*. That is the first and the most important principle of comforting.

And once she trusts your graceful presence, then seven other principles may be engaged:

1. *Name*, when she is able to hear it, and *explain* as simply as possible her particular stage in the drama of grief. She will need assurance that her behavior is not unnatural. She may forget your explanation; be ready to repeat it as often as she asks. The words themselves may be her stay against an utter confusion.

2. By your uncritical responses, *grant her permission* (and the time and the space) to perform what her present act of grieving demands of her. Don't force things, but *listen* to any mood in her, even her rages. These may be hidden in shame or else overt and powerful. Let them occur even if the anger is against God. On the one hand, be not

aghast; on the other, do not echo what she says. If you are startled, she loses an ally now. If you agree with her furies, she loses the ally in the future when she she will need to believe that God is good.

Rather, *listen* with honest attention. Restate her sentiments, asking if that is what she meant; and so she'll know that listening (so much a salve to the torn spirit) is happening. If she needs to be sad for seven months, allow for sadness. Affirm it. Trust that (in almost every case) the griever's instinct is accurate, and she does need the time. If she wants to repeat certain memories over and over, let each repetition be new to you. The point is not to learn something you hadn't known before. The point is relationship, manifest in plain listening.

3. *Attend,* especially during periods of distractedness, *to her basic needs.* Grief can neglect the body, its food and dress and cleanliness. Grief forgets the requirements of society, bills, lawns, kids, gas, taxes, voting. But if these things are not accomplished, chaos comes indeed.

With the help of the whole community, maintain these other relationships until she's ready to take them up again. In order to learn what duties need to be done, pretend you are she; but when you do her duties, let it seem a matter of course and no big deal. Don't let your kindness cause her guiltiness. And surely do not patronize her, as though you reached down to her from a lofty health.

Always watch for signs of revival—so that the instant she's able to shoulder her load, you slip away and vanish from that particular juncture.

(So critical is it that you "expect nothing"—especially here. Your hope for some gratitude might communicate itself and double her burden: guilt for her failure, obligations to thank you equal to your work.)

4. Always, *express confidence in her.* Find ways to gesture your undiminished appreciation. She should know that you never cease to believe that her worth, her abilities, her goodness—her particular virtues—will rise at the right time, and resume her life again. In you she will have a sort of savings account; in you she will find evidence of her faith and strength and good purpose, especially when she can't find them in herself. You'll create certain phrases that characterize the best of her, and you'll repeat them till she trusts them: "I know you don't feel it now, but you're the finest architect I know." "The wisest parent." "A singer that gives me joy."

And this: "I love you, Gloria. Nothing will change that. I love you."

5. *Stay with her,* stay with her, stay with her: abide.

The whole world gives a griever only so much time as the world itself can stand to be sad. Short time. Abbreviated grief. And then it demands that she get on with it. The world will attend a funeral; but two weeks later, when she sits in her kitchen staring at her empty hands, it doesn't know. It's back at work, wondering where she is. Stay with her: holy stability and the human touch. Stay.

6. And though you learn from her the amount of time she needs to complete any single act of grief, the genuine love in you (not a snifty pride in you) will notice when it's gone too long. So you will *encourage her* to move to the next act simply by presenting its next actions as reasonable possibilities.

"Are you angry these days?" you say. "When you sit all alone, what do you feel?"

"Are you sad?" you say. The question does not trouble you, and so it doesn't trouble her.

And always you indicate that you're willing to hear whatever the furnace in her soul casts up: whatever.

7. But throughout the process, comforter, *take care of yourself.*

You will need an emotional support of your own. Earnestly I suggest that you surround yourself with a group of people not involved in this matter. Let the group covenant:

—to pray with each other for each other;

—to praise one another in knowing detail, and to offer a continual encouragement;

—to do something *else* than your various ministries together, like playing bridge or tennis, laughing loudly, gathering regularly when there is no crisis at all, on holidays, for feasts, with all the children, looking forward, perhaps, to a unifying worship—gathering simply to prove the commitment of this group, the unity and love.

If you are to be life to one bereaved, then you must find nourishment from others unbereaved. And so this support group must be yours, not the griever's. It can't be a body of people as large as a congregation but one well able to name you in love. It needn't know the confidential details of your ministry; but it will affirm you nonetheless, and hold you up to God.

This is common sense. It will establish your own life and health so that you maintain a realistic perspective from which to comfort them who have lost exactly that perspective.

Oh, comforter! The peace of the Lord be with you, that it might be with them whom you serve and console. Amen.

14 Death

Stella Mayes is no stranger to us. She's Mary Moore's mother, Gloria's aunt, sister to little Marie and to Sonny Boy Hopson. She's a member of Grace. Stella, a stick of a woman, her tongue as salty as pork cracklings—I know her well.

Nevertheless, when suddenly she appears in the door of the lounge, we freeze for a moment and stare at her as if she's an intruder.

We make an odd scene, I suppose. I'm kneeling down to Gloria; Mary's at my shoulder; poor Marie has rocked herself so far around she's facing the corner, humming *Precious Lord* as loudly as she can.

But Stella isn't laughing.

Mary breaks the silence. Softly: "Mamma."

Stella snaps: "What's 'a matter?"

Now we move. Gloria sits up and smoothes her skirt. Marie whips around to see who spoke. I stand and sweep coats from the only other chair in the lounge.

"Hello, Stella," I say. "Sit here."

"What's 'a matter!" she demands. She has a shrewd eye, a woman mostly bone and gristle and gritty thoughts.

"Oh," Mary says. "Well, Gloria had a sort of charley-horse—"

"'Sa *matter!*" Stella hasn't budged. She's fixed on a purpose, like a ferret burrowing. "What they doin' to Sonny Boy?" Ah, *that's* the matter she means.

Mary steps toward her. "The best they can, Mamma. Rest your coat. Sit—"

"An' what do Sonny Boy have to say about it?"

So then we are silent a moment.

"Mamma, Sonny Boy's not talking."

"What?"

Marie, in the corner, screams: "BY-PASS SURGERY!"

Stella's offended. "I know that," she says, and for a moment her fixation is forgotten in a pout. Without removing her coat, she sits. She seems all at once to notice Gloria. "An' why you poppin' yo' lip at me?"

Gloria has the same fierce expression she had when I first entered; but her face is a mask. She doesn't answer.

In a sudden rush of anguish, Stella Mayes spreads out her arms to the whole room and cries: "*Why* ain' Sonny Boy talkin'? What you not tellin' me? What's 'a matter?" And then she shrinks to an old woman's size and whispers: "Is my brother dead?"

"Oh, Mamma!" cries Mary. She goes to Stella and gathers the poor small head into her bosom. "No, he's not dead. The doctor has some things to do yet, but Sonny Boy's not dead."

Raggedy mother of Mary, suddenly stricken, accepting the hug— this old lady is tough. She walks the city, whatever the season. In winter she pulls net stockings over her boots in order to cross the snow and ice. All year long she feeds four generations, never gaining a pound herself. She lives in the "Projects." So does her sister Marie. They are an outrageous pair, filled with sass and laughter when the living is good and no one they love is dying.

"My brother," she says, "he ain't dead?"

"Mamma, Mamma, the only reason he can't talk is 'cause he's 'sleep. It's a long operation."

Suddenly Stella straightens. "Well, an' I'll tell you somethin' else," she shouts, knocking her daughter away. "It's hot as a pot in here. Thi'shere hospital's like to fry me to death."

That tickles Marie. "HAW!" she barks.

Gloria's fierce mask slips a bit.

"I ain' lyin'." Stella's shaking her head, tremendously offended: "If the knife don't kill Sonny Boy, the oven will."

"HAW!"

Mary says, "Oh, Mamma!"

"What?"

"Nothing," says Mary, as in *What's the use?* "Take off your coat."

Marie bellows, "*And* your sweaters, *and* yo' shirts, *and* yo' flannels. HAW!"

Stella frowns. "It's cold outside. It's a fall wind comin'."

All at once Gloria stands up, staring at the door, her face flushed black with high blood. Stella looks at her. "Wha'?" she says, and turns, and then, like the rest of us, rises to stand at a silent attention.

The surgeon has returned, gaunt, unsmiling.

He says, "If you wish to do anything . . . well, I think it's best you do it now."

Gloria has no hesitation. "I want to see him," she says.

"Yes. Yes," says the surgeon. "For the moment, Leroy is in recovery. Um, I'll lead you—"

"Who?" says Stella.

But we are already moving. The force of Gloria's request has driven the doctor backward through the door. She follows immediately, then Mary, and then I snatch my communion set and go.

The surgeon's leading: "Down the hall. You can have as much time as—"

Stella is stuck in the room behind us. "Who? Who is that? Who's he talkin' about?"

Mary steps quickly ahead and takes Gloria's arm, two sober women, their bodies bending toward the thing they're going to see.

"What did he say?" cries Stella. "Who was—"

Far, far behind us, in a murmuring misery, her sister explains: "Bypass surgery."

Mary Moore is the first to enter the recovery room. She gasps immediately then covers her mouth. I walk around her. It's a small room choked with chrome equipment. Sonny Boy lies on a narrow table between machines, his feet toward the door.

Mary whispers, "He's swole."

Gloria follows me, stops at his feet, and begins to stroke them.

"Pastor," Mary bleats, "he's swole."

There's a tube thrust up his nostril, forcing air into his lungs and jerking each time it clicks into action. The man is draped in a pale green sheet, but his feet are naked, sticking up. The soles look wood-stained. I move toward his head.

"Sonny Boy!" Mary's tone is pleading. "How can you dance if you're fat?"

She's right. His arms lie thick on his stomach. His cheeks and his lips hang like a rubber, his mouth gapes, his teeth are gummed yellow, his eyelids droop over half the eye. Half the eye: his face is like an icon carved in wood and turned toward eternity.

He's breathing.

I call his name softly: "Sonny Boy?"

He breathes. That is, his chest jumps at the sudden pressure from the nasal tube: CLICK! Then it subsides with a slow rush of air in the machine behind me: *Whisssssss.*

I place my hand on his forehead, feeling moisture. "Sonny Boy Hopson, Gloria is here. So is Mary. The surgery is over."

CLICK! goes the valve, and his chest swells. *Whisssss,* and the chest deflates.

I can't be sure, but I think he's trying to swallow. He doesn't turn his eyes toward me. "Are you all right?"

Nothing. CLICK!

"I am Pastor Wangerin, Gloria's pastor." I stroke his brow as if he were my father. "We've come to pray with you—"

Whisssssssss.

Mary moves near me. I am grateful for her presence. I lower my face to Sonny Boy's, as if to kiss him—but even as I speak the following words a disastrous sigh arises in the room. "Sonny Boy," I say, "I've brought communion with me—"

"Pastor! Pastor!"

It's Gloria. She is kneeling and pressing her cheek to the soles of her uncle's feet.

"Gloria," I say, "come here."

She says, "I think he's dead."

CLICK! *Whisssssssss.*

"Gloria, please, I need you here."

Well, and then it breaks my heart how meekly she obeys me. The dark woman stands and comes round the table. Like a child she creeps close between Mary and me. We stand in a row at Sonny Boy's side.

"Take Mary's hand," I say, and she does. The cousins hold fast to each other. "And touch me too," I say, and she does: she encircles my waist with her right arm. "You see? We're a fortress for Sonny Boy." But her face is drained, her color ashen. "Gloria, don't let me go. I need your help."

So I open my communion set and place the articles on a flat surface: the tiny cup receives a drop of wine; a tiny wafer is fractured tinier.

I bend down. We all bend down. "Sonny Boy Hopson, listen: in the night when Jesus was betrayed, he took bread—"

Gloria murmurs, "Jesus!" Mary puts her left hand on her uncle's hand. And so we make a circle together, the four of us.

I dip a flake of wafer in wine. I carry this morsel on the tip of my finger to his mouth and touch it to his tongue, and there it sticks. "—shed for you for the forgiveness of your sins—"

But his mouth hangs open.

Oh, I wish he would smile, like the man in the cream-white suit—that dazzling, audacious African whose manner was so imperial, that short man, that dancer, him!

I lay my hand again on the moist forehead of Sonny Boy, and I begin to pray: "Our Father—"

Gloria seizes my waist with a terrible strength and joins me: "—who art in Heaven—"

CLICK! His chest swells. *Whissssss—*

Collapses.

Mary prays with us: "Thy kingdom come, thy will be done—"

O Sonny boy, you gaze so far away. Your eyes are golden. Do you hear us?

"—forgive us our trespasses as we forgive those who—"

There comes a moment in the ritual when Gloria goes to the feet of her uncle and gently kisses each swollen sole, the right and then the left. *Your feet are so cold, my beloved.* She draws the green sheet down over them, then she faces me with smouldering eyes and sorrow, then she turns away and departs on a silent tread. As she goes I see that angel's wing of black hair down her back. Gloria mournful, Gloria is so dark and lovely, Gloria. I can scarcely breathe.

Mary follows.

CLICK! That fleck of bread is still stuck to the poor man's tongue. *Whisssssss—*What shall I do? He hasn't swallowed it. He isn't eating any more. Ah, let it be. The glory of God is upon him now. I leave.

—lead us not into temptation, but deliver us from evil—

Gloria is the first to return to the lounge. She doesn't sit. When I arrive, she's standing just inside the door.

"Mamma," she says.

Marie turns away from her daughter and starts to rock again; Stella glares at Gloria.

"Mamma," says Gloria still to Marie, "Sonny Boy is dead."

—for thine is the kingdom—

The surgeon is standing behind us. I had forgotten about him. "I'm sorry," he is saying. "We couldn't persuade his heart to start again. I'm sorry—"

—for thine is—

Little Marie, facing away, clutches the sides of her head and starts to wail. She is crying with her eyes wide open.

—life is—

Mary Moore walks over to me, her hands stretched out in appeal. She is shaking her head side to side. She hugs me mightily and whispers into my ear, "Pastor, you should have seen him dance."

Stella Mayes is furiously buttoning her coat.

Gloria hasn't moved. She does not cry. She does not speak. The shadow has fallen across her. She seems to feel nothing at all. She does not think.

—for thine is the kingdom and the power and the glory, forever and ever. Amen.

15 Grief I: Shock

S he does not cry. She does not speak. She seems to feel nothing at all. She does not think.

Sonny Boy is lost. The word *apollumi* applies: he's cut off from the world. It's an objective fact and, as a fact, irreducible. Gloria knows it. She can even express it. *Mamma,* she says, *Sonny Boy is dead.* She is like most grievers (before they enter the stage of active denial) who respond to the raw external detail.

But Gloria, like most grievers when first they encounter the reality of their loss, also needs time in which to prepare the deeper parts of herself to receive the same news. She becomes a woman divided.

Mamma! Sonny Boy is— Look closely at her face. She has raised her eyebrows very high; she droops the lids; she lifts her chin and pouts her mouth. The effect is arrogance, a nearly aggressive indifference, as if she were saying, *Do you think I care? Well, I don't care.* Let no one blame her. The gesture's not altogether true: she cares so much that the caring itself is intolerable now. Therefore, neither is the gesture false: at the moment something within her is choosing not to care. So: she knows, and she does not know—and the difference between knowing and not knowing is shock.

She accomplishes the internal division this way: although she can say, "Sonny Boy is lost," she cannot say, "Sonny Boy is lost *to me.*"

Again: although she knows he's cut off from the world, she refuses the knowledge that *she* is cut off from Sonny Boy. He is dead. That is sad. And she expects to be sad for him. But she herself has not yet felt the sundering. That she has died in Sonny Boy's death; that unto her too the hard word *apollumi* may be applied; that she who shall cry for Sonny Boy must likewise cry for herself—all this is benumbed.

The first actions of grief can seem so unlike genuine grieving that others may grow concerned or impatient or angry. They blame the coldness. Even the griever may doubt the depth of her love because her sorrow lies seemingly on the surface. Or else some friend wants to force the griever to face the "truth." Don't! Trust the griever's instincts. When the heart is ready, the mind will allow the knowledge down.

More than normal, shock is merciful. The knowing and the doing that is still to come must require the griever's entire store of energies: she has withdrawn in order to prepare. She needs the time. Wait.

VARIOUS BEHAVIORS OF SHOCK

If the relationship sundered was significant, then here, at the beginning of grief, most of us will simply be unable consciously and immediately to process the gross bulk of fact or else to comprehend its dreadful implication.

But we fend off the facts in different ways.

Terra Johnson remembers the series of emotions she felt as the family drove home from evening worship. Her oldest son, sixteen, was driving; he had a learner's permit. Her husband sat beside him in the front, she in the back with their daughter.

A fire engine came wailing behind them. Terra's first thought was to wonder if her son knew what to do. He did. He pulled to the side and switched on the flashers. She felt proud of him.

And then, as they re-entered traffic behind the fire engine (she remembers) she felt curiosity mixed with sympathy for strangers: "I wonder what's burning?" she said.

Closer to home, she saw the night sky glowing orange, and pity sharpened within her. This must be someone she knew.

Suddenly her husband—heartlessly, it seemed to her—commanded their son to stop: "Now," he cried. "Right now!" He rushed around the front of the car, pushed the boy aside, took the wheel, and drove fast, saying nothing. Terra felt his fear with a certain amusement: he always takes charge.

But when they turned and she could see down her street, all in an instant swift impressions flew through her:

—*The road is wet, reflecting fire-light.*

—*Black smoke is blushing above the flame.*

—*Flames actually do "lick." Like tongues. Through windows. The outside of the house.*

—*This is my house!*

And such horror overwhelmed her then, that the smoke and flame seemed actually to be *inside* her, blackness thickening in her head, the fire inside her breast. An inversion of things. Disorientation. Dizziness. She gulped air once and felt that she would faint—but then did not faint. Instead (all this occurring in seconds) she heard her daughter screaming beside her, saw her son grab the dash and lean forward, noticed with a distinct irritation that her husband was not parking at a curb, but stopping in the middle of the street. She did not faint. Instead, as her husband leaped from the car, she said to herself, *What does he think he can do? He always wants to take charge.* She felt embarrassed for him. On the other hand, she would, in her quieter manner, keep the important things together, the children, the family, their health and spirit and peace. That particularly: they would have peace in spite of this disaster. And she would see to it.

They got out of the car. She took her daughter's arm and squeezed it. The girl could not stop crying. She put a firm hand on her son's shoulder. It was evident that the house would be a total loss. Even now the fire was gutting it. The three of them walked slowly forward, confronting this thing together. Together. Terra determined to hold it all together.

Taking a Part for the Whole

Terra's son is called "Will" to distinguish him from his father, William.

Her daughter's name is Jessie.

Of the four, Jessie cried the most, unashamed of her behavior. But curiously, she was crying *for* one thing only. A photo album. As soon as she knew for sure that the house was burning down, she thought of that album. She could think of nothing else.

She told her mother that she wanted to save the album. Her mother replied that it was impossible, that Jessie's life was more important. She screamed to a fireman, "Save my photograph album!" He didn't even hear her. She quit trying and just cried.

It had pictures of vacations and of her dog—and the best picture of her grandmother.

This is the only thing Jessie could think of. She consoled herself for a while with the thought that maybe it survived, and they'd find it in the ashes. She even imagined where it might be. She saw the place in her mind. But when they went looking for stuff that might be saved, she couldn't find it. And so she began to cry all over again. Her pictures were gone.

The album, then, haunted her for weeks. It seemed to her the single real tragedy of the fire.

Jessie's response is one form of shock: the loss too huge to be grieved at once is reduced to a size one can cry for. In a child this behavior is acceptable; in an adult it is judged childish, silly. Adults are not supposed to confuse the values of things, grieving the loss of something incidental while remaining oblivious to losses truly grievous.

But in shock we return to strategies of our childhood.

If a hundred relationships break all at once, shock shuts down awareness of all but a manageable few. These we suffer consciously. These alone we seem to mourn. But these are symbols for the whole. Childish? Yes. Silly? Of course not.

I know a woman for whom the greatest outrage of her husband's death was that he died with a hole in his sock. His big toe stuck out that hole. The man was a farmer. He was mowing ditches in front of the house when the tractor turned over on him. She ran and arrived just as others did. There was much to grieve a widow in such an accident; but his boots were removed, and there was her husband's exposed big toe, and that's all she could think of: she spent endless energies explaining to people that he didn't need to wear torn socks. She wept for his socks.

Some neighbors wondered why laundry should bother her much at that moment. Grist for gossip. She seemed more concerned for her reputation that for her husband's life. In fact, humiliation was an easier emotion than the woe that must sooner or later follow. Socks are fixable. Death is not.

Objectivity

Terra's son, sixteen, at first said nothing. He watched fire-fighters break holes through the roof of his house, through which they shot streams of water. He saw the constant drenching of neighbors' houses, producing steam. Finally he said, "Hmm. So this is what a house afire looks like." He smiled. "Get it, Mom? A house afire." She didn't return the smile. But Will found himself fascinated by every detail of the event, almost a scientific interest, he thought. He'd never seen so big a fire before. Listen. It even made its own wind.

Later his sister told him he didn't belong in their family because he didn't care what they were feeling. "All you do is laugh and make jokes. I hate you, Will!"

In fact, shock may depersonalize the experience of dying, may generalize it into a phenomenon to be observed: anybody's house, anybody's fire. That which is too great immediately to be grieved is not perceived as one's *own*. The personal and passionate participation is stalled for a while. Distance is established.

The "disinterested" intellect can drive a cold wedge between the griever and the event. Thus, many people protect themselves *from* the death by a very precise scrutiny *of* it, perhaps by describing it in a journal or a letter.

An ironic (even a cynical) humor, likewise, causes distance between the griever and the thing to be grieved. Imagine how little this behavior is appreciated. Understand how much it is needed by the one who is laughing.

Even a sort of philosophizing—a cool generalization of this death as the fate of all human flesh—forestalls the sense of a personal blow. The griever takes an Olympian view, a godly superiority, abstracting his own experience, making it but one illustration of many such in the cosmos. "Ah, me," sighs the divorcée. "How many people divorce these days! It's a characteristic of the age." Civil tears for the culture at large are easier than the anguished and helpless howl for a personal devastation.

Passivity

On the other hand, shock may suddenly leave the griever pliable, robbing her of an independent will. She can make no decision; she can't pursue a thought to its conclusion; she can't identify alternative courses of action, compare them, and choose one. She seems weak, infantile. She may sleep longer and deeper than usual.

She jumps up in the middle of a conversation and smiles and turns elsewhere, as if the conversation were done after all.

She gets an idea. Right away, she walks into the kitchen to find something. But as soon as she's there, she bows her head and stands still, utterly distracted: she has forgotten what she came for.

As a result, she is grateful to anyone who will take charge, and she will be mindlessly obedient.

"Mindlessly": in this case, the intellect has been disengaged. The heart and the mind of this particular griever are too intimate; what the mind knows, the heart feels; so shock must stun the mind to silence a while.

Therefore, they say to a divorcée, "Go," and she goes. They say to the man who has lost his dream, "Come," and listlessly he comes. In this state the griever is vulnerable to bad advice or evil cunning. Surely, she needs a comforter now, not so much for comforting as for protection.

Pragmatic Activity

Terra Johnson herself did much and did it very well, so that she might feel nothing. She would *be* order in a world drifting toward chaos. By competent action she'd keep all things together. "At least we have our lives, and we have each other."

And the people at church said, "Look how well she copes."

Already while she stood facing the fire, Terra was planning: where the children would sleep, what clothes she could get in their sizes, whom to call about insurance, where to rent lodgings, whether to rebuild. Oh, yes—to rebuild!

She scarcely felt the heat on her face any more. The fire required response; and when she responded with lists and proper calculations, why, the fire was diminished before her.

Terra's in control! No need for sorrow now.

Actually, Terra was choosing to confront those problems that had solutions in order not to confront, not even to acknowledge, the Problem That Hath No Solution At All.

This form of shock seems least like shock, both to the community and to the griever. It is dry-eyed. It's unaware of itself *as* shock. So the griever, surprised by peace in the midst of trouble, marvels at herself and gives thanks to God for such reserves of strength. "Things won't be as bad as I thought. Lean on me. I'll keep us together."

But she is deceived.

Every other form of shock prepares the griever somewhat for its own ending, the transition to the second act of grief. Generalized tears finally become poignant and personal tears.

But when the griever is forced from that shock wherein she thought she fared well, the transition is sudden, astonishing, and violent. Neither Terra nor anyone in her family was prepared for the storm that broke in her soul when that pyramid of oranges came tumbling down, when she went down among them, unable to rise again. Terra Johnson, when finally she began to sob, could not stop sobbing for days.

Distractive Activity

William Johnson had irresistible desires to do, to do—to *do* whatever could truly be done. He who had leaped from the car on the night of the fire and rushed toward the disaster, by the next day seemed as obsessively rushing from it. He's an architect. He became a hermit for work. Although he'd been producing plans for two projects reasonably on schedule, he now drove himself to exceed their schedules. He worked twelve hours a day. He visited sites of other plans he'd made. He fussed the drawings to perfection and beyond, ornamenting them unnecessarily.

He washed his car.

He tuned it himself.

If his basement or his garage had not burned down, he would have cleaned them out.

He wasn't disassociating himself from trouble. He knew what had happened. He was just *doing*.

Shock may pitch itself with manic energy into activities that, although they have value in themselves, are nevertheless irrelevant to the death one has experienced. It intrudes the raw busy-ness of the body between the griever and his bereavement. It fills time. It redeems this particular day, if not the death it cannot touch. It tries hard to exhaust the griever so that he might sleep deeply when he lies down.

Thus, an elderly woman, newly widowed, can't help it: she begins to clean house. Room by room. At two in the morning. With a headlong passion. As if her life depended upon it. It does.

"Mother." Her children are upset. "Mother, you need your sleep." They are afraid for her sanity. Her face is so compact, so closed. Her eyes dry. Her manner merely pragmatic. Among themselves they worry: "Mother needs help," they say.

The only help she needs is a little more water in the bucket and privacy. The obsession is necessary. She's scrubbing death away, though only for a while. Shock is distraction.

But Terra Johnson, who was mightily holding all things in the world together, one evening commanded William to take a break from his furious labors. "Come," she said. "Please. Let's just spend one evening grocery shopping together—like we used to do when we first got married. Please, William. Please."

Physical Diversions

And shock, when one relationship has broken for sure, is the sympathetic breakdown of many relationships. It's the stunning of these others so that the full knowledge of bereavement comes but slowly into the griever's consciousness, bit by bit as she is ready for it. This stunning occurs not only in Communal and Natural Relationships, and not only in mental and emotional sorts of Internal Relationships—but also in the body itself.

So, the employee who was laid off suddenly develops a blinding headache.

And homesickness is *sickness*, producing insomnia, digestive disorders, rashes.

The griever experiences cramping, strange paralyses, vision trouble.

The retiree loses his hearing with unreal speed.

A student fails her graduate oral exams and then goes straight to the infirmary with nausea and the flu.

Folks may consider these afflictions manipulative or hypochondriacal. The griever herself may disbelieve the symptoms and feel embarrassed. But they are real. They are the eruption of sorrow in the body itself. That which cannot be healed has been translated into something that can be served and salved and nursed—and the best response is to minister to the physical hurt.

When I massaged the tightened muscles of Gloria's legs, it was to touch her heart. It was to companion the woman through this first precinct of grief. It was to comfort her.

COMFORTING SHOCK

Surely, in experience the various behaviors of shock are never as neat as they are in the explanation. Grievers may swing from one protective method to another, or muddle them all together, or skip shock, having no need for it. Nevertheless, knowing the reasons for these behaviors can comfort the comforters and help interpret the griever: shock itself *is* her passage toward realization.

Aware of that goodness and the need, the comforter will not force a griever to confront facts, but will rather facilitate the business of this first act and will open opportunities through which she can *by degrees* come to the knowledge of her dying.

Sonny Boy's surgeon, as gaunt as Abraham Lincoln, offers an excellent model. His method of announcing her uncle's death both honored Gloria's sorrow and permitted a period for the heart's preparation: he broke the news in stages. First he indicated that things were critical. Sonny Boy's heart wasn't beating on its own, he said. But he offered a little hope—then left and allowed her to process the news. Gloria's legs went into spasms. When he returned the second time, he implied that death was imminent. But he didn't say so specifically. Rather, he granted her the chance for positive action. He gave her something to do, a means for the expression of love and sorrow. And only then, after she had fulfilled the mournful act, did he confirm the death—even when she herself had already perceived it. His ministrations were unobtrusive and invaluable. As much as he could, he obeyed Gloria's personal timetable rather than his own. Here, briefly, was a comforter.

Let every comforter recognize that shock may properly last a very long time—that it may take a young widow months before some little thing loosens the woe she had dammed in her soul. Such sudden emotion, coming so late, may cause her to think that something is terribly wrong with her. But the comforter (who waited in patience for any development) will not be surprised, and he will tell her so.

Neither will he be disappointed, though she seems to reverse an otherwise healthy progression. Instead, he will serve the belated grief as if the death had occurred just yesterday. In her heart, it did.

Read the griever. Perhaps someone else will need no time for shock. It may have accomplished its purpose already *before* the final separation actually occurred. If a parent dies of a lingering cancer, for example, his offspring shall have had time to prepare, and the event of the death may, then, *be* the confrontation that the heart is ready for—so shock will be done with the dying. In that case, the comforter will not want to distract the griever from her deeper suffering and from the second act of grief, as if the period of ignorance (shock) were still necessary. Any distractions may feel irritating to her, even offensive. Remember: shock returns to the strategies of childhood. If a comforter suggests such strategies to a griever who no longer needs them, he implies that she *is* a child, helpless and dependent. This comforter will lose her trust thereby, and she will lose a comforter.

❦

The Grace Church parking lot starts at the corner of Elliott and Bellemeade. Bellemeade is an east-west thoroughfare. Gloria Ferguson lives with her mother and most of her children on this same street, three blocks east of the church. Just one block east, at Garvin, is a traffic light.

Generally, when I come from the west I'm blind to activity at Garvin and Bellemeade. My attention is already making a right turn down Elliott, to the church and a score of duties.

And so it should be this day too. Well, I've spent the whole morning and part of the afternoon at the hospital—a necessary business, to be sure, but unscheduled. My Septembers always require huge amounts of office-work, preparing lesson plans, outlining worship, writing agendas and goals for the autumn season, which is really the start-up season of the year for me.

Therefore, I am, right now, traveling Bellemeade at a good clip eastward, and thinking of a hundred jobs to do. Automatically, I slow down to turn south on Elliott—

—when a long line of cars wakes me up: I *can't* turn onto Elliott. I can't even get that far. Traffic is backed up more than a block from the light at Garvin. Okay: I'll reverse my vehicle and take the earlier cross-street. But here come cars behind me. And I'm blocked.

And when I've stopped altogether, I can hear a violent, blasphemous, bitter, continual stream of screaming. Someone is angry about something. The voice is high, but the manner is male, a cursing, verbal attack and an *I'm gonna beat-choo!* attitude. Well, well. Neighborhood. As Talitha would say, "Word." Me and the traffic can wait a bit.

But a new voice joins, and I recognize this one.

"GO HOME!" it booms. "GO HOME TO YO MAMMA!" It has the strength to rattle windows more than a block away.

The nastier cursing does not cease.

I get out of the car, letting it idle in the street, and peer forward and then begin to trot forward.

Gloria's enormous Buick LeSabre sits at the intersection facing east but going nowhere. The light is green. No matter. Her car is not moving. In the street on the driver's side a long-legged, high-backed, goose-necked youth is jumping and screaming. He throws back his head as if cocking a gun and pours vituperation toward the skies. Then suddenly he tucks his head, spreads his arms, and flies at the car. He bangs the roof with the heels of his hands, which bounce up like rubber—*BOOM! BOOM!*—and which open into a gesture of outraged supplication. Then the whole boy springs high into the air, absolutely taut with fury, screaming, screaming:

"You gon' kill me, Bitch! You *aimed* to kill me. You done it on *puhpuss!* Murderer!"—*BOOM!* "Murderer!"—*BOOM!*

On the other side of the car, scarcely able to see over it because "all us Hopsons is short," Marie Landers has emerged to challenge evil face to face. She too bellows, making gestures of potency and wrath. But she is a grandmother and a great-grandmother with access to different authority:

"BOY!" she booms, rattling windows, "BOY, AH KNOW YO MAMMA. AN' IF YOU DON' SHOW SOME RESPECK, AH'M GON' *TELL* YO MAMMA, AN' SHE GON' *WHALE THE* RESPECK INTO YO SITTIN'-DOWN, TILL YOU *CAIN'T* SIT THAT SWEET BROWN SMILE DOWN AGAIN!"

And so forth.

A truly memorable scene. Marie in church, rocking to a strong song, can raise her hands and roar glory to God. Well, the voice that reaches heaven with praise can also meet wickedness with weaponry, in this case the marvelous cannon, YO MAMMA!

Just as I arrive, Marie decides to hobble around the nose of the Buick—so the furious boy (taller than either of us) is flanked on two sides, and neither the old woman nor the white pastor is impressed by his cursing.

Cursing still, then, and vowing monstrous vengeances, he backs up, turns, and retreats with his slickery-fingered, loop-necked, knee-popping pride.

Gloria sits in the driver's seat, staring straight ahead. No expression whatsoever. Her hands are locked to the rim of the wheel, her small mouth pinched. I lean through the window beside her.

"Gloria, how are you? What happened?"

Without the slightest motion, scarcely parting her lips, she whispers, "He's right, Pastor. Somethin' in me wanted to run that poor boy down." Her face is ashen, drained of its blood.

"Gloria, do you want me to drive you home?"

Her hands are locked to the wheel. "God help me," she whispers with awful quietude: "He was eatin' an apple. He was amblin' 'cross the road. An' then he up an' grinned at me, an' he winked, an' my car just jumped forward like my foot slipped. But it didn't."

Traffic is creeping around the Buick now, grazing me behind.

"Come, Gloria, come—we've got to get out of the way. Move over. I'll drive you home."

She doesn't move.

But she turns her head and looks up into my eyes, her face a mask of amazement. "How can they jus' go on an' do, Pastor?" she begs with piteous appeal. "Sonny Boy *died* today. Sonny Boy *died*. But folks don' notice. They walkin' 'round, gettin' on buses, goin' 'bout their business. Something should be different. Something should . . . Pastor," she whispers with slow astonishment: "Nobody's crying. Nobody's holding his hat for sorrow. Nobody's even walking slower. An' here comes a boy, strutting and smirking and eating an *apple* an' spittin' the *seeds*—"

Abruptly she faces forward again.

She whispers, "I almost killed him."

And then, again, she whispers, "I am so scared—"

16 Grief II: Wrestling the Angel

T he increasing awareness of pain is itself our waking from shock. Pain: the direct sensation of the break; pain in every place where we had enjoyed relationship, the house we inhabited, the bedroom we slept in, the holidays we celebrated with him who died. Pain makes real this death, and this death makes real our human mortality. With pain the drama of active grieving begins.

We hate this present death.

Moreover, we hate its vaster implication: that we are ourselves not limitless in scope and importance and power, that we *can* die. And though that word but lurks at the boundaries of immediate sorrow (and though the response is unconscious in us) we reject it. We will resist the facts of our personal finitude by acting still as gods of our personal circumstance. That is to say: with all our (limited) resources, truly believing that the effort must have some effect, we fight the dying—

—with all our strength, by the bare force of will denying death: "I will not have it!"

—with all our heart, by the brute force of angry emotion seeking to overpower death: "I hate it!"

—with all our mind, by the insinuations of human reason arguing death away: "If only things were different. . . ."

The second act of grief, as focused and total as any wrestling match, may have three rounds, till the Self has been tested against immutable fact and found wanting. Death is death. It neither flees nor changes, however we attack it. We aren't gods, but creatures after all. In the *experience* of the struggle we are forced to confess an essential helplessness in the universe, for we in the extremes of strength and heart and mind have accomplished nothing. This is the more elemental anguish behind the specific pain of a particular dying. This is why grief is more than a physical, emotional, psychological experience: it is metaphysical.

All night long on the banks of the Jabbok, all alone, we are Jacob striving with a mighty angel. We think this is the Angel of Death. And there are moments when we think we might overpower him, learn his name, and command him. In the end, we learn nothing from the angel. Rather, he takes our measure. He takes our names. Undefeatable, he defeats us. He schools us in an abject humility. We bow and are ready to die.

Only in the morning—when the struggle is done and we have not died the final death—do we know who the angel has been all along. Against so mighty an Opponent it was fated from the beginning: we could not change him; we would surely lose; and our loss should have been our dying. We should have been clean cut off. But we who could change nothing may, in the mercy of that same Opponent, *be* changed.

So Jacob called the name of the place Peniel, saying, "For I have seen God face to face, and yet my life is preserved." The sun rose upon him as he passed Penuel, limping because of his thigh.

EPISODE I: THE OPPOSITION OF THE WILL

Like a child who would change things by defiance alone, flatly denying the fact of a death, the griever cries, *No!*

No, this divorce is not happening.

My son is not an addict, no!

And for a while she believes the cry. The very intensity of her desire persuades her to feel as if this life had not ceased to exist. Like a creating god she commands the dead relationship to rise, and then she behaves accordingly. This isn't shock anymore. Shock was numb to the truth. Now the griever defies the truth, and the source of the life of her sundered relationship is from within herself.

❦

You enter the front door of Gloria's house directly into a living room as wide as the building itself; then you pass through the kitchen on your right to a small bedroom at the back. This is her bedroom. This is where she sits. This is where she has been sitting since yesterday when she came home from the hospital, carrying Sonny Boy's effects in a plastic bag.

She left once. This morning. To travel with Mary Moore to the funeral home. But the experience must have hardened her; because she sits, it seems to me, with a willful immobility, eyebrows halfway up her forehead like flags flying against disaster. She doesn't frown. She doesn't knit the brow. She keeps her hands in her lap as if posing for a portrait. She breathes through her nose. Altogether, she seems to be sailing, self-composed, by an absolute act of will, between the heaves of storm. She does not cry.

We are discussing the funeral service. Mostly she's been accepting my suggestions. Mary Moore has just left the room to answer the doorbell, but even in our privacy Gloria gazes forward formally. She seems prepared to resist the intimate word. I think she wants to be alone. I should go.

"Gloria, I'll be back tonight, all right?"

She nods.

I yearn to touch her with tender effect, as at the hospital yesterday. But I say, "Folks from church will be here then. If you don't mind, I'd like to speak a word of devotion to them—"

All at once, enormous in the doorway, Mrs. Alma Jefferson appears. "Honey!" She lifts up hands of helpless sorrow. "Honey, honey!" she wails, crossing the bedroom floor. "Oh, honey, I know what you're goin' through, yes, I do." And down she comes like a mud slide, covering Gloria in mountainous sympathy. "I recollect how I felt when James Jefferson Senior had his surgery. Scared! To death! Honey, I'm so sad for you."

And so Mrs. Jefferson breaks into tears on Gloria's neck.

Gloria, her black hair pulled taut and gathered at the neck, her head both noble and expressionless, pats Mrs. Jefferson's back. "It's all right," she murmurs, comforting the comforter. "Everything is all right."

Mrs. Jefferson pulls her huge self up again and sniffs. "Ain't it just the way, though?" she murmurs a condolence. "Listen, now: if it's anything I can do for you, honey, you don't hesitate, hear? You jus' let me know. Okay?"

Gloria nods. Gloria dark and solemn—she strikes me suddenly as a Byzantine icon, not unkind but unbending.

"I brought some fried chicken," says Mrs. Alma Jefferson. "Mary said leave it in the kitchen, so I did. I'm just goin' out here to set a while," she reassures the bereaved, dabbing her eyes with the corner of her sleeve. Without warning she pokes her hand in my direction. "Hello, Pastor." We exchange a brief handshake. She puts a knuckle to Gloria's cheek then bustles from the room.

There are six or seven women sitting in the living room. People will come and go the whole day through. Wakes with us are lingering affairs, swelling to their just proportions in the evening.

Mary Moore returns.

Gloria doesn't look at her either.

In fact, throughout my entire visit this afternoon, Gloria hasn't addressed her at all, and Mary has suffered the silence.

She scans the room. Her eyes light upon underwear in the corner. "I could do your laundry," she says.

Gloria turns and looks out of the window, presenting Mary with her profile.

Yes: it's time for me to go.

But before I can make a proper departure, Mary moves behind her cousin and begins to massage her temples. "Remember when we used to braid the other's hair, Gloria? Skinny-legged little girls? Remember?"

Gloria gazes out the window.

"What do you think?" says Mary earnestly. "Can I do it again? Baby? Feels so good. I'll warm your head. I'll make you calm. I'll steal that headache away till you're small and safe and sweet again—"

Gloria says, "Don't."

"Shhh," says Mary. "You know you need the comforting."

Gloria reaches up and pushes Mary's hand away. "Don't," she says.

So Mary clasps her hands together and thrusts them against her chin. "Why not?" She is wounded.

"It isn't necessary."

"Please, Gloria, don't shut me out."

"I ain't shuttin' no one out."

"You know I'm here for you."

"Thank you. I don't want my hair braided. I am not a child. And I am not going to Sonny Boy's apartment with you. No!"

Suddenly a gulf yawns between the women, and I have the sense that this is a troublous subject.

Gloria retreats from it. She mumbles again, "It's . . . it just isn't necessary."

But Mary herself is provoked. "Some things *are* necessary," she scolds. She moves to the dresser, where Gloria can see her, and she touches the plastic bag brought home from the hospital. "Look, Gloria! Look at this here," Mary commands. "You haven't inspected Sonny Boy's things. You haven't even opened the package! You don't know what he took to the hospital, and you don't know what you brought home; you don't—"

"I don't want to!" Gloria snaps, twisting her head away. "I don't have to!"

"Oh, yes, you do. It's his identification in here, his most personal things, his wallet. You need to check for papers—"

"No! I don't. You do it. Not me."

Mary pauses for a hot second, then narrows her eyes. "Fine," she says. She takes the bag and starts to open the drawstring.

The sound frightens Gloria, who turns and yelps, "*Not now!*" But then by a mighty effort she restrains herself. She whispers, "Not here."

"When, Gloria?" Mary's eyes are flashing with feeling. "And where, Gloria? And why not now? Can you tell me that?"

Quietly, Gloria whispers, "Because I don't want to be smelling his cologne. If you open that package, I'll smell his cologne. No, no, I don't want to be smelling my uncle now."

That explanation devastates Mary. Her face crumples with guilt, and the woman herself sinks down to her knees by Gloria's chair, murmuring, "Baby, baby, I never meant to push you to sorrows. I just . . ." She breathes deeply a moment, looking up at her cousin. "It's just, some things need doing. We *had* to shop today, is why I went with you. We *have* to do what the funeral director says. And I'll be with you when you get ready to go to Sonny Boy's apartment—"

"Stop it," says Gloria in a cold, articulate tone, gazing out of the window again. "Mary, stop that nonsense. I am not going to Sonny Boy's apartment. I will not go in there. I won't. Now, I want you to put Alma Jefferson's fried chicken in the refrigerator. Tommy can eat some when he gets home tonight."

Mary, stricken, obeys. She withdraws in silence, and her departure permits my own. Then Gloria is left in the bedroom, severe and upright, a sufficiency unto herself, silent and dry and alone.

❦

The Signs of Denial

We repeat the principle: life is lived in relationship; and relationship requires the mutual participation of two beings.

When the relationship breaks, however, and one is left alone, she might sometimes *pretend* the presence of the other and act as if she were *re-*acting. She might fulfill both roles, creating the signals of the departed herself, so that the circuit *feels* unbroken for a while. In this manner she refuses to admit his absence.

A mother might keep the room of her daughter precisely the way it was before the girl left home (marriage? run-away? war? death?)—all the dolls, all the posters, all the dainty things still in their places. She might dust the room weekly, as if the child were about to return any day now. With her mouth the mother says, "She's gone." But her heart and her imagination pretend a presence: she is a mother still, awaiting the spirit of her child.

But it is such exhausting work, playing the parts of two.

Or sometimes the griever spends energy simply avoiding the evidence of the break: if she does not see and cannot feel the separation, then it hasn't occurred. By desire alone she strives to abolish certain facts in the universe—as though her very awareness (like God's) made or unmade things.

There is a part of Gloria Ferguson that knows which symbols of death must destroy her illusion of life. The particular scent of her uncle *must*, without his smile, without his voice, without his body, prove him absent indeed. (Such personal signals, you see, are promises that charge the heart with anticipation, but that cannot be kept; and the disappointment that follows cries *Death, death!* to the trembling heart, and kills it again and again.) When she went with Mary to buy clothes for Sonny Boy—underwear in his size, socks for his naked feet—she almost lost control altogether. Well, then: what if she should enter his apartment, the very walls of which would clamor the name of the man, and what if she should find it empty? What then? As long as she does not go, she holds the horror at bay. She preserves for herself an emotional latitude—in the secret of her soul pretending the presence that hasn't been completely disproven.

But even as the day gives way to night and the house fills up with people come to mourn with her, Gloria grows wearier.

Dramatically, passionately, against all reason, the griever may express her disbelief of the separation: *It cannot be!* And the expression itself may be so consuming of all her attention that the very gestures of denial can become the evidence she chooses to believe in, rather than in fact. She is consoled—for a while.

—So the widow awakes one morning, suddenly convinced that a mistake has been made. Records were confused. Somebody else died, not her husband. Hope springs in her breast, and she actually feels happy for an instant.

—She may spontaneously make breakfast for two and only notice what she's done when setting the table.

—The floorboards creak in the next room, and she looks up smiling, truly expecting her husband to enter. She thinks ridiculous things in the interval: *He's coming, but he's testing how much I love him.*

—Or in the midst of pain, the griever actually cries aloud the lie: "He is not gone." The divorcé: "She loves me still. We will get together again." The parent pronounces the name: "Matthew! Matthew!"—and a marvelous thing occurs. The declaration itself feels real! The lie *out loud* suggests a presence after all. Language replaces reality, and there is a brief, immediate respite: the griever has discovered the means to invoke the image of what is gone. At night she whispers over and over, "Matthew, Matthew, Matthew," until she falls asleep.

—More commonly, the griever will talk about the beloved in detail, over and over, to anyone willing to listen. The talk itself makes the relationship continue. Let every good friend realize that the words are not meant to inform the listener, but rather to be *experienced* by the *speaker*—and then no one will grow bored or worried for her. Sometimes the talk falls into the present tense: "Yes, he likes beans cooked in bacon fat—" Sometimes the talk looks toward the future, making plans as if no break occurred. If some officious friend points out the fallacy, well, the griever agrees, looks sad, and apologizes—but then (so long as denial still is necessary) she may avoid that particular friend thereafter. And she can become angry (as Gloria was with Mary) for the challenge to her illusion.

—And this can be a sign of denial too: that the griever feels an unfounded ebullience, a lightness, even a joy, as if the break were a good thing after all and she, in its goodness, has happily skipped the deeper anguish. Between the announcement of an impending divorce, for example, and the actual serving of papers, between the first pain of knowing and the dead-fall crush of reality, there may be a period of irrational gladness. Any sort of break we suffer might be explained as containing an ultimate good ("a blessing in disguise"), and the griever, hungry for order in chaos, *chooses* to believe it. She seems in no way to deny the separation. Rather, she busies herself putting her life back together. She cleans house. She buys new clothes. She sleeps well and considers herself fortunate. She does not consider (does not even suspect) the enormity of her loss nor the confusion of the grieving to come. And the proof of the goodness of this separation is in the miraculous peace she feels. Until the papers are served. Until the court declares divorce. Until the body lies still in its coffin. Until the oranges come tumbling down and she cannot put things together again. Until the therapist comes into the room holding before her eyes the prosthesis that must take the place of her breast forever and ever hereafter.

Until she must enter the apartment of her uncle and smell his smell and feel the absence.

❦

The people of our neighborhood—friends, kin, members of any church, folks close to those that suffer—they don't even think about it. They gather. They're not invited. They don't call ahead. They know no alternative. There is always a wake in the home of the bereaved. And this precisely *is* the wake: that the people gather there.

They talk. Sometimes it's the genial noise of many conversations all at once, the natural wash of the community when it's death that wants a cleansing. Sometimes the mood of the whole room goes low and laments. Then sometimes it rises to hilarity, and someone is telling a story, and everyone's remembering the same silly thing. So they laugh and they laugh till they weep again. Because this is what a wake is: the command review of a life, the immediate and living response to the life that was, helpless laughter, helpless tears, both. And this is what a wake has always been: the motion of one dead spirit still among the living; the chance for the most bereaved to admit and to express her grief in the company of others, in the safety of their presence.

So Gloria's house is crowded when I come, faces in a ring around the living room, nodding, gazing at me, waiting.

It's after nine at night. No matter. Likely no one has left since seven. And now that the pastor's here, things turn formal. It's his job to pray. Talk pauses a while till people can judge whether he intends to do his job sooner or later.

Well, later.

As a matter of fact, I always feel a bit uncomfortable praying on demand or praying with people whose spirits I don't yet know. I always need some time to adjust. Half the people here are strangers to me. Therefore, later.

Right now I adjust to this group by greeting those I know, the members of my congregation.

Mary Moore helps me. "This is our pastor," she announces. And then to me she says, "Can I rest your coat?"

"Oh, Mary, thank you."

While she does that, I make a circuit of the room, and the talk resumes; the room returns to its jumble of sound.

"Margaret Wiley," I say to a dark and dignified smiling woman— ever present in our parish when her presence can be healing. And the daughter beside her: "Hello, Linda." And the granddaughter: "Stephanie." Stephanie's name means *crown*. We look directly into one another's eyes, each grateful that the other is here. I'm beginning to feel better. "Rosemary Smith," I say around the circle, and "Lillian," and "Rozaline," "Aida, Jim, I'm so glad to see you," "Cassandra, Shirley, Sherry—" These last three I greet with particular care. They are children of Gloria Ferguson. Another daughter, Deborah, isn't here. And she has a son: "Where's Tommy?" I ask.

"With Mamma," they say.

"Is your mother in the back bedroom?"

"Yes."

Mary Moore touches my shoulder and leads me from the living room into a kitchen full of food. Suddenly she turns and hugs me and breaks into silent tears. A hard day for Mary. A hard time altogether. She is both a griever and a comforter. I return the hug as long as she wants it.

"Oh Pastor! She's still pinching her mouth. She's so mad at me."

"She isn't mad at *you*, Mary. Not at you. Just mad."

"Well, well, it feels like me, and I don't know what to do with it. You want coffee?" She pulls back now and stares at the food. "Or fried chicken? Or beans? Or tuna casserole? Hoo, it's a bunch of food." She sighs and smiles. She runs cold water into the sink and washes her face.

The conversations grow louder in the front room. —*was dancin' the two-step*, someone is saying while others are grunting agreement: "*Yep, the two-step—*"

Mary whispers, "Thank you, Pastor," and we go into the bedroom.

"Gloria?" says Mary. "Pastor's back."

Tommy is sitting on the side of the bed by his mamma. Huge and young and helpless: a boy in middle school but seemingly strong enough to play on a high school football squad. He flaps his hand at me without smiling. He would serve his mother if he could. If he knew how. But she is sitting erect and independent. She has indicated no need to anyone. Therefore Tommy sits in sad silence and waits.

Gloria's face is ashen grey.

She does not acknowledge Mary's announcement. Mary, quietly, leaves.

I move to shake Tommy's hand. I admire this child, his rooted loyalty to his mother.

Gloria says toward the empty doorway, "You going to pray?"

I don't sit. I stand next to her. "Yes," I say.

"Well, you better."

"Now, Gloria?"

But she draws a sharp breath. "Mary says I have to go to Sonny Boy's apartment—"

"I know."

The voices in the front room suddenly swell in laughter. *I told you, didn't I? Ha ha! He carried her like a flop-doll for two hours straight an' they won the dance 'cause he never quit smilin'—but she was stumblin' drunk! Ha ha ha! The two-step!*

"Pastor, you don't think I need to go there, do you?" Now she looks toward me. "I've done about all I can do." She drops her eyes to her hands. "You going to pray?"

"Yes, Gloria. It's the main reason why I came." I wish I could hug her as naturally as I hugged Mary; but her features refuse it. She's solitary now.

"You better," she says. "Tommy, Pastor's going to pray."

And I would. Immediately. The boy beside me glances up, then lowers his head—but Gloria's talking again:

"This is what I know. I know I did the right thing yesterday. Went to Gaines Funeral Home. Mr. Lawrence George took us down to where he's got coffins. But when I saw them open—Oh Pastor, my heart started kickin' *hard!* It hurt. I couldn't breathe. Pick a coffin for Sonny Boy! I couldn't—"

—*one more person!* Suddenly someone is angry in the front room. I recognize that voice because it makes a diphthong of the word "person" and it rattles the windows: Marie Landers, Gloria's mother, must have just come in.

If one more pour-son say, "Let me know what I can do for you," I'm gon' spit in his eye. I hate that! How do I know what you can do for me? Figger it out yourself!

Tommy cocks his head, listening to his grandmother.

Someone cries, *Preach it, sister!*

There's a moment of silence, then Marie barks, *Yah-ha!* She caught a glimpse of herself. She's laughing. *Ha ha ha!*

Gloria, wearily, shakes her head. "Oh, Mamma."

Tommy looks at her with a speechless concern.

Softly she says to me, "Mr. Lawrence George said get good clothes for Sonny Boy. So we went to Sears for the underwear and a white shirt and argyle socks, and I said to myself, 'For Sonny Boy to dance in,' and Mary said, 'We have to get a suit.' I said, 'We'll *buy* one.' She said, 'We don't know his sizes.' I said, 'We'll *buy* one.' She said, 'We have to get it from his apartment.' I said, 'No.' I said, '*No!*' I said, 'No, no, no, no—' and I walked out of Sears and left her there."

Gloria is staring down into her hands. She whispers, "You going to pray now?"

—*seen that boy eat fish!* Someone has started a story in the front room.

"Pastor?" Gloria says, "you don't think I have to go into Sonny Boy's apartment, do you?"

—*seen him pop a whole filet in his mouth at once. Bones and all!*

That's Margaret Wiley's voice. Gloria stiffens, listening suddenly.

He's a little man, you know, but he could cram the longest, fried-est fiddler into his mouth. Then he'd roll up his eyes and chew and chew and swallow down the meat and finally, phoo-phoo, spit out them fishbones like darts, clean as needles, ha ha ha!

During this story, Gloria lowers her face into her hands. Her shoulders begin to shake. Tommy sees this. He reaches toward her, then changes his mind and jumps up and runs from the room. She begins to turn her head left and right. Her breathing grows labored, and I too want to reach toward her—

That boy, cries Margaret Wiley, *he deboned the fish inside his mouth. Artist of the fish-bones, ol' Tom Cat—*

Tommy's back. "Mamma?" He's carrying a glass of water. Gloria's shaking uncontrollably, and Tommy is frightened. "Mamma! Please!"

But all at once she lifts her face and gulps air and splutters into laughter. She's laughing! "I—" she chokes. "I—" But she can't say more.

Tommy draws his lips into a silly, bewildered grin.

I start chuckling in spite of myself.

It sounds so beautiful, to hear my Gloria laughing, like water coming down!

"Oh!" she shouts, aching at the stomach. "Oh! Oh! I've seen him eat fish! Oh, Sonny Boy!" She wraps her arms around her abdomen and leans forward, laughing, "Oh, oh, oh—"

The whole house has heard her. The living room holds still, listening.

Gloria, bent forward, draws another enormous breath, and I keep grinning, expecting another burst of laughter.

It never comes.

Instead, a high, thin, pitiful note arises from Gloria Ferguson. A long, long wail goes up. She slips forward out of her chair. She kneels. She is weeping: "Sonny Boy, Sonny Boy, Sonny Boy." She raises her face. The tears roll down. She rocks back and forth, "Oh, Sonny Boy, don't go 'way from me. Don't leave me, please." She is kneading her stomach as if the pain in that place is more than she can bear.

All at once she cries at the top of her lungs, "Daddy! Daddy, I miss you!"

And then she sinks, sobbing. None of the sadness is secret now. Tommy, holding a glass of water, is crying with wide-open eyes. People are creeping into the bedroom, gazing at Gloria in merciful kindness. And I myself—I have the right, finally, to go to the woman to touch her.

So I kneel beside her and brush back the hair with my hand, and then I put my arm around her and I hug her, and she turns and clings to me. "Pastor, it hurts so bad, so bad."

Here comes Margaret Wiley and Linda behind her, and Stephanie. Here come Cassandra and Shirley and Sherry. Here comes the community.

I can pray now.

So I say, *The Lord is my shepherd; I shall not want.*

The people begin to take one another's hand. They make a great chain of hand-holding. It winds out of the bedroom, through the kitchen, into the front room, into the universe, till all of the people have a hand and hold it. And Mary Moore takes Tommy's hand. And Tommy kneels by me. And I hold Gloria.

He maketh me to lie down in green pastures: he leadeth me beside the still waters. He restoreth my soul: he leadeth me in the paths of righteousness for his name's sake.

Now Tommy, muscular son of his mother, touches her cheek for attention. She looks up, tear-streaked. He offers her the glass of water. Gazing at him, she takes it. She drinks.

Yea, though I walk through the valley of the shadow of death, I will fear no evil—

And suddenly, while I am praying, I can hear the deep notes of an organ swelling around me. A soft, sustaining, lovely music. It is the people. All of the voices. Murmuring, remembering, reciting the psalm with me:

—for thou art with me; thy rod and thy staff they comfort me.

Holy voices. A holy congregation. A holy cup in which to carry my

Gloria's grieving. She has finished drinking. She is crying freely now. But we are the tolling of one great bell around her:

Thou preparest a table before me in the presence of mine enemies: thou anointest my head with oil; my cup runneth over.

Surely goodness and mercy shall follow me all the days of my life: and I will dwell in the house of the Lord forever.

Amen, say all of the people.

"Amen," I say in the ear of my sister.

Amen, sweet Gloria, whom I love so tenderly. The terrible pain has arrived. But my arm is around you now.

Amen.

❦

Denial is, at bottom, the supreme effort of the human still to control his world and to maintain the lie inviolate: "You will not die." Denial is an active refusal to accept the natural limitations of the creature.

God said, "Let there be light," and there was light.

In denial we cry, "Let there be life" where there is no life; but so long as we cry it loud enough, we may delude ourselves—until we lose our breath and must confront the truth that we are limited.

When the divorcée received her papers and burst into furious tears; when the widower saw his wife in the coffin; when Gloria began to wail, "Daddy, Daddy, I miss you"—then sorrow rose from the hidden places, and the pain was greater than they had imagined it could be. They were crying for the immediate break of a dear relationship. They were crying for the sudden sense of impotence in the universe. They were crying for all whose fate it is to die, for all who cannot change that.

They were crying for the race.

They were Rachel, weeping for the children since now they know what awaits them all—and like Rachel, they would not be comforted.

Instead, they found another resource in themselves: bitterness. Brute emotion.

There is something satisfying in the complete release of a seemingly righteous wrath. And, feeling the force of a personal rage, the griever has found her second strategy against the angel of death. If willfulness fails, she shall enlarge herself with anger.

EPISODE II: THE OPPOSITION OF EMOTION

The failure of the will leads to, and intensifies, the effort of emotion. Simply, the obduracy of death frustrates us. It angers us. Anger is the reaction of the unreconciled.

First, like children, we cry: "I don't *want* it."

And when we must swallow it anyway, like children we cry, "I don't *like* it!"

"I hate it!" Such hatred itself feels very like power within us.

1. We are, after all, exercising a certain genuine strength, realizing and releasing an internal resource.

2. And rage persuades us that we are independent in judgment at least, able to make up our own minds and to exert our own criticisms.

3. And it is often characteristic of anger to believe that one has been dealt a personal injustice. Anger feels righteous in the face of our foe's unrighteousness. Moral law seems on our side, giving us the right to even greater rages: *out*-rage!

With the opposition of our will we tried to be the Creator and failed. We are not God.

With the opposition of emotion, now, we admit as much; but then we take up an adversarial position against the Deity (for the fact that he *is* the Deity and we are not) and attack him—as though we might be equal to God in our fury if not in our nature. Moreover, like Job we believe that our case is just in the courts of the cosmos: anger indicts God for our particular pain and then for the misery of all flesh. No: we do not always name God in the indictment. Rather, we may depersonalize it and "rage against the dying of the light," or complain about "the way things are," or fly in the face of a human authority, or accuse the impassive skies. But these are symbols or dodges. God is responsible. God is our opposite. Jacob is striving with God.

There is a grandeur in the expression of emotion, here at the limits of existence. Humans confronting the Deity, whether in the assizes or with swords, do always seem heroic. And for a while the poetry of the thing, the epic stature, swells us. And we are strong.

For a while.

The day is grey. A dreary, drizzling autumn day. "Nasty," the neighbors say. On such a day, people wear sweaters.

But Gloria stands in the center of a small room, her back to the windows—and the windows are open. So is the door to the tiny terrace behind her. So is the apartment door in front of her. The wind is billowing curtains and blowing through Sonny Boy's apartment into the hallways of Buckner Towers.

Her arms are folded, her shoulders hunched, the lights are off, the room is dark.

When they had first entered, Mary Moore wrinkled her nose and said, "Faw!"

Gloria stalked straight to the windows.

"Honey?" Mary said. "It's cold outside."

"Musty!" Gloria snapped, yanking windows open. "Smells moldy in here."

"It smells like Sonny Boy."

"It smells like death."

So Mary said no more. She went into the bedroom while Gloria took up her chilly position in the living room, her arms folded.

The light is on where Mary went. Hangers click in the clothes closet. Mary is busy.

Gloria, unmoving, glares around the place. Blaming it with her eyes.

Sofa on her left. Big TV on her right. Coffee table in front of her. Everything quiet, except the wind flutters pages on the coffee table.

Kitchen alcove next to the apartment door. A fry-pan on the stove. Cold grease and bits of potato in that. Sonny Boy's meal. *Damn you, Sonny Boy Hopson!* Gloria narrows her eye and curses him because she has begged him and begged him to give up his fried foods.

But then she sees something else and her heart breaks: *Oh, Sonny Boy!* By the sofa two slippers lie side by side, squashed and empty. She thinks of her uncle's bare feet. She feels so guilty that she cursed him.

Ain' no one here but the slippers. And he can't dance no more. Oh, Sonny Boy.

"Gloria?"

Mary Moore is calling from the bedroom.

"Gloria, he's got a bunch of suits in here. I don't know which one to pick." Suddenly she gives a little squeal: "Well, lookee here!"

Mary appears in the doorway, grinning, holding high a cream-white suit. "Remember this? Remember Buddy's wedding? Sonny Boy trifled with the Pastor that day—wouldn't take off his hat in church—"

"Not that suit."

"Oh, honey, yes it is. At the reception Sonny Boy danced in this exact same suit." Mary lifts an empty sleeve and begins to sway, to dance. The motion makes a tiny *Clink* in one of the pockets.

"Not that suit," Gloria repeats through her teeth.

Mary stops. "But I know I'm right—"

"I don't want him buried in that suit!"

"Oh! No. I didn't mean that either, honey," says Mary, crestfallen. "I was just remembering."

"Put it back."

Poor Mary obeys. She lowers the suit and turns back into the bedroom. A pocket hits the doorknob: *Clink!*

"Wait," Gloria says. "What's that?"

"What's what?"

"That." She breaks position, walks to the bedroom, and begins to pat the white suit until she causes *Clink, clink!* in a side pocket. Her face maintains an intent expression; her heart, however, is bucking against her chest. She reaches into the pocket, panting slightly, and finds and feels and draws forth two tiny bottles, two amber vials filled with tablets.

The women look at one another.

"Nitroglycerine," says Mary. "Prevents angina."

"Heart attack."

"Yes."

"He kept them close, didn't he?"

"Yes."

"Oh, Mary! Oh, Mary!"

On impulse, Gloria goes to the closet and pats the pockets of other suits. *Clink! Clink!* From every suit she takes an amber vial filled with tablets. Five bottles.

"Oh, Mary! This is so pitiful."

Now her eyes are adjusted. Now she starts to see bottles everywhere. On the table by his bed. On the dresser. Her stomach grows tighter and tighter at the multiplication of tiny bottles. She rushes back into the sitting room. There are bottles in the corner of the windowsills, behind the sofa, in the kitchen, in the cupboards, by the telephone. Gloria trembles. She throws the bottles together in the center of his bed.

"He was so scared! Mary, don't you see? He was fearing an attack at any time, in any place—and he was alone! He was alone! He was all alone!" Gloria can't control the mood now. Her face twists in anguish at the discovery. "He—" There must be two dozen bottles gathered like roaches on the bedspread. "He didn't have no one else to depend on! Only on his own self to reach the nitro! Damn it!" Gloria cries.

Mary is standing perfectly still, her head bowed down, holding low the cream-white suit. It drags on the ground.

Gloria raises her face to the ceiling. Her chin dimples and quivers. Her eyes are brimming. She does not want to weep now. She does not want to be *weak* now!

She can't help herself.

"Damn it!" she cries, and the shuddering overwhelms her, and the tears stream down. "He didn't deserve this! He was a good man! He didn't deserve to stow his life in medicine bottles, fearing death at every step, alone! Alone! I'm going to tell you, cousin! I'm going to tell you the God's truth: *I hate this! Oh, dear God, I hate this!*"

Mary can't look up. She's crying too, but in silence. The white suit slips from her fingers, slumps to the floor and sighs and collapses upon itself.

Gloria notices.

In a sweet articulation, almost lisping—as if instructing a child—she speaks slowly now, word by word: "There's an old man sits down in the lounge of this apartment building. I say he's ninety. Skinny switch of an ol' white man, runny blue eyes, brown blotches on his face, plain bone an' a bit o' skin. You seen him, Mary. You know who I mean, an' you *know* I'm right.

"Well, when I knocked on the door for someone to let me into the building, that ol' stick jus' stared at me and didn't move. Nasty ol' man. No kin anywhere. No friend to mourn *his* passin'."

Gloria lowers her voice to a witchy hissing. She pinches her mouth and glares at Mary and draws out her every word in black African vowels: "An' so what I say now, I say that if things was truly fair, that ol' man—he'd be daid, an' my uncle Sonny Boy 'ud be livin' now.

But ain't no fairness, Mary. Now, you *know* that! Ain't no sense, ain't no kindness, ain't no love or righteousness a-tall. Nasty ol' white man lives, an' a good man dies. So," she whispers, lower and lower and meaner than ever, "so what am I gon' do? Listen me, Mary. You listen me: Ah'm gon' resign religion. An' Ah *do*!"

Mary, altogether still but dreadfully alert, whispers, "You don't mean that."

Gloria purses her mouth. "Try me."

❧

The Signs of Anger

Death is death, now, in the open. This is the natural progression of grieving, that there comes the time when the griever cannot doubt her separation any more.

But she doesn't *accept it*. Knowing the truth does not mean that she submits to the truth. Rather, the struggle is openly engaged and feelings all come to the surface. Emotion grows mighty and strong.

And grief becomes grievance:

"Why is this happening? What did I do? I did nothing to deserve this—mastectomy, divorce, betrayal, criminal child. Well, then, whose fault is it after all?"

More broadly: Why does God allow such things to happen? Why do bad people hurt good people? Doesn't goodness count?

And because anger presents itself as a passionate questioning, friends and comforters feel that they must answer the questions, that healing will come with the "right" solution. (Like Job's comforters, folks think that grief is a problem to be solved.) So they quote Scripture or offer philosophic anodynes. It does no good. These answers only make the griever angrier. So friends and the foolish comforters speak of biological necessities. Or else they mouth platitudes: "Nothing lasts forever." "We all have to go sometime." "Accept it." "Look on the bright side: you're not losing a daughter; you're gaining a son." Yet nothing consoles the griever. She continues with fully as much passion to ask her questions—because these come not from an inquisitive mind, but from a disappointed soul. Let every wise comforter understand: questions asked in anger have no answers. That is the point!

The griever feels herself to be terribly wronged. Her questions aren't questions at all. They are accusations. And if she is seriously seeking anything by them, it is redress. She doesn't want evil explained. She wants it punished.

Therefore, as the anger increases the language changes, invoking universal codes by which to lodge the grievance: "It isn't fair!" she declares. "No one deserves to suffer so. It just isn't right."

There may come, then, a point where passion persuades the griever that she can *make* things right. No: she can't raise the dead. No: she can't restore the failed marriage or grow a new breast or regain her job. But she *can* restore a moral order *by making someone pay*. Vengeance follows naturally as a personal force, a private power, a means at one's own hand for solving the outrage of this dying.

More than mere talk for its expression, now anger has something to do.

She sues her physician—and means it! Or takes a whole corporation to court. The criminal justice system is harried and driven to do its job. The death penalty (if it applies) looks very righteous right now. Ecclesiastic rules come down on the heads of enemies. Or if there is no obvious culprit and if no legal system applies, she picks her own foe and avenges herself in subtler ways: by bitter gossip, by a deep, unspoken, smoky hatred.

Here is where families break apart over minor matters. At the death of a parent, brothers and sisters cease to speak *to* each other but continue to speak *about* each other with a raking criticism. Someone is blamed because he didn't visit mother before she died. Someone else skipped the funeral. Someone else took a brooch she had no right to take. Little sins are magnified, because the griever is seeking fault for the death itself, a place to lodge her rage: upon the head of a brother or sister are heaped the wrongs of the universe. Oh, heavy burden!

Vengeance is the effort to create meaning and order where there is chaos and pointless suffering. Hurt for hurt: this is the re-establishment of a rough justice, a comprehensible world, after all.

But the real foe is no *one*. At least no one *else*. Her real enemy is the limitation of human flesh, that people die. None of her passionate action changes that. No matter, then, how sweet the vengeance tastes at the start, in the end the griever is no more satisfied by this than by the answers offered her accusatory questions. Vanity of vanities: she is little in the universe, and the One with Whom her real grievance lies, He remains supreme, seemingly indifferent, untouched by her furies.

He: God.

It is good finally to admit the ultimate object of anger. To direct it elsewhere is dangerous, destroying friendships and families and relationships that do not deserve the attack. To direct one's wrath at God may not be righteous; but it is right. Now the drama of grief can move properly through its pattern toward healing.

And God alone is able to take the griever's anger and turn it to good.

Anger, Seeking its Object

Comforters, anger is natural. It needn't frighten you, however vehement. But it wants a focus, always, in order to manifest itself, and it *can* mistake its object.

Your best service at this juncture, then, is (1) to recognize when the griever is aiming her fury in the wrong direction, and (2) gently to re-direct it till she knows that her deepest grievance is with God.

Here are signs of a proper anger improperly placed:

—*Anger Diffused*, when emotion simply drowns the griever.

"I go home," a woman told me, "and scream. I just scream, loud as I can, till I break down and cry, and the crying makes me tired, and I sleep. What else can I do? I scream."

This is the simple discharge of emotion. Maybe kindness keeps the griever from blaming anyone. Maybe she's unable to think: rage erupts, inarticulate and unfocused. Or maybe the destructive force of her fury frightens her too much to fault another person, *because I could kill him*, she thinks. The griever scares herself, goes home, and screams.

Or else she represses emotion altogether, feeling absolutely nothing, walking stiffly, speaking coldly, refrained from any expression of anger—but burning herself on the inside as with an acid.

Help her to take this anger to the Lord.

—*Anger Socially Directed*, when whole categories of people are held accountable for the griever's sorrow.

Because of his divorce a man may hate women generally, or a

woman men. Then any member of the enemy group can trigger anger, and the griever lashes out at innocent individuals.

Because a mugger was black, his victim unconsciously blames the race. The anger is right and necessary; its object is wrong.

Because it was a cop who caught her son and sent him to prison, an impoverished mother is enraged by any blue uniform.

I know a man whose wife died on the night his supervisor required overtime. "If I'd been home," he told me, "I could've called 911." He grew grim at work thereafter. He nursed a bitterness against the entire plant, though he didn't recognize the cause of his feeling. Sullenly he resisted every suggestion his supervisor made. His performance suffered. And when he was finally fired, the man was not surprised: to him this was proof of the intrinsic evil of that plant.

Or sometimes the scope of the griever's emotion grows large enough to embrace people in general, and anger manifests itself by antisocial behavior. She separates herself. Her clothing and her action demonstrate scorn for the conventions of her community. Because she has suffered a singular hurt, she wants all people to pay.

Gloria's fury at that "ol' stick" of a white man is, in fact, fury at any who survive, though seemingly less worthy than her beloved Sonny Boy.

Such misdirected judgment is neither realistic nor helpful; it forestalls healing. Let it go to him who is greater than any group, greater than societies and civilizations together: to the Lord.

—*Anger Directed at Any Authority*, at those who seem to the griever responsible.

Doctors and pastors are often the object of a griever's criticism, the former for their knowledge of the body, the latter for their knowledge of the spirit. Whole families may contemplate leaving their churches because the pastor, by some infraction, seemed to fail his duty.

It is too dreadful to approach the judgment seat of God (whom the griever takes to be the one responsible for "the way things are"). Therefore she taxes God's representative, anyone she believes an authority below the heavens: lawyers, governments, bosses, teachers, parents, strong-willed and confident people.

—*Anger Directed at Intimates*, since those who love the griever are softest to her criticisms and vulnerable to her attacks.

Well, (1) they register the wound quicker than others; and anger, seeking tit for tat, wants to witness the pain it inflicts.

By instinct (2) the griever knows where the stroke will hurt them the most, and this anger is never planned nor rational; it is always instinctual.

And (3) the tight interweaving of their lives to hers makes them available for the sudden outburst. Anger comes suddenly. And looking for an acceptable cause, it will easily recall some old offense and charge the intimate person all over again, but with a renewed and astonishing wrath.

Here is most dangerous ground. This misdirection of anger can damage dear relationships forever. Quickly, quickly teach the griever her error and aim her guns where they are safer, at her God.

—*Anger Directed at the Deceased* is not at all uncommon, though shocking and troublous to the griever when she discovers it in herself.

Gloria was thunderstruck that she could curse Sonny Boy or blame him for his own death. Yet there occur to the griever a hundred ways by which the dead could have preserved his life. He didn't *have* to smoke. Or work twelve hours a day. Or carry so much fat.

More shocking still is the notion he did it on purpose. Sometimes in anger the griever condemns the dead, wanting to punish him, angrier still that he's past retribution, being dead.

Well, then the anger seems shameful and crazy and cruel. Nevertheless, it is natural still, though altogether hopeless to charge the dead with dying.

Turn it toward the Lord.

Or when the dying is a divorce, the "dead" is walking about on two legs. Hatred never experienced such violent excesses as in a divorce: the griever becomes a shrieking harridan of rage, singularly enjoying the release of vitriol. It feels good. It feels, at the same time, sick and horrible. And finally it must cease, or it will embitter the divorcée's life ever thereafter.

Turn it from the living individual, whose suffering, no matter how great, will change nothing of death or the world.

Turn it to the Lord.

—*Anger Directed Inward* is the griever's blaming herself for the circumstances of her grief. It is guilt. It goes nowhere.

"What could I have done differently?" she begs. "Where did I go wrong?"—as though to determine that might give her the chance to make things right again.

This is anger. It is the same emotion as that which the griever projected at others. It is identified when she finds relief in self-inflicted pain—for such anger still seeks, though by an internal effort, to restore order in chaos. This sort of guilt knows nothing of the mercy of God, knows only the law. The griever chooses to punish herself to balance the records.

These, then, are some signs of a futile, self-directed anger:

That the griever lets her home grow filthy, that she doesn't eat well, or wash, or sleep; that she creates an environment almost calculated to make her sick—because she feels she deserves no better.

That she fails her professional duties, arriving late at work, performing haphazardly, resisting help, almost forcing her superiors to contemplate releasing her.

That she consistently offends or neglects her closest friends—almost destroying the community that supports her.

That she descends into substance abuse, or a libertine lifestyle, sins never sinned before, surrendering to the evil image she has of herself and "proving," as it were, how bad she is.

Stop it!

Comforter, help her to stop such ruinous behavior. She need not accept this kind of fault.

But *stop it* doesn't mean that she should shut the anger off. Rather, identify it as anger, a natural reaction to pain, and then re-direct it.

Take It to the Lord

Her anger must be expressed—not so much to relieve herself of the pent emotion as to *experience* the emotion unto its conclusion. It is by experience that she shall be confronted again with the truth of her created self.

Anger is the second assault against death. For all of us who suffer separations, emotion is our second resource. But it is as limited as was our will: our potency is impotent, our strength is weak, our raging changes nothing, and we are not equal to God, no, not even in heroic furies.

But few of us accept this by the hearing of the ear. We require the suffering of experience. Finally, the failure of brute feeling becomes for us a revelation. *Ecce homo!* Behold the human that you are.

Not all of us experience anger to the degrees I've described above.

Everyone's grief goes its own course, and if you feel no resentment at all, God bless you!

But if the anger does rise within you, name it, accept it, and send it to God!

Why?—because God is responsible for the tragic quality of human existence? Of course not. We are responsible.

Then why? Well, for two reasons.

First because we *think* God is responsible. Even when we fear to admit it, God is our final antagonist. God the Omnipotent, Sheer Infinitude, the Holy Other, by his mere being and by the contrast to ourselves, teaches us our tiny-ness. It is plain honesty, then, that carries the anger to God.

But second, because God can take it! God, who understands us better than we understand ourselves, will not be destroyed by our most passionate rages. In fact, he sees already the fury and its intended object before we confess either one. And it hurts the Lord when our anger hurts his people.

Better, then, to give it to God.

It doesn't matter that we are wrong to accuse him for our sorrows. God will not give tit for tat. Instead, he is glad for the chance to communicate. When we speak, we are also inclined to listen. When we confront the Lord we open ourselves to divine response—and then the Lord can engage us in dialogue, and *then* he can heal us.

Even so did he do for Martha when Lazarus died. She berated Jesus for that death: "Lord, if you had been here my brother would not have died." She was wrong in the accusation but right to take it to Jesus, because no one else could do what he did. First, he named himself before her: *I am the resurrection and the life.* Next he required from her the confession that could both change and save her: *Do you believe this?* And only then did Martha answer with faith, "Yes, Lord, I believe that you are the Christ, the Son of God, he who is coming into the world." In this way Martha's wrong was made right, and she was brought into relationship with her Lord again.

Best to take the anger to him.

As Jeremiah does. In his despair the prophet blasts God in dangerous language: "O Lord, thou has deceived me! Thou art stronger than I, and thou hast prevailed. I have become a laughingstock all the day; every one mocks me. Why is my pain unceasing, my wound incurable, refusing to heal? Wilt thou be to me a deceitful brook, like waters that fail?"

Terrible words. Jeremiah accuses God of lying, as though he were drawn into the desert, trusting a certain stream to be there, but the stream was dry. To him, God is that deceitful stream. But God isn't hurt by the charge. Nor does he hurt Jeremiah for it.

Instead, God engages the prophet in dialogue and brings him to healing. *If you return*, says Jehovah, *I will restore you*. And Jeremiah, hears, and Jeremiah confesses, and Jeremiah returns.

Even so, take it to the Lord. Express the anger over and over in prayer until you've gotten the feelings exactly right. If it helps to have a friend sit with you, invite a friend, someone who knows God's forgiveness, who loves you and will not be shocked by the sharpness of your wrath. Detail the accusations against God. Don't compromise the emotion, but pour it forth wholly and clearly. In this way, present yourself before God *exactly as you are*, so that he might deal with the genuine *you*, not some falsely pious you, not the you whom others know: you. Do not be afraid. Do not be deceitful. Do not be a religious hypocrite. You.

And God will respond by loving you. He will acknowledge your anger. He will not call it just, but he will call you to himself and will himself empower the coming.

The opposition of emotion must fail in the end. We cannot but suffer the finitude of all creatures. But if we experience the failure in the presence of the Creator, we will know who is God and who is not.

Thus, Gloria's truculent dismissal, "I resign religion," is both wrong and right. Religion is not the enemy, yet to pick on religion is right, because when her suit fails, she shall not be stuck in grieving (still blaming some human whose punishment would be pointless) but ready to stride toward God himself and like Job to reason with him.

EPISODE III: THE OPPOSITION OF THE INTELLECT

Finally we are reasoning creatures. The mind that defines us becomes the third means by which we wrestle the angel of death.

The will said, "I don't want it"—but failed to change a thing. Emotion said, "I don't like it"—and likewise failed.

Now the intellect says, "Come, let us reason together"—and the event is probed, analyzed, detailed, and divided while we seek some way to comprehend the tragedy and make it less the sorrow that it is.

Exactly so we "bargain" with God before an imminent death, begging that we, like King Hezekiah, might be given fifteen years more of life. We'll exchange pieties for time, prayers for days, and praise for the chance to see another Christmas.

In the same manner, *after* a death we philosophize the stark event, placing it in various lights of analysis in order to change its effect on us—or else to change its nature: the consolation of philosophy.

Or compulsively we rehearse the details of the experience, those causing it and those caused by it. After all, we've solved lesser problems by reducing them to their parts and re-assembling those parts differently. So we seek to re-assemble this differently, telling the story over and over, but adding: "If only—"

❦

We brought nothing into this world, and it is certain that we can carry nothing out.

So I say. So I read from a small black book. I am walking slowly in front of a casket borne by six men, which is followed by a train of people. We wind through the tombstones, moving toward a yellow canopy and chairs arranged in rows beside a new grave.

Sonny Boy is in the casket.

I read: *The Lord gave, and the Lord hath taken away; blessed be the name of the Lord.*

George Ray is one of the pallbearers. A man named Jim. A man named Cyril. The buddies that traveled with him to Fly's and watched him dance in days gone by. Cyril is balding, ears protruding. George Ray is stocky and deeply contemplative. I never met the man before today, but after the funeral service, leaving church, he turned back to look at the building, and then said to me, "I'm going to join this church before I die."

The statement might mean several things.

They that sow in tears shall reap in joy.

I enter the space beneath the canopy. It's chilly. We all wear coats. A gleaming aluminum frame above the grave awaits the casket. Mr. Lawrence George, funeral director, indicates with a wave of his hand that the men should set it center there, and they do, and they back away self-consciously. Sonny Boy's friends are in their fifties and sixties. "Been knowin' him now, well, mos' the century, yep. Yep."

Here comes Gloria. And Mary. Mary has a husband. Gloria, though her children walk solemnly behind her, is essentially alone. They side-step to seats in the front row of chairs, their knees near flowers and inches from the casket. I am standing at its head, to Gloria's left. All this morning she has maintained a noble silence. Others have wept, and some wailed so loudly in church that I had to raise my voice to be heard; but Gloria has borne the day with serenity.

Mr. Lawrence George places flowers on the casket, removes a blossom and crushes it in his left hand while with his right he salutes me: my signal to begin.

I do. I bow my head and read: *Man that is born of a woman is of few days and full of trouble. He cometh forth like a flower, and is cut down; he fleeth also as a shadow, and continueth not—*

Gloria is gazing absolutely nowhere. Her marvelous face is composed. She holds a handkerchief knotted in the palm of her hand. I haven't noticed that she has actually used it; but she's been carrying it ever since the limousine brought her to the church and she entered to take the family's place, front pews, right side. I was standing at the church door when she entered. I put forth my hand to shake hers, but her hand was occupied by its handkerchief. Instead, she turned and walked into me as a blind man might walk into a post: she bumped hard against my chest, then stopped and stood that way for a moment, her forehead pressed against me, her arms straight down, her hair exuding an odor of coconut, and a shining below my eyes. I would have thought she was crying, but she wasn't. I put my arm around her and patted her back. She said, "It ain't nothing, Pastor. No reason to feel bad for me." She stood back then and looked up and I saw that she held herself straight and dry and serene. She said, "'Cause he's comin' back, Pastor." I smiled. She said, "He's comin' back for the buffalo."

Forasmuch as it hath pleased Almighty God, in his wise providence, to take out of this world the soul of our departed brother, we therefore commit his body to the ground; earth to earth, ashes to ashes, dust to dust—

At precisely this point Mr. Lawrence George lifts his left hand and allows the petals of the crushed blossom to fall upon the casket.

Marie Landers raises her hands too: "Lord!" she sighs aloud, "O

Lord! O Jerusalem!" She sits in the front, extreme left. She is having a hard time. She is very sad and doesn't know what to do. Her sister beside her is glassy-eyed and thin and gritty and mad. But Marie— she feels like shouting; at the same time she feels it wouldn't help. So she allows the words to slip out in husky sighing: "Jesus, Jesus. He'p me, Jesus!"

May God the Father, who has created this body;

May God the Son, who by his blood has redeemed this body together with the soul;

May God the Holy Ghost, who by baptism has sanctified this body to be his temple, keep these remains unto the day of the resurrection of all flesh. Amen.

Suddenly the wind gusts over the canopy, which bellies above us and snaps like a sail. Its poles shudder, and Marie Landers leaps to her feet:

"OH, JESUS!" she yells, her eyes rolling. She looks terrified, yelling, stressing the first syllable: "OH! OH! JEEE—"

Behind her, good-hearted George Ray makes feeble motions to stand, to sit, to help, to avoid the outburst.

But it's Gloria who serves best. She stands. She sidles between people's knees and the casket. She reaches her mother and takes the woman's face in two hands—one of them holding its hanky: "Mamma," she says with strength and a gentle coontrol. "Mamma, listen to me. He's coming back. You go on and cry; but he'll be back."

Marie stares at her daughter and then sits again. So does Gloria.

Everyone prays the Lord's Prayer.

And then I face the family and raise my right hand.

The grace of our Lord Jesus Christ and the love of God and the communion of the Holy Ghost be with you all.

It has always been my custom, at the conclusion of this little committal service, to speak immediately and individually with the people closest to the deceased.

So, now:

I take the single step toward Gloria where she sits, and I kneel on the ground in front of her so that she bends her head down to look upon me. I take her hand.

"Gloria?"

"Yes, Pastor?" she whispers, calm and watchful.

"But Sonny Boy did die. He will be raised to life again. He will come back when we all are raised. But we do all of us die first. Yes?"

"Of course. Yes."

"Then what do you mean, *Sonny Boy's coming back for the buffalo?*"

Gloria smiles down upon me. A childlike radiance suffuses her whole expression. She loves me. She pities me a bit. "The buffalo nickel," she says.

She touches my cheek as she did her mother's, and she makes a soft sound meant, I think, to soothe me: "Shhhh, Pastor."

Nobody is moving yet under the canopy. Though they can't hear us, out of respect they will not move until we've finished this private conversation.

Now Gloria begins to unknot the hanky. "I saw him last night," she whispers to me. "He was standin' at the foot of my bed. He smiled with white, white teeth. And he reminded me about the buffalo. When I was a girl, when he entered the military, he gave me the buffalo nickel and told me not to worry, that he would come back for it. As long as I had it, he said, I should know that he was coming back."

Gloria opens her handkerchief and shows me a nickel, one side an Indian head, one side a hump-backed buffalo. She leans very close to me so that our faces form a sort of tent together.

"Well, when he was gone, I got up from bed and went to see if I still had it, and I did. Here it is. It's my way, Pastor. It's just my way. I say: He'll be back for the buffalo. Because he told me so. Twice."

Now it is late October, Saturday morning.

The telephone is ringing even while I unlock the doors to enter the church, and although I don't rush, it keeps on ringing as if waiting patiently for my arrival.

"Hello."

"Pastor?"

"Yes? Gloria?"

"I been sitting here," she says slowly, "looking at pictures of Sonny Boy. Photograph album, you know. Picture of him when he *was* a boy. You know."

She pauses a long time. I can hear her breathing. The breath is labored. I wonder how long she let the telephone ring in the faith that I would come and answer.

She speaks: "Well, I been sitting here thinking. He was so pretty then. Pastor, what if Sonny Boy had accepted Jesus into his life *then*? Would everything be different today?"

She waits. It is a dead-serious question.

But before I can frame an answer, she hurries ahead with explanations: "I mean, he was always good to me. Don't get me wrong. And he *passed* in the arms of Jesus. But what if his whole life was lived that way? What if Sonny Boy danced all of his dances for the sake of Jesus? What if he went to church more than goin' to Fly's on weekends? What if, maybe, he married somebody and stayed married? Maybe he would'n'a been so lonely at the end. Maybe he would'n'a had to care for himself alone. Maybe he would'n'a ate fry-grease. Do you know what I mean? Pastor? Maybe he would'n'a died yet—"

She falls silent. Gloria is sad. It is six weeks since the funeral. She doesn't do this usually, make sudden, wandering calls like this; the woman is by nature gracious and quiet and reasonable. She raised all five children on her own—the husband and father having left them to their own devices years and years ago. She told me once that she accepted her straitened circumstances and chose to keep away from men for the sake of her children. She *chose* morality. I remember that particular conversation. It was at night, and the light was low, and her hair was loose in those days: she reminded me of a medieval saint, heroic in faith and restraint, ascetic, poor, and holy, and devout.

She says now, "You should come and see these pictures. Sonny Boy has pretty eyes. He's so happy."

"Gloria?"

"Yes, Pastor?"

"What about the buffalo nickel? Where is it?"

"Oh, I put that away. It was just a notion."

"Gloria?"

"What."

"Are you crying?"

"Yes. Yes. Yes. Yes. Yes. Yes—"

❧

The Signs of Intellectual Resistance

When anger passes, the change can be dramatic. The griever is no longer defiant, but docile, reasonable, seeming submissive. Comforters sense victory. And foolish comforters leave, thinking their job is done. Society, uncomfortable with death anyway, considers grief concluded and will be irritated if the griever acts like a griever anymore. Which, of course, she will.

Because even her reasoning now is grief.

She feels compelled to talk about the death (whatever sort of dying it is, whether divorce or retirement or surgery or burglary or the dream that was killed by reality). She discusses the details. She seeks any related information. She reads books, speaks with experts, watches TV shows that deal with the subject. And she talks, talks: she talks about anything connected with this death. She wearies her comforters with the talking.

She doesn't use the present tense. She is no longer in denial. Neither does she use belligerent tones. She is not angry.

But with earnest and winsome intelligence she begs agreement from those she trusts, affirmation for her effort.

She's revising history. Writing a new script. Rewriting the story of this death. And the more she can with precision and scholarship elaborate that story, the more she may actually *experience* the re-telling. By taking thought, the griever is creating alternative worlds; and while shaping that thought in words, she dwells in these variations for a while.

For a while.

This is the action of the intellect: to identify clearly the causes of this sorrow, to learn the sequence of events that led to it, and then to select one particular detail and wonder whether changing it would change the world entirely.

What if, she says again and again, living within her changes. *What if* her son had waited two more minutes before leaving the house? Couldn't she have kept him here?

And: *If only.* She reads everything she can on cancer and says, *If only* he hadn't smoked. *If only* they had recognized that lump much earlier. Odds are, he would have lived. *If only* he had paid more attention to his wife when he was beginning his career, she wouldn't have run with another man, and they wouldn't have divorced.

What if he had accepted Jesus into his life when he was a boy?

The logic is not syllogistic, but conditional; yet it is a logic, the function of the mind. And though she repeats herself, exasperating comforters by the redundancy, she needs these logistics a while. She must go over the ground again and again until every possible alternative has been named and spoken, tested and discarded. For, bit by bit, the death is entering her mind, becoming more and more real even unto her intelligence as every alternative is proven a fiction. Is it really so? she's asking. Is he gone indeed?

At the same time, the griever (still, still—but by a third and different resource) is trying to gain ascendancy and power over her sorry circumstance. It is human nature to believe that by comprehending something totally that one takes control of it. The mind arises to a cool level of contemplation and gazes down, then, from a distance. Free. Unaffected, however the body may suffer. This Olympian region of thought feels godly. Indifferent. Mind and body separate. Mind survives by a supernal understanding.

Therefore, the griever researches. She wants to know everything about the separation she has experienced: what others were thinking or feeling. Divorcées probe the minds of their ex-spouses. War-widows read everything on Viet Nam, imagining the final moments, imagining *life* in the face of death, banishing mystery, taking control by thought alone. It is an intellectual dominion.

When, however, the rewriting of history fails, and when the mere comprehension of events fails also to change events, she may attempt a third strategy of the intellect: that is, to change the context in which the death occurred. Create a world in which "death" is not what it seems in this present world to be.

So Gloria changed the meanings and the values of her uncle's departure by means of an old promise and a buffalo nickel. So people apply to mediums. So false religions abound. So philosophies teach grievers to abstract themselves from the facts of their dyings, making of the real world a "seeming" after all. And even so the Christian faith sometimes pretends that there is no death, but merely a "passing." A "crossing." As if we could skip the dying part of the story and slip sweetly into heaven. As if there never was the rebellion that caused dying in the first place.

But the dying part forces itself finally upon the griever. The absence gapes here in her world, her material and fleshly world. And the effort of the mind must come to nothing. Death is death. Dying cannot be reasoned away. Above the animals, indeed—but man and the son of man is less than God.

Memorial

It is during this period of grieving that certain efforts, though they cannot change the dying, do ennoble humanity. The mind is not unlimited; yet it is a grand and subtle gift of God; its opposition, then, can leave remarkable signs behind.

If a mother is able to imagine the last moments of her child's life, she may never forget the imagined memory. Even after her grief is complete, it may remain a memorial to him in her. A homage. The stuff of poetry.

Or one may actually go to the place where death occurred, go there in ritual fashion, walk the grounds and grieve: and then the *having done it* memorializes the one who died. Often such a single act evolves into an annual ceremony. Crystal-nacht. Veteran's Day: *We shall never forget thee.*

And so we erect stones above graves. Or build buildings in memory of good people. Or established institutions in their names.

At first these may be desperate efforts to control the uncontrollable; but in time the memorials no longer dispute death; rather, they honor one who died and so maintain a part of the relationship that was life while he lived. They are beauty born of anguish. They are that sweetness of grief that deserves to survive. Therefore I memorialize my dear ones in literature. Soon enough I shall myself be reconciled to the death; but the literature remains, the issue of a truly engaged relationship, the infant of my pain. It is a human record. The world is marked by the sighings of single souls.

And here is a mother whose child was killed by a drunken driver. While wrestling in grief she conceives an idea. She wants to rewrite the story of her son by rewriting the stories of other mothers' sons, preserving them from the death she suffered. Therefore, with her mind and her administrative talent she creates M.A.D.D.: Mothers Against Drunk Driving. Her creation becomes both a political and a social force, and a memorial to her child.

What her effort does not do is protect her from the final onslaught of sorrow. She has changed neither her bereavement nor the progress of her grief.

But what her effort does do is (1) grant her something tangible when she shall finally arrive at an acceptance of death—a stepping stone to life again; and (2) give her the means of expressing love for the child so long as she shall live; and (3) benefit society at large: for one woman's grieving always has the potential to become a community's wisdom. It has ever been so, from the beginning of time.

Grief creates a cornerstone of human caring.

Wrestling the Angel

Finally, the second act of grief leaves us stripped. Thrice we've assaulted the angel, with strength and heart and mind. Thrice we were forced to take our measure, the limited will, the limited emotion, the limited intellect. Finite. We are not gods.

> Behold, thou hast made my days as an handbreadth;
>   and mine age is as nothing before thee.
> Verily, every man at his best state
>   is altogether vanity.

Experience persuades us so; and the harder we wrestle against the truth, the truer it seems when we fail. No doctrine is so real as that which we must feel.

Therefore, neither the process nor the pain is wrong. It is not wrong that we resist. Even in the extreme. Nor are our failures wrongs for which we should be ashamed. The process is right and necessary— if "rightness" is determined not by success but by our coming to the truth.

This is the truth: that we are creatures.

And this, too, is the Truth—and the Way and the Life: Jesus Christ.

But we will neither encounter nor honor that latter Truth until we know our need.

It is grief that teaches us the need, exploding the old lie that we are independent and eternal.

It is grief that strips us to a genuine humility.

It is grief that reveals our proper proportion in the order of things.

Lo: we thought we were striving against a single Secondary Dying. In fact, that dying was but a catalyst. We were striving against another adversary all along. And he is not the one who must change, but we ourselves.

"What is your name," says the adversary.

"Jacob," we say. "The trickster, the grabber, the usurper; Jacob, the self-sufficient; Jacob, who works his will on all around him," we say.

"Well," saith the mighty adversary whom we took for death, "your name shall no longer be Jacob. But Israel! For you have striven with God with humanity, and you have prevailed."

With God!

We have been wrestling God, even from the beginning. From the Primal Dying through every Secondary Dying we've made the eternal God our foe. Our defeat will *feel* horrible, a sudden reduction, a loss of the self we had cherished. But that defeat will be most blessed. For the Lord is merciful. By our mortification he draws us back to himself and becomes again our father and our God.

To those who think they are gods, God must be an enemy.

But to those who are dying, he is Life.

We may not yet realize it, because there are two acts of grief still to be experienced; but the terrible blessing of the second act is Peniel:

> *I have seen God face to face,*
> *and yet my life has been preserved.*

17 Grief III: Sadness Only

S truggle is done. The griever looks different to her comforters. Empty. Life's spark seems altogether quenched. When the fight was lost, the fight went out of her. And the comforters may be a bit bewildered since during her period of questioning/reasoning they had thought she was approaching acceptance.

So, what is she doing now?

Nothing.

What does she want now?

She doesn't know. She doesn't care.

How does she feel?

Sad. Simply sad and hopeless.

How long has it been since the cause of her sorrow was made known to her?

As long as it takes to defy it and fail. As long as it takes to be convinced of the personal defeat. And now she looks defeated indeed.

Though the comforters worry, she does not. The comforters say, "What happened? You were doing so well."

She doesn't answer. There's no point to it. She doesn't read the papers. She doesn't watch TV. She sits.

But what is she doing now, truly? Deeply?

Dying. Finally, she is experiencing her own death in the relationship sundered some time ago. Finally.

❦

Catty-corner from Gloria's house is a softball diamond. A little farther west is a bare park with swings and slides behind a chain-link fence. It's a dreary place. It's dreary December. The child who slouches alone on one of the swings—not swinging but scuffing his shoes in the dirt—is dreary too. It's the middle of the morning and the middle of the week.

"Tommy?"

Tommy Ferguson, son of Gloria. He and I are both wearing coats. It is very cold.

"Tommy?" I say.

He looks up, flaps his hand in greeting, then grabs the swing chain and drops his head again.

I've parked on the north side of Bellemeade. I walk in through the gate.

"No school?"

He shrugs.

"Tommy, it's Thursday."

He nods. He knows.

"How were your grades at mid-term?"

He shrugs.

"You keeping up with studies?"

He shrugs.

"Can I sit by you?"

I truly like Tommy Ferguson. He will be a massive man one day, dark, a low center of gravity, stumpish, immobile, strong. His loyalties are as burly as oak. If one doesn't know him, one can be baffled by such staunch simplicity. But if one knows him, one weeps because his loyalties are love.

I sit in the swing by his.

"Tommy? What's the matter?"

He flashes a glance in my direction and then looks down. "Nothin'."

"You bought that swing?"

"What?"

"Monday, Tuesday. Not Wednesday, but today again. Three days in one week."

"What?"

"Tommy, I drive down Bellemeade every day. I see things. I say, 'Yup, there's Ferguson again, sittin' on his swing.' On Wednesday your swing was empty. Where'd you go on Wednesday?"

"School."

"Good for you, Tommy Ferguson!"

"Mamma made me."

"Ah."

"So I went."

"Yes. But not today."

"Didn't make me go today."

"So. Then it's school that's the matter, hey? School's makin' you sad."

He checks to see if I'm mocking him. I'm not. I like him. So he puts his head down and continues to scuff his shoes. "No," he says. "Ain't school."

He starts to blink. He makes a fierce face. He does not want to cry.

"Tommy, are you missing Sonny Boy?"

"Yes. No. Mostly no."

"Then what's the matter?"

"Mamma!" he shouts. Suddenly he lifts his face and shouts, "I'm missin' Mamma!"

And I feel the heaviness on my shoulders again.

Sometimes I am so sad to be a pastor.

This is a most dreary December.

Tommy shouts: "She goes to work, but she don' work. How do I know that? I know. Mr. Sullivan comes to the door and says to me, 'We be prayin' for yo' Mamma. For her spirit,' he says. But he's the ol' man she's s'posed to be helpin' at the Salvation Army, right? So I know."

Tommy doesn't like what he's saying. He keeps jerking his head as if arguing with someone. These are sentiments he's been considering for a while, and he sounds angry, but he looks guilty. He feels disloyal.

"Mamma," he says and lowers his head.

Gloria.

Now he murmurs, "She comes home, but she ain' home neither.

She sits in her bedroom. I say, 'Mamma, what you doin' now?' But she don' even answer. An' so what? So yesterday I made a fist and busted the window out. Smashed the back window."

Tommy's eyebrows are up, exactly like his mother's. It gives a cool belligerence to his face. But he wants to cry.

He says, "Didn' plan on it. Jus' did it. But Mamma, did she see? No. She says, 'Go to school. Go to school, Tommy.' Not mad. Not nothin'. An' when she comes home from work, nothin'. So the window's busted, an' the house is cold, and no one ceers, an' I'm hungry, an' Mamma ain' cookin', an'—"

He stops.

He puts his face down, black to black earth. "I don' ceer either," he says.

But he cares.

He's crying. Man-tough, boy-broken, he's lonely and he's crying.

"Tommy," I say, "she's sad."

"I know that."

He shrugs. It isn't the sadness but the length of sadness that bothers him. Sonny Boy died in September. This is December.

"Tommy?"

"What?"

"I'll talk to her."

"Talk to a ghos'."

"Tommy."

"What."

"Look at me."

He looks at me.

"I know your heart. I know you love your Mamma. And I love her, too. Listen, can you be her Daddy for a while? Her own Daddy died. Can you watch out for her? Can you? And if you will get off that swing and go with me now, we'll fix the window together."

❦

The third act of the griever—like the first, seemingly no action at all—is a direct consequence of the drama and the closure of the second act.

1. She is confronted now by the fact of death, immutable, unappealable. No illusions are left. She knows.

2. She is sad for the loss. There's no complexity to this mood and no disguising it: she is missing something that was dear to her, and she's lonely, and her feeling is exactly as it seems. Sadness is so complete that she can imagine no other way to be, no end to the sorrow. She feels that it must go on forever.

This is hopelessness. This is despair.

3. And so she is finally dying the secondary death herself. The third act is her own full experience of the separation that caused her grief in the first place, that roused her valiantly to resist this death—till Death exhausted her altogether and ruined her resistance.

Now a real part of her person is mortifying.

Almost always there's a lag between the actual event of a death and the woeful realization of that death. The actual event is the withdrawal of one partner from relationship. The realization, sometime thereafter, is the other partner's private withdrawal. Now *she* dies. And the dying is painful. And that particular pain is sadness.

But many relationships are breaking right now, so death seems everywhere around her; the whole world is plunged in gloom. Look at the number of relationships which suddenly the griever feels she's losing, and understand thereby that it is no figure of speech to say that she is dying. It's a fact. She is dying:

Internal relationships: The exaggerated and false image she had maintained of herself, by which she had defined herself, shatters. The "I" she once knew has ceased to be. The present "I" is weaker, dependent, crippled, a creature limited and helpless.

It is a radical fall to realize that one is dust. Death is not only extrinsic, something suffered like an attack from the outside. Death is intrinsic, a condition of one's own nature. She is Job, abhorring herself in dust and ashes, chagrined by the "I" now emerging.

Communal relationships: And if she knows no worth in herself, she's likely to remove that miserable self from those who had loved her, from those whom she thinks she's deceived by being unlovely and a liar to boot.

Likewise, she may withdraw from family and from those who have proven themselves incapable of real help. No one (she believes) can understand the depth and the quality of her pain. Sadness is by its nature an intensely private affair, impossible to communicate. She has neither words for it nor the energy any more to try. She takes isolation as her due, neither expecting nor hoping for anything else.

She drops commitments at work. Well, she doesn't trust herself to accomplish even simple tasks any more. She lacks motivation.

And the whole world, which once seemed to lie before her "like a land of dreams, so various, so beautiful, so new, hath really neither joy, nor love, nor light, nor certitude, nor peace, nor help from pain. . . ." She doesn't trust it either. If the devil's a liar, so is the world he rules.

The Primal Relationship: And she withdraws from God. For God is a grim, victorious Deity, having just beaten her into submission by doing nothing at all, by merely being—but being Omnipotent to her impotence. (Always we know God's greatness before we know his mercy.)

Or else God seems impersonal now, the watchmaker Deity whose grand design dispassionately kills small things.

Or else God is a supernal Parent whose love she dearly seeks, but who must be disappointed now in so false a daughter.

The griever may feel, in this third act, bereft even of her faith. She may fear either that she's stopped believing or that she never believed in the first place. Her soul feels dead as stone.

She is dying.

Signs of the Dying in Sadness

Comforters, please realize that this act is as natural as any other. When lightning flashes, thunder follows. Cause must have its effect. The break of relationship at the beginning of grief is like lightning that splits the sky asunder; this present mortal sadness (however late it comes) is the thunder. It is the death come home: this death is completing itself.

Don't look to the grave to find the decay; look in the face of the griever.

Her face grows slack. She doesn't complain of sickness or lethargy. She scarcely speaks at all. Her manner is desultory. She doesn't respond. You talk; she doesn't. If she were truly alert, this would constitute an insult. In fact, she's breaking apart inside and is mostly unconscious of the image she presents to the world right now. She just doesn't know what she looks like. Please, comforter, don't blame her: many others will. Especially those with whom she works. Especially those inclined to self-centeredness. But you: touch her often. Hold her tight (realizing that in this act there are no sexual yearnings, despite the asinine interpretations of the world). Murmur. Your voice is more crucial to her than your words: *that* you are is more helpful than what you *do*.

When she speaks at all, it will be in simple sentences. Literally: no subordinate clauses. Or else she uses incomplete sentences, fragments of thoughts. She forgets the point before she's finished. She sighs often and to no particular purpose. She starts an action, then can't remember the rest of it. She feels she's losing her mind.

Comforter, do not express frustration. She feels the frustration in herself. Likewise, don't think it's necessary to finish the thoughts she started, ending all her sentences for her. Healing here shan't be in making sense of the senseless, but (especially during this period of grievous self-recrimination) in being. Being *with* her. Not avoiding her as all the rest of the world will be doing now—for it is in this act that the world decides that she ought to be done with her endless sorrow and get *on* with it! The healing, comforter, shall be in your gentle perseverance: you stayed. You stayed.

Also, she may apologize often, abjectly, and to embarrassing extremes. Well, and she may have much to apologize for: missing appointments, forgetting commitments, growing unkempt, allowing her house to get dirty, crying at inappropriate times. When she apologizes, she is truly sorry; but she'll make the same mistake again. Guilt roots and flowers in her.

Comforter, when she apologizes, forgive her. Genuinely. And when she apologizes again, forgive her again. As often as she asks it, she needs it; you have it: give it. You are now the mercy of the Lord God for her. You, in the flesh, in all your behavior. *You.* This is ministry. Service. Grace. Goodness.

And she will cry very much, now, though not with fierce emotion. It will be as if her eyes kept leaking. Little things will cause these tears, the slightest bump (physical, emotional, spiritual)—because she is now altogether without resources. You are her resource. Hold her.

And in this sort of sadness she may become immodest, dressing in anything handy, sitting in slouched and revealing positions. Civility has lost its meaning. She who does not honor herself no longer honors her body. Dying (the breaking of many relationships) means that she is less affected by cultural mores and public censure.

Comforter, what you can do for her, do; but do not criticize and wait in patience: soon enough she will cease such carelessness. But comforter, I beg you: do not take advantage of her! It is also during this act that the griever is most vulnerable. People may steal, people may touch her, people may rape a woman of low esteem. You must protect her not only from "people," but also from any sinful inclination within yourself.

And now she may cease to pray, may cease to worship. It isn't a spiritual choice, really. It is mere hopelessness.

And at night she may suddenly suffer terrors. Dreadful descents, unfocused dread, as if the world were about to stop and fall apart. Then, like a child, she may whimper, and the whimpering might give her a certain solace; but she yearns for her mother to come and hold her, just to hold her. But there are no mothers any more. And childhood is past. The age when sorrows could be fixed is past. Innocence, credulity, goodness—all, all are gone. So she whimpers. Her eyes leak.

Comforters, finally, don't interrupt. Don't try by any means (whether by pious sermons or by rough commandments) to stop this process as if it were wrong. For the first time in her grieving—for the *first time*—she is attending exclusively and honestly to death. The attention will come to its own conclusion. In the meantime, be near, be available, be uncritical; but let her be. Clean her house. Put air in her tires. Repair the window smashed in her back door. And wait.

Wait upon her. Wait for her. Wait.

Despair

This particular sadness is perhaps the worst stage of grief. There are a hundred ways into it; there seems no way out of it. For the griever is bereft of all that she held good. Not only has she lost her beloved, but with him she's lost her reason to live, her connection to the world, her own value, and her God.

There seems, then, no alternative to this sorrow, no possible change, no future save sadness alone—because everything that might have revised it was tried and failed.

The worst moment of grief, then, is hopelessness.

To be altogether without hope is to despair.

When one despairs, she has died indeed.

For this state must go on forever.

And so the griever has come to the Hebrew *tehom*, the deepest chasm of sorrow in the Psalter: "Out of *tehom*," cries the psalmist, "out of *the depths* have I cried unto thee, O Lord!"

The griever has entered *sheol*, the pit, the unillumined gloom of the dead. This is all that she can imagine for herself forever hereafter. She has no strength to climb out. She has no talent nor goodness. All has been weighed and found wanting.

Hopelessness has no ending she can name save death.

No ending *she* can name.

But God can name another ending.

And that, finally, is the point: God, who was always here, becomes evident to us by the gravity of our need. And resurrection comes from *outside* ourselves. It comes even from outside our knowing. It comes as the stunning surprise, the thing we could never imagine, illogical, implausible, the absurd solution—arising from no system we know or control. It's source must be God alone. Grace. It is a gift. But it would not be a gift if we thought that we had, in any way, caused it.

Therefore, it was necessary that we come to nothing in order to know God's love as grace.

The griever *had* to suffer hopelessness in order to be astonished by her new life.

We *had* to die to experience resurrection.

And it is in grief that we die. The third act finally is our dying.

But the fourth act—the action we do not do, but that God does for us—is that we rise again. We rise not only from this present death, the separation recently suffered, but also from the Primal Death! Pause and consider this a moment: our separation from God, the Source of Life, is healed when we return to him in faith. Grief is the path of our return, for it teaches us to know ourselves truly, and truly to know God. Grief is the Way that reveals the Truth and thereby grants us Life again.

The highest good of the process of grief is to turn the prodigal back to his father.

Child, child, O my child!—now that you know the need, come home. Where else can you go? Come home. Beg, if you wish, to be my servant. But I will make you my daughter again. And my son. And I will love you. Come.

III
THE DRAMA OF
REDEMPTION:
FROM DEATH TO LIFE
AGAIN

Jesus' Story

18 The Readiness Is All

T he "Mr. Sullivan" who visited Tommy is one of his mother's regular clients. Gloria supervises the Senior Citizen's Drop-In Center for the Salvation Army. On any day she might have forty people scattered through their basement rooms, singing, sleeping, reading, sewing, playing cards, watching TV, fighting.

Mr. Sullivan is old and slow, white-haired, huge at the middle, peaceful in spirit, clad in bib-overalls, heavy on his cane. His skin is the color and texture of hickory. He hollered at me yesterday. "Rever! Rever! When you comin' down to the Center?"

He never remembers my last name, and *Rever's* as close as he could get to Reverend.

I crossed the street. He was standing in front of the old Post Office. He is always solemn, a man borne down by grave contemplations. When I drew to him, he told me that people were praying for "Miz Glory," that no one blamed her negligence these days since old folks understand the sorrow of a "passin'," and that most were, as he said, "catchin' her slack. Pickin' up behind her."

"Course," he continued, "here's one'r two biddies unhappy wif anything. Always a cackler, you know. Ah set down on 'em. They don' mean no harm. Jus' irritated by ol' age. Rever," he said, peering at me. "When *you* plannin' to drop by the Center?" No question *whether* I planned. Just when. A mandate.

Yesterday I heard him, and today I obey.

As I descend the steps into the old building's basement, I can hear the dear Mr. Sullivan himself, roaring down the hallways: "Miz Glory? Miz Glory, I prayed for you las' night!"

She is nowhere in sight. That doesn't trouble Mr. Sullivan. He roars: "You feelin' som'at better this mawnin'? I got a serprise for you—" He disappears into her office.

At the same time, she appears in the hall before me. I smile. "Hi."

She hardly seems to recognize me. "What do you want?"

"Oh, I just had a notion to see how you are."

"How I am—" Abruptly she looks down and walks away.

"Gloria? Gloria, wait."

I take a step to follow her, but suddenly my coat is yanked from behind.

"What you want wif Miz Glory?"

Here is a woman sitting on a hall bench, glaring up at me, angry. She has iron-gray hair and an iron spine: skinny, inflexible, willing to kill for Miz Glory.

The woman beside her is bent by embarrassment. "Callie," she hisses.

But Callie evidently will not be deterred: "What you want wif Miz Glory?"

I say, "Just to talk."

"Ain' no one gon' grieve Miz Glory, hear?"

"No, no, all I want—"

"You the Insurance Man?" Callie yanks my coat so hard I fear a rip. "You comin' to pester her fer payment?"

"I'm—"

"You comin' fer yer damn dime?" *Yank! Yank!*

It occurs to me that to be loved by Callie is to kissed by the U.S. Marines. It'll ruin your face.

The woman beside her hisses, "Callie!" patting her wrist.

Callie cries, "Why, you ain' even delivered on her uncle yet." *Yank!*

"Callie! He ain't insurance."

"What?"

"It's her pastor."

"Her what?"

"It's Miz Glory's preacher come to see her."

"Preacher? Preacher? Well, why'nt you say you were her preacher?" Suddenly Callie's voice is honeysuckle, and her iron spine is piety. "You gon' pray wif Miz Glory?"

"If she's willing."

"Oh, honey, she's willin'!"

Callie rises to her feet. She is thin, taller than I am—and I am six foot one. She grabs my hand and pulls me down the hall toward a small storage room at the end of it.

"Miz Glory!" she booms. This woman could clear Europe by a cry. "Miz Glory?"

Mr. Sullivan appears and joins us, an ocean-going vessel in suspenders. He adds his roar to Callie's. Other folks come out of the side rooms, yelling Gloria's name, and altogether we become a bellowing chorus. "Miz Glory, here's yo' preacher come to pray wif you!"

By the time we arrive at the storage room, I think the entire population of the Salvation Army Drop-In Center has surrounded me. "She sits in there when she's feelin' lowly," whispers Callie. "G'on in. You're allowed."

I do.

I admit myself by opening a door in which a clouded pane of glass rattles; it rattles when I close it again.

"Shhh, shhhh," say the people outside.

And I beg her pardon. "I'm sorry, Gloria. I didn't mean to force myself on you."

She sits at a beaten desk. She doesn't even raise her face. "It's all right," she says. "They're just being kind."

"The, ah—the tall woman thinks we should pray."

"They all do. They believe in praying."

This is a narrow room with a high ceiling, a single window, and shelves up the walls. The one chair Gloria uses. I can't sit. I've intruded in a private space.

I say, "I'm sorry. I'll go."

She says, "Don't."

"Do you want me to pray."

"Maybe later."

"Shhhh, shhhh," say the old folks just outside the door.

Their noises empower me. Their untroubled love for this woman teaches me.

So I kneel beside her desk, look up into her face, and say, "Do you know that Tommy did not break the window by accident? Do you know he did it on purpose?"

She says nothing. The color of her skin is a deep reddish brown, and her lips are defined by ridges, and her eyes are as dark as midnight. There are stars in midnight. I love Gloria. I wish I could tell her as much.

"He's been skipping school," I say. "He says he feels forgotten. Lonely, I think. Guilty, too. He's suffering, Gloria."

She keeps her head down. She looks like a truant in the principal's office. I place my hand on her forearm. "Gloria, I wish my word were a buffalo nickel and your heart were a purse, so that I could tuck this into you, and you would never lose it: God loves you. God loves you, Gloria. God loves you."

Softly, without raising her head, she whispers, "Where is he?"

"Here!" I say. "He has always been right by you. Always."

Now she looks at me. "Who is here?"

"God."

"No, Pastor," she says. "Where is Sonny Boy? Where is *he*?"

Suddenly there rises in the hallway a sort of stifled screaming, a score of antiquated voices breaking into song.

"SILENT NIGHT!" they shout and bellow and quaver and beep. "HOLY NIGHT!" they scream. The senior citizens of the drop-in center have decided to carol Miz Glory. A little Christmas cheer. "ALL IS CALM! ALL IS BRIGHT!" And if it isn't bright, by God, they'll terrorize it into brightness.

For my own part, they've granted me a little respite before I have to answer Gloria's question. She shifts her glance from me to the door then back again.

Her eyebrows go up. "Oh, dear," she whispers. Her hands cover her cheeks, and her shoulders shake, and the tears come down like rain. Her lashes grow bright with the shining. "Oh, dear."

"ROUND JOHN VIRGIN, MOTHER AND CHILD."

Gloria Ferguson stands up, the tears streaming down her cheeks. She goes to the door and opens it. And there are the ancient faces, every color God can imagine, every splinter of wood grown old. "HOLY INFANT SO TENDER AND MILD!"

Yes, I love Gloria.

She stares at her clients, whispering, "Dear, dear, dear."

"SLEEP!" the old people shriek in her face, "IN HEAVENLY PEE-EACE! SLEE-EEP IN HEAVENLY PEACE."

Then Mr. Sullivan comes through the people pushing ahead of him the stumpish and loyal Tommy Ferguson, who is carrying a gorgeous poinsettia. Gloria takes the plant and sets it aside in order to hug her son.

Mr. Sullivan has been busy.

"The flower," he announces, "is from all of us. The boy is yours."

His mother notices then a massive bandage around Tommy's finger, consisting, it seems, of an entire cotton diaper.

"What did you do?" she says.

"I fixed a broken window."

Gloria, her hands on the sides of the young boy's head, buries his face now in her bosom and begins to smile with her eyes closed.

"AWAY IN A MANGER NO CRIB FOR A BED"—woofing and whistling and groaning and tweeting, the old folks are tearing down the roof with Christmas carols—and Gloria spreads her nostrils and sings along: "The Little Lord Jesus lays down his sweet head—"

Where is Sonny Boy?

This is not the time to answer her question, but that time is coming and I know even now what I'm going to do. I'm going to write a book. For Gloria. About Gloria. For all who suffer the separations, Gloria's Story.

And looking about myself, listening to Christmas in the shrieks of the elderly, I think: this will be one of the latter chapters; and I know already how I will entitle it: *The Readiness Is All.*

The Readiness

Even from the beginning of grief, the Lord Jesus has been with her. Born a baby in human flesh, heir to every death we die save one, then printed with all the deaths because he died them all, Jesus Christ has always been with her. There was no sorrow she suffered that he hadn't suffered. There was no death he couldn't himself remember. There was no solitude he did not breach. There was, therefore, no real solitude after all. There was always, always relationship for Gloria— for always, there was Jesus.

And relationship is life, even in the midst of death.

She just didn't know.

She just couldn't see. And lamentation deafened her.

Blind, deaf, ignorant, the bereaved has been very involved with her self. Her wounded, severed self.

But that is the nature of the race entirely: the problem was never the absence of God. The problem has always been that seeing, the self-centered do not see, and that hearing, the self-pitiful do not hear; proud hearts are dulled by the thick redundancy of flesh.

From the beginning we robed our souls in a royal lie and believed that the lie *was* the self!

So the goodness of grief is that it dramatically sheers the self away. By degrees it reduces the arrogance. It silences the clamor. It strips the false image of autonomous strength to one bare bone of truth: Behold the human, how small she is and how needy! Ah, but she has been made ready by grief to listen. She is ready, now, to see the Truth that walks beside her everywhere.

The readiness is all.

"I LOVE THEE LORD JESUS LOOK DOWN FROM THE SKY—" Mr. Sullivan's head is thrown back, his voice booming from a big chest and an open throat as if he were a cannon.

Gloria looks about herself.

Tommy verily shines. In him is the spirit of God the Comforter, the boy unaware of the holiness of his recent sacrifices, but no less effective for all that. In him God has continued to dwell, near to Gloria—because he loves you, Miz Glory.

Do you see that yet?

AN' STAY BY MY CRADLE TILL MAWNIN' IS NIGH.

Gloria, he loves you.

19 The Four Sacrifices of the Christ

I write directly for you now, Gloria, trusting the readiness.
Having heard the sweet word, that he loves you, and having felt by holy force the presence of that love, my griever can now consider the more difficult word of *how* it is the Lord Jesus loved and loves and will forever love.

Every death we die, Jesus died: we cannot go where he has not gone. He companions us even in darkness and sorrow. And he leads us to light and life again.

Every death we die, he died in the flesh. Not merely "in the spirit" or by an imaginative sympathy, but in our world, in diurnal time, among us, in historical fact.

Every death except one. He did not die the first death, the Primal Separation. Jesus never rebelled against the Father; therefore, Jesus did not deserve to die any death whatsoever. Death for him who didn't sin could only come *by his own choosing*. This is an unspeakable mercy: that in order to seek and to save the lost (*apollumi*) Jesus volunteered to experience what we are required by our sins to experience.

Every death he died, then, must properly be called a "sacrifice."

And excepting that first death, he died them all: every Secondary Dying we suffer because of our sins, he suffered as a sacrifice. And the

251

third death, the Corporeal Dying, was his bodily sacrifice upon the cross.

Every death we die, I say, he died: but then he died yet one death more which, because of him, we need not die. He suffered the fourth, the Dying Absolute. This is the Greatest Sacrifice. He *perished in our places, that we need never come near this extremest sort of perishing.*

Lo, the faithful shall never descend into hell! They shall live in the presence of God eternally.

But all this is a story.

Of course: God loves us by *doing*; when we tell what God has *done*, then, we must be telling stories. God enters human *experience*, the living in relationships, the dying of sundered relationships, the resurrection of renewed relationships; we meet him, then, in *experience*. That is to say, our stories and his story merge. They become the same story. And what Jesus did at the climax of his is the climax of mine as well. And of yours, Gloria. And Sonny Boy's. And my daughter Talitha's. And my father's, Walter Senior.

I shall write many, many stories yet before I leave this earth. But no story is more important than this one, for none could be hopeful apart from this one. Except for salvation, every tale the world would tell must end in death, cold and sober and eternal. Every play must close in an absolute darkness. And all the universe must resolve itself into a spinning cinder no one knows, and none remembers.

Listen, Miz Glory. Marvel at the depth and the persistence and the power of Jesus' love for you. And believe in what you hear: this is our story.

HIS FIRST SACRIFICE: THE INCARNATION

So the first deed that Jesus did on our behalf—the very first act, you see—was to suffer a sort of dying. It characterized the quality of his love forever thereafter.

Oh, yes: our Christmas commemorates his first significant separation! He came down to us not burning with heavenly glory, the very sight of which made Moses' face a fire that frightened Israel. We couldn't have tolerated the First Light directly. So the Son of God gave up the glorious relationship of omnipotent authority for the lesser relationships of the flesh. He gave up his eternal life for the temporal life of humanity. Who can measure the depth of such love?

No one. Because we cannot measure the distance between heaven and earth.

Down, down: he who never disobeyed did not count his parity with God as something he must preserve. He emptied himself, down and down. He severed himself from deific power, took the form of a servant, came down to us in human frame, went down beneath the rule of death, humbled himself into obedience even unto death on the cross.

Immortality became mortal.

And the story starts exactly as do all our stories: we enter as infants. Sonny Boy was a baby once. So was Jesus.

"In Him Was Life"

Even on earth Jesus didn't *have* to die. He was by his Deity and by his continued righteousness the very model of perfect life. He was what the first Adam had been before sin: the Creator's unsullied handiwork, God's best intention.

Jesus maintained all his relationships, then, perfectly.

—*The Primal Relationship* was whole and healthy, because Jesus was obedient, trusting utterly in the Word of God, praying continually. His will was God's will. He was the true "Israel," the child that Moses had exhorted to "choose life."

—*The Communal Relationships* were not marred by selfishness on Jesus' part, but were ever centered on the other. Which is love. He loved the people, pitied them, served them, called them sometimes roughly to account, but called them nevertheless, called them and never did anything *not* calculated to benefit them.

—*The Natural Relationship* never knew more harmony with a human than now—not since the sweetness of Eden. For Jesus spoke to the wind and the waves, and they obeyed. He murmured to fish, and they rose to the nets. He made blind eyes see. He took a seemingly dead flesh by the hand and whispered, *Talitha cumi,* and the damsel stood up looking for lunch. Most of what folks called "miracles" weren't so much miracle as the restoration of the loving relationship between God's Image on earth and God's Handiwork. This is how things were meant to be in the first place!

—*The Internal Relationship,* modeled in Jesus, was whole and healthy. He knew himself perfectly. He knew his person and his purpose upon the earth; he knew precisely the willing limitations on his power; he knew without self-deceit what he felt and what he thought. Between his image of himself and that actual self, there was no difference. Between the Christ and his own knowledge of the Christ, there was no separation.

In him, then, there was no death.

Of all who walked the earth, this one didn't deserve to die, nor could anyone truly condemn him to die apart from his choosing.

He chose.

HIS SECOND SACRIFICE: THE PASSION

The passion of our Lord is that he suffered all the Secondary Dyings in full consciousness, in their extremes. Even so is he able to walk with us wherever we go: he broke the trail. He knows it intimately.

Gloria, he knows every step of the grieving you've just traversed. He knows you. You have never been alone.

On the other hand, *his* experience was solitary. It is the hauntingly unique quality of Jesus' dying that he suffered every death in a perfect isolation: no one knew what he was going through. No one could companion him.

"Behold, Your King"

What good to him was all the praise with which the people met him in Jerusalem? "Hosannah!—yeah! Messiah!—you bet! Now, show your stuff, you Son of David, and cut our enemies down! Yo, we shall all rise up in victory now! Hosannah!"

But he was riding to town to die. And he knew it. Not one of these cheering supporters understood him. Not one.

I suppose we are able to sacrifice ourselves for those we love; but we desire that someone should know the value of the act; we hope that there will be at least one person who admires and approves. Or what's the value? What's the worth? How would it feel if no one approved? How would it feel if absolutely everyone criticized the act to one degree or another?

How must it have felt to enter Jerusalem in order to save it by going down to defeat before it?

How must it feel to know that one can count the days until his death? And the minutes?

But everyone's yelling, "Hurrah!"

It's a holiday.

It's a separation as broad as a gulf between the people and the Christ. It is already a Secondary Dying.

"You Will All Fall Away"

Every sort of human separation, treachery, lying, the loss of intimates: "I will strike the shepherd, and the sheep will be scattered." For Jesus, part of that strike *was* the scattering of his beloved; part of the dying *was* their desertion.

Midweek, Judas slips away to effect a betrayal. Judas supposes he acts in secret. But Jesus knows. He hasn't the comfort of ignorance. Jesus knows all things. He must in his mind's eye follow Judas with grief.

Look at his face on Thursday evening, while the disciples eat but do not know they eat the Lord's last supper. His heart grows heavier and heavier. "One of you will betray me."

Does it cheer him, then, to receive vigorous protests and promises of "relationship" forever and against all odds?

Simon Peter: "Though they all fall away because of you, I will never fall away."

The first time I received such a promise of goodness and life from my son, I believed it; it made me happy. He failed to keep the promise. But the second time he made such a promise, I gave him the benefit of the doubt, believing that he had learned from previous error, and I believed him, and it made me happy. But he failed again.

When my son makes the same promise again, now having made it and broken it so many times that I can no longer count them, it tears me up. He hurts me because I love him, but he doesn't even know himself. Or else he cares so little as to lie to me. He will hurt me when he breaks the promise again; but he hurts me right now, because of the futility of his own character, of his will and his virtue and even of his love: it is all dross and he does not know it. I know, and I grieve.

So, then, does Peter's promise cheer Jesus?

"Truly, I say to you, this very night, before the cock crows, you will deny me three times."

Peter says, "Even if I must die with you, I will not deny you."

So say all the disciples.

Jesus' solitude, even within the ring of his closest friends, is complete.

"They Went to a Place Called Gethsemane"

"My soul is sorrowful, even unto death," he says softly to Peter and James and John, now in a private darkness, a separated garden. "Remain here and watch."

They fall asleep,

Sundered thus, he turns to the Father in prayer. Jesus turns from the Communal Relationship to the Primal, and he who has ever been obedient begs now a particular boon:

"Father, father, take it away. Please, take it away from me."

Take what away? What terrorizes Jesus, even in the anticipation? The whip? The hatred of the people? Yes. But more than that.

Then what? The cross? Death on the cross? Yes, of course: but this must be more than a merely mortal death, or what is the difference between Jesus and any other good person cut down?

"Let this cup pass from me!"

Jesus is agonized by the only death that can save humanity from its right and righteous, just, judicial conclusion: Hell. To drink this "cup" will mean to bear the guilt of the whole world, even from Adam to Sonny Boy, from Gloria to the last morning of time before the Maker returns in judgment. To drink this "cup" means that Christ *becomes* the full history of the sins of humankind. In consequence, he shall die the fourth death, the Dying Absolute.

"Take," he begs a second time and a third time, three times only, "this cup from me."

He truly fears such an extremity of death.

And what shall I say to you, Gloria? How shall I describe the love of the Lord at this instant? For though he loathes this death worse than any other can loathe it (since he alone can truly comprehend it), even now he remains for our sakes perfectly obedient to God. In him the Primal Relationship never, never breaks. He whispers, "Nevertheless, not what I will, but as thou wilt."

Obedience! From the beginning, obedience would have maintained the relationship between us and God, would have maintained our lives forever. Disobedience caused all our dying. But now again, it is obedience in the person of Jesus that interrupts history and snatches us from the final dying.

This is how much the Lord Jesus loves Sonny Boy: he obeys the most terrible and the most merciful of all commandments:

Give your life as a ransom for many.

He does two things we could not or else would not do: he lives a righteous life; and then, even as a result of his righteousness, he goes to die the Absolute Death.

The Father refuses the suit of the Son. Jesus' Secondary Dyings now outstrip anything we mortals have felt on earth.

From this point forward, Christ is alone in the cosmos.

"He Was Despised and We Esteemed Him Not"

Judas comes. Judas kisses him. The crowd that arrives with swords and clubs now grabs him and binds him and leads him away. And yes, we all forsake him.

We do, all of us, flee.

Every age crosses at this age. Every person has sinned this sin. Every story is woven into this story right here. For even now, Jesus knows the names of Sonny Boy and Gloria and Tommy and Walter Senior, Walter Junior. His heart contains us all; his life combines, his death relieves the reach of the entire race.

We are here.

And we flee.

And every institution of the human community which was established to administer godliness and justice and health and protection and truth (that is, *relationship*) now cuts off Jesus too, killing him bit by bit.

The religious community, far from effecting an atonement, far from keeping the two great commandments upon which all the law and the prophets depend, arraigns him before a mock trial, destroys truth, admits false witnesses, accuses him of blasphemy, and sentences him to death. All relationship is severed here: "His own received him not."

Separation: he suffers the death.

The judicial community is now manipulated by malevolent forces to prosecute the sentence of death.

On one side stands a legitimate criminal. On the other, Truth. But the crowd and the Governor choose to release the criminal and to execute Truth. Jesus, now, is solitary. There is no system of the human community prepared to understand or else to serve him. None.

Separation: he is suffering all deaths.

The universal community, all humanity: the Christ cannot have been ignorant of the timeless vastitude of his separations. We all, says the prophet, "esteemed him stricken, smitten by God, and afflicted." This is the uttermost of Secondary Dying, when not one created soul stands in relationship to Jesus. Now do we reject him; we feel righteous doing so; for pious people exercise their piety by separating themselves from one who is *smitten by God*. Obviously, God separated himself first. We good people only do the godly thing.

And this is the reason why we hide our faces from him: "The Lord has laid on him the iniquity of us all." His ugliness is our ugliness. The sin we see in him is ours. This is a sight we refuse, a picture of ourselves too loathsome to admit. If we stand in relationship to *this* Jesus, you see—the one approaching the cross, not the one glorious in resurrection; the one befouled, defeated, sickly, unpretty, contemptuous because he bowed his head and accepted it all, while we desire our heroes to be triumphant—if, I say, we looked upon this Jesus we'd risk ugliness all over again. Too great a risk. This is not a Jesus we can know. Or love.

Give us another sort of Christ. Give us another religion.

We will have nothing to do with this cringing, pitiful wretch.

Thus, when Jesus gazes out from the Roman courtyard, his vision pierces history, even to today; and even in this day he finds no member of the human race willing to acknowledge him. No, not one. Not *this* Jesus. We know not *this* Lord. Another master, yes. A great teacher, perhaps. A miracle-worker, to be sure—one who can get us into heaven: him. But not this monster obviously on his way to hell, hated by all, rejected by God. No, we neither know nor understand such a one.

"But you are one of the followers of Jesus."

We deny it.

"Certainly you are; you've got the same defects, the same sort of ugliness. You're as simpering as he—"

God, strike us dead if we're not telling the truth: we do not know this man of whom you speak!

And immediately the cock crows a second time.

All are gone. Even the best have left him.

Separation: the Son of God and the Son of Man is solitary in the universe.

HIS THIRD SACRIFICE: GIVING UP THE GHOST

We too shall die the third death. But we shan't die it as Jesus does now, altogether alone.

When Sonny Boy went into the yonder room to die, the Lord went with him. When Sonny Boy slipped beyond the reach of the physicians and into the quietude of coma, Jesus went with him. For Jesus does in fact, in history, in our world die the death.

And so it comes to pass:

They whip him. He feels the lash, and he bleeds. They plait a wreath from tough briar weed; they press it upon his head. He feels the thorns, he feels the derision, he knows.

They force him to bear the cross-beam outside the city. All their action declares him an "exile" now, a Cain in everything except that they couldn't kill Cain. They will kill this Jesus.

They drive the spikes through his flesh into a grainy wood. He feels the dull separation of cartilage and bone. They hoist the wood to an empty space between heaven and earth; when it drops in its socket, his own weight begins the final business of killing him. And the natural elements will hasten the end.

As with us all, the corporeal dying of the Christ is the breakdown of every relationship essential to life.

The Natural Relationship is made his enemy: exposure to the hot sun, to the cold night, to any weather the wind may bring. On the cross, even his Internal Relationship turns invidious; for as his arms lose strength and his body hangs down from his shoulder sockets, the weight must close his rib cage. He cannot breathe. His body is suffocating itself. Humans who make a profession of killing other humans do it very well, with a sharp awareness of pain, and even with fine irony.

Jesus whispers once or twice while he hangs on the public hill.

"Forgive them."

"Woman, behold your son."

"Yes, today you will be with me in paradise."

"I'm thirsty."

He utters a phrase that confuses people. They think he's calling for Elijah.

"Into thy hands I commend my spirit."

Then suddenly he makes a loud, inarticulate shout: a human roar in darkness. It has been dark for six hours. And Jesus screams one scream—which sounds oddly like a warrior's cry of triumph.

And so he lowers his head between the wings of his two shoulders, and he leans forward, and he faces the earth, and he dies.

He dies.

The Lord Jesus Christ expels the little wind left in his lungs, and he dies.

For Sonny Boy.

Yet this is not all he does.

HIS FOURTH SACRIFICE: FORSAKEN

It is by his final death that Jesus changes for us the third death into something that we may hate, but through which we may yet have hope. It is by this sacrifice that Jesus takes the sting from death and the victory from the grave. It is by this death that he completes the long cosmic drama which we began by rebellion and which *had* to end in an absolute dying: Jesus accepts that dying himself.

He finishes what we started.

Jesus dies absolutely the fourth death; and so the church confesses: "He descended into Hell."

Communal Relationships, Utterly Sundered

Hell begins, as we described it above, when all the world turns away from the defeated, iniquitous Jesus.

In that time all times are one, and this becomes the very center of human history. In this moment, no one loves him, no one believes in him, everyone self-righteously separates from him and cries for crucifixion—because every human among us desires the annihilation of our sins, our guilt, our wretchedness, and in this moment Jesus *is* our sin, our guilt, our wretchedness. "Take it away!" we beg the Father. "Please take my transgressions away!"

And God does. God answers this most humble and serious prayer. How often have we prayed it? God hears it every time and grants it:

He lays upon Jesus the chastisement that makes us whole, and by those stripes we are healed.

This must be stated in the extreme: for Jesus there is, in this sole and eternal moment, not a single communal relationship. This is what Hell is, to be despised by everyone.

The Internal Relationship, Utterly Sundered

And this is what Hell is, to despise oneself.

Jesus *agrees* with the world's rejection. He does not dispute it. He accepts it and loathes himself more than anyone else could loathe him, even his enemies.

For the righteous Christ hates sin. The righteous Christ has been obedient unto the end. Righteous and perfect and obedient, Christ is the antithesis of sin.

And yet at the same time, Jesus on the cross *is* sin—the very thing itself.

Sin is more than a burden he happens to be bearing, more than a job he must accomplish, more than is a single characteristic of his person. If it were merely a heavy load, he could hate it without hating himself. If it were merely a duty or a quality, he could hate it with a hatred that needn't encompass his self.

But the Apostle Paul writes: "For our sake he made him *to be sin* who knew no sin." At this moment, Jesus is himself the thing his entire divinity and his goodness must utterly reject. He *is* the thing he abhors. The Savior is sundered in two.

All the world is crying, "You are guilty!"

And Jesus whispers, "Yes, you are right, I am guilty." Our sins are now his person. "Yes, I deserve to die." He has not even the mild reprieve that an innocent man forced to die an unjust death might feel. For the death is just. Nor can he take solace in the fact that he is performing a wonderful love on behalf of the world. There is nothing lovely about him now.

"In order that in him we might become the righteousness of God," writes Paul, he became sin.

The Internal Sundering is complete. The fourth death is not unknowing, but full of knowing: Jesus knows what he has become. He knows himself very well, even now. And He hates it. This is Hell.

Natural Relationships, Utterly Sundered

Let it remain a mystery but let it be written nevertheless:

In the fourth death Jesus is separated not only from the material elements of the created world, wind and earth and sun and water; he is cut off as well from its most basic elements, time and space.

That is to say: in the moment when Jesus dies on behalf of humanity, there is no time by which the moment may be brought to an end. It is, paradoxically, an eternal instant. Even though he shall surely arise again, *in that moment* the resurrection is no comfort, because *in that moment* death is the totality of his experience. That moment, while Jesus dwells therein, is clean cut off from all creation, divorced therefore also from the changings and motions of time. It is, while it is, forever.

And this is right! This is the full penalty of the Primal Rebellion, that our sin should be banished finally and altogether from the realms of the Creator, from time (which would otherwise allow for hope, even the imagination of a reprieve) and from space (which would otherwise imply some small relationship somewhere to exist, and life thereby—a cool drop of water, say, on the tip of a finger).

Between this absolutely dying Christ and all the rest of the cosmos "there is a great gulf fixed; so that they which would pass from hence to him cannot; neither can he, who would come thence, pass to them." That gulf defines what Hell is, one's utter separation from every *thing* of God, creation, time, space.

Now Jesus is in a Nowhere. And there he must be timelessly. Nothing but "this" can be for him, ever and ever.

This is what we deserved.

This he bore for us.

This is what makes the thought of any death so terrifying.

But this is the death we need not die—the fourth death.

The Primal Relationship, Utterly Sundered

Finally, it is not only from the *things* of God that Jesus is separated, but also from God.

The logical end of our abandonment of God is that God should accept our act of and give us over to our dishonorable passions and, in effect, abandon us. But in the eternal instant of his greatest sacrifice,

Jesus *is* the sin of all humanity, which God now gives over unto itself, unto its self alone. God departs from Jesus.

This, then, is a cry from Hell: *Eli, Eli, lama sabbachthani!*

His solitude is, in every spiritual precinct, now perfect. Nothing remains for Jesus. He has drunk the cup completely. God is gone.

"My God! My God! Why hast thou forsaken me!"

So the damned do howl. And when no answer comes, when the cosmos is altogether silent, damnation is accomplished. "It is finished." It is done. This is extremest dying.

This is, therefore, the absolute solitude that causes terrors in our every Secondary Death. This is what we contemplate when we are lonely and sad in the third act of grief. And this is the curse that every human somehow understands and anticipates.

Ah, Gloria, but *It is finished.*

And you have been made ready to hear this. The grieving itself has prepared you to depend upon another, not upon your self, and to believe in the accomplishment of that other:

IT IS ALL FINISHED

Now listen: the resurrection of Jesus Christ upon the third day comes like a trumpet blast, a bright cry of triumph. By raising Jesus bodily and glorified, God declares to all the world that he accepts the sacrifice. He is satisfied. In Christ the old account is closed.

There is now no Hell for those who hide in Jesus!

No longer is God the indifferent Deity whom my griever knew in the horrible period of her despair. Neither is God sheer Infinitude to our miserable finitude. Nor is he the just Judge executing sentences we know we deserve but which we cannot tolerate.

Now God is seen in the face of Jesus, the Shepherd who calls us by name: *Gloria, do you love me?*

Yes, Lord. I love you.

Feed my lambs.

Now there is forgiveness for all the separations we've caused in the past—forgiveness for the First Death, the denial of our God.

Sweet savvy Gloria, do you love me more than these?

Lord, you know all things; you know that I love you.

Tend my sheep.

For the third death has been transfigured now into a "sleep." And this sleep shall have its awakening. Jesus rose; so shall we. And rising begins as soon as we see the living Lord around us, living in spite of all his dyings, resurrected here and now.

Gloria?

What, Lord.

Look at your son.

Tommy? At Tommy?

How do you think he's been able to forgive you through your long neglect?

Oh, Tommy, I am so sorry. I didn't mean to hurt you when I hurt.

Gloria, open your eyes and see! I have been in Tommy all along, forgiving you. And look at your cousin, the longsuffering Mary. And look at these people who form a bulwark around you.

I have always been here, comprehending your sorrow, embracing it, understanding and outrunning it, healing it altogether.

Gloria, Gloria, sister, do you see me now?

20 The Cherry Tree: A Parable

E piphany fell on a Sunday that year, the Twelfth Day, the last of the days of Christmas. We acknowledged it in our morning worship by reading Scripture lessons devoted to the bright exposure of God in Jesus:

Arise, shine; for thy light is come, and the glory of the Lord is risen upon thee—

And again:

Behold, there came wise men from the east to Jerusalem, saying, Where is he that is born King of the Jews? for we have seen his star in the east, and are come to worship him.

After church Gloria lingered in the pew—praying, I thought. She hath ever been a mighty assaulter of Heaven; and I am moved by the long, dark rivers of language with which she rows toward God.

As I walked up the aisle to my tiny study, she said, "Pastor?"

I turned into her pew and sat.

She was quiet a while, gazing toward the altar. There stood upon it a tall brass crucifix. Above that, filled with southern sunlight, was a stained glass window in which Jesus knelt at a stone, praying in Gethsemane.

She said, softly, "I been knowin' Jesus since I was little-bitty. And I have loved him. And I have called upon him. Why did I hurt so bad

265

when Sonny Boy died? Why does it take me so long, so long, I mean my whole life long until now—"

She fell silent again.

What is the matter with me? Don't I really believe?

There was much that I did not say aloud that morning.

I didn't say: It takes the poor adult forever to become a child again, able to make her bed on the bosom of Jesus.

I didn't say: We resist falling completely and helplessly into his arms. Helplessness scares us. We wish to keep a little control. The lack of it leaves us blind; and a *blind* trust feels like death to us.

I didn't say: It takes forever to become nothing in Jesus' Everything.

To deny ourselves altogether.

To die into him.

But the third act of grief *was* dying for you, sweet savvy Gloria. Grief brought you down unto him not only in knowledge, but also in experience.

No: I said none of this. I told her a story.

❧

When I was a boy (I said), I told people that my father was stronger than anyone else in the world.

He was a handsome man in those days. He had a curl of hair at the middle of his forehead, and brown eyes, and a pulsing muscle in his jaw. And he loved me.

So I would go out on the front porch and roar to the neighborhood: "My daddy's arm is as strong as trucks! The strongest man in the world."

My mother came out and said, "Are you trying to start a fight with someone?"

I said, "Nope."

She said, "Then what do you mean by shouting?"

I said, "Robbers beware. A strong man lives in this house."

"Well," she said, "*Wally* beware. Big words, big deeds, you know."

When my mother went back inside the house, I bellowed, "My daddy's the strongest man in the world. Big words, big deeds, you know!" I had no idea what that meant. But momma did.

In those days a cherry tree grew in our backyard. This was my hiding place. Ten feet above the ground a stout limb made a horizontal fork, a cradle on which I could lie face-down, reading, thinking, being alone. Nobody bothered me here. Even my parents didn't know where I went to hide. Sometimes Daddy would come out and call, "Wally? Wally?" but he didn't see me in the leaves.

I felt very tricky.

Then came the thunderstorm.

It was usual for me to dream in my tree and therefore not to notice changes in the weather. So if the sky grew dark or gave any warning, I didn't see it.

One day suddenly, a wind tore through the backyard and struck my cherry tree with such force that it ripped the book from my hands and nearly threw me from the limb. I locked my arms around the forking branches and hung on. My head hung down between them. I tried to wind my legs around the limb, but the whole tree was wallowing in the wind.

"Daddy!"

The sky grew absolutely black. Dust whirled higher than the house. I saw a lightning bolt drop from heaven, then there was a perfect calm, and then the thunder crashed.

"Daddy! Daddy! Daddy!"

The whole tree bowed down and rose again, and the wind blew my shirt up to my shoulders, and the rain hit like bullets, and I thought that my arms were going to slip from the branches.

"Daddeeeeeeee!"

There he was. I saw his face at the back door, peering out.

Lightning stuttered in the sky.

"Out here! Up here! I'm here! Daddy, come get me!"

The branches swept up and down, like huge waves on an ocean— and Daddy saw me, and right away he came out into the wind and the weather, and I felt so relieved because I just took it for granted that he would climb right up the tree to get me.

But that wasn't his plan at all.

He came to a spot right below me and lifted his arms and shouted, "Jump."

"What?"

"Jump. I'll catch you."

Jump? I had a crazy man for a father. He was standing six or seven miles beneath me, holding up two skinny arms and telling me to jump. If I jumped, he'd miss. I'd hit the ground and die.

I screamed, "No!" At least I could feel the bark of the branches against my body. "No!"

I made up my mind. I'd stay right here till the storm was over. I closed my eyes and hung on.

But the wind and the rain slapped that cherry tree, bent it back, and cracked my limb at the trunk. I dropped a foot. My eyes flew open. Then the wood whined and splintered and sank, and so did I, in bloody terror.

No, I did not jump. I let go. I surrendered.

I fell.

In a fast, eternal moment I despaired and plummeted. *This*, I thought, *is what it's like to die—*

But my father caught me.

And my father squeezed me to himself. I wrapped my arms and legs around him and felt the scratch of his whiskers on my face and began to tremble and began to cry. He caught me. Oh, my daddy—he had strong arms indeed. Very strong arms.

But it wasn't until I actually *experienced* the strength that I also believed in it.

And I myself did not choose so frightening an experience. The storm did.

Horrible storm. Wonderful storm.

It granted me what I had had all along, but what I had not trusted. A father with arms as strong as trucks.

❦

THE FALL TO FAITH

Not every time a person grieves will he be brought to deeper faith by the experience. But he might. The opportunity, at least, exists in all our grieving.

We are all the boy who clings to an idealized view of the world— and also to his own devisings. No matter how "realistic" we believe ourselves to be, if a Secondary Dying takes us by surprise, then we have been ignoring some piece of reality.

So the storm hits. What sort of a storm? Any separation that causes sorrow. Any of the countless dyings to which our flesh is heir: divorce or human treachery or surgery or retirement or the leave-taking of a child or the death of one beautiful dream or a dreadful personal failure or guilt. The storm hits.

God does not send this storm! God desires the death of no one! Rather, human sinning inaugurated conditions invidious to life. And sometimes a particular sin will clearly be the cause of this dying; but often no sinner at all can be charged: it is the groaning of the whole creation in travail because of the transgressions of the children of Adam.

The storm hits.

Now, in such a storm the tree which was our stable world is shaken, and instinct makes us grab it tighter: by our own strength we grip the habits that have helped us in the past, repeating them, believing them. We'd rather trust what *is* than what *might be*: that is, our power, our reason and feeling and endurance. Though the Secondary Dying is a single and seemingly finished event, the storm continues. The storm is the world, now, which we would resist. We spend a long time screaming *No!*

Oh, best let go. Jump. Accept what is and fall upon the bosom of the Lord. *Be* the baby that you are. Let go and let God. Jump.

No—with all our will. And with all our feeling. And with all our reason, *No!*

But always, God is present. God has always been present. And it is God who says, "Jump."

But we hear, *Die*. We hear, *Choose death*, and such a call runs exactly counter to the sweeter call of the world and our own sinfulness. We hear, *Leap into the darkness. Abandon yourself*—whereas the whole world has said, "Exalt yourself!" And such a leap of utter faith is unreasonable; it is antithetic to reason and caution.

Jump.

Are you crazy?

Jesus calls the helpless lamb to jump.

And even while the Savior "waits to be gracious to us," we cling to the little branch. And some of us never do nor ever can jump.

Rather, the branch breaks.

And we fall.

That is to say, in the third act of grieving, we die. Not because we are suddenly wise; but because we had no choice any more.

Everything we had trusted in failed. It all proved vain. For a period of time, then, we despair. We suffer knowledge of the annihilation of all our strength. That is, we quietly confess: "I am nothing."

We expect to hit bottom and we expect to die.

But at the bottom of the pit—even where he went in his own most grievous dying—waits the Lord. Christ Jesus descended into death in order to meet us exactly there, in death!

Lo, then, how strong are the arms of the Lord! And how astounding that this is the place where we encounter God.

All of this is right and proper. Except we go down to the Pit *expecting nothing,* anything would seem our doing, or our deserving, or our due. In that case, God would not be acknowledged as the pure giver; rather, we would think some exchange had occurred, and we would salvage thereby our old value. But since we truly believe that we have come to the end, any life hereafter must be seen as gift, an utterly undeserved gift, the grace of God.

Any life:

In the fourth act of grief, having bowed our heads expecting death, the smallest event of daily existence astounds us. It seems bright with a holy glow: it is Jesus, catching us, and now we know the breadth and goodness of his arms not by doctrines or by sermons, but by experience.

We have felt him here beneath us.

Others may not see the simple things of creation as marvels. But for us they are relationship where we had sincerely expected solitude.

❦

The sun comes up in the morning, Gloria, and you notice the common event. The air smells sweet, and you take note. One bird sings, and the song transports you: all music is in the mockingbird's throat. Each small spasm of life now seems unspeakably precious, simply by being, just by persisting.

And Tommy had a bandage on his thumb the size of Oklahoma, and you laughed to see his boyish extremes, and you wept to receive his loyalty. He stayed. He forgave you—though you expected no forgiveness, no continuing son. This persisting love-child is your own Epiphany, Gloria.

In the person of strong, staunch Tommy, God comes to you. You have had a very great fall; but in Tommy's returning, the Father is catching you.

It's just that we adults take so long to fall.

But now let me tell you an even deeper wonder: the relationship which God had intended from the beginning of time, full and free between himself and you, he now renews. He who catches you, keeps you. This is life eternal. But it is different from what it was. For in the beginning the relationship was to be maintained by *your* righteousness, your complete obedience to God. Now, however, it is your faith in *Jesus'* righteousness which preserves the divine relationship. Gloria, rejoice: righteousness has been replaced by faith. The new covenant in Christ has replaced the old covenant of the law.

And you, now humbled, know it.

"For this my daughter was lost and is found; she was dead and is alive. Somebody run out and kill the calf and let's have a party!"

So faith springs from sorrow. And grief prepares us to believe.

Sister, let me kiss your lovely cheek. The church is empty. They've all gone home to their busy existences. And your Epiphany too is outside this place—back in the world and at work. Arise, shine; for thy light is come, and the glory of the Lord is risen upon thee.

21 Grief IV: Resurrection

T his too is part of grieving—not as the end and the absence of it, but as its purpose and its success—this: Rising to life again.

As were the first three acts of grieving, so is the fourth a process. Though it can produce a change spiritual and deep and lasting, this particular act may be slow, internal, scarcely evident to watchful comforters. Well, the griever is cautious about her emotions just now: not ready yet to trust them or to show them. She is healing; but the healing should not be gauged by any intensity of emotional behavior, by gladness or gratitude or relief or serenity. Her health shall be revealed betimes.

Let comforters slowly retreat, just now. Let them go quietly, shifting responsibility to the griever as she signals the readiness. But let them keep patient even now—and now, more than ever, keep faith. It has been a long road; the last turning is no quicker than the first or the third.

Moreover, "rising" and "healing" do not mean that sorrow is finally abolished. Wounds leave scars, and deep wounds scar the soul.

Whatever the death, if it has caused a drama of grief as complex as the full four acts, it shall never be forgotten—nor shall the grieving ever altogether pass away. Something lingers. Gloria will always miss

Sonny Boy. Always. Missing him has now become a part of her person.

The man who marries a widow ought cheerfully to realize that the woman whom he cherishes was shaped in relationship with another man: he marries her past; he marries her present remembering; he marries someone refined by grief; he marries a marvel of experience. Let him anticipate and welcome ghosts. They shall enrich the present relationship.

And an anguished divorce will teach the divorcée anguish forever: she has become an initiate. She understands sorrow. She shall be sorrow's intimate hereafter—not necessarily in morbidity, but in sympathy: seeing it and knowing it in others! She who was comforted has learned how to comfort—just as Jesus suffered to know our suffering—and this is surely to the good.

But grievers do not, in the end, return to their "old selves." The "old life," "that old sparkle" are gone.

Resurrection blots out neither death nor the long sorrow it caused.

Resurrection is not the sweetening of bitter truth.

Nor is it a pious sentimentalizing of disaster, as if one suddenly surrendered common sense by saying: "Well, it was the will of God. I've learned to accept that now. I'm a better person for it"—or some such simplification.

Resurrection is this: that though she was sure she would die, she lives. And though she *knew* she'd never feel again, she feels. Against all reason, against all evidence—a consequence that was impossible to any who entered the Pit—she is alive, breathing, feeling, thinking, making decisions again, again!

She lives *in spite of death*. Now, if death were forgotten at the end of grief, the preposterous nature of life would likewise be lost, the flat miracle of the thing, the miracle of her own being: she is the miracle!

She lives in spite of death: that is, Gloria remembers Sonny Boy, missing him so truly that there is a "Sonny-Boy" lump in her womb, an everlasting heaviness. The dead and the living continue one within the other; but the equation changes. Now it is not Sonny Boy dragging his niece into death; rather, it is Gloria celebrating Sonny Boy with life. She is bearing his memory back to the daylight. Indeed, that she is living at all becomes a memorial to her uncle.

And now she can't help it: she will look at life with new eyes. No longer can she presume that life is maintained by her own strength—

not since her crash into personal impotence. Life comes *in spite of* her frailty. It must, therefore, be given. And it must be received as a gift.

Therefore, this too is resurrection: that she both lives and is *grateful* to be living. An essential characteristic of the resurrected life is gratitude.

Which is relationship.

To whom does the griever, now rising, give thanks? Like anger, gratitude seeks an object. Its nature is outward; its yearning is to identify a Someone Responsible for this conundrum of life in spite of death; and (if gratitude is genuine) that One must be Someone Greater Than the Griever's Self, must be the Source of Life, Creator, Deity—

The transcendent God.

But God comes near to us in the Word made flesh.

Gratitude seeks the Christ. Even if she knows not his name or his story, the griever now seeks the Lord's Messiah.

Humbled as never before (not abjectly so, not beaten down, but full of astonished thanksgiving and praise) the griever is ready to see his glory now.

In small things. In common things. In the persisting, daily things.

It is precisely because the Lord inhabits ordinary things that she did not see him there before; but she has changed, and absolutely everything (since anything now is undeserved and all is unexpected) seems extraordinary in her sight. Simple sunrise is like the solo of God at the dawn of creation, a splendid *Fiat lux!* And a loyal boy with a monstrous bandage is the temple of the Lord.

Holy! Holy! Holy is the Lord of Hosts: the whole earth is filled with his glory!

The whole earth: each piece of creation. Now the griever may see divinity in any common thing, and so renew relationship with the Almighty Creator even as she renews relationships with the bits and pieces, the handiwork of God.

SIGNS OF THE RESURRECTION

Since the renewal of life (the renewal of relationships) is slow and small and internal at first, the comforters might miss its signs. But you, my griever, should be aware of them; and you can accept them as an Easter inside yourself. Honor them. Don't try to manufacture them; they will arrive on their own as gifts from God. But neither should you belittle or doubt them: they are from God.

Natural Relationships Renewed

One day you're hungry. You eat. And while you eat, a remarkable thing occurs: you taste exquisitely—you do thoroughly appreciate—the food. It's just a french fry! But you think, "I've never had a better french fry! Oh, I've been missing french fries." And you find yourself chewing with something more than mere pleasure; you are chewing with a distinct feeling of gratitude. You want to thank someone.

But it's just a french fry! Isn't it silly to be moved to tears by a french fry?

Not silly at all. The goodness of this moment (of the spasms of renewal) is not to be measured by the material thing that caused it, but rather by the passion in you that receives it, and then by the glory of him who gives it. If you are compelled by a french fry to give thanks, by all means—give thanks to God.

Of course, by tomorrow your heart may be cast down again. And then you may feel the worse for a moment of gladness that didn't last. No matter: the rise is always fitful at first, with fallings again when sadness returns, and fallings when you doubt the signs of life. Be patient. Wait. The gift will come again; and again—despite setbacks—you will feel the rush of thanksgiving.

One morning you wake, and you look, and here after winter is the spring! Lo, the breezes are warm and the land is loamy and the trees have gathered a green wool with their fingers; crocuses stand at tiny attention; there is sound, there is glad sound, there is the birdsong sound—and the distinct response in your heart is that all the world has clothed itself especially for you. On this particular morning, nature's no longer indifferent, but friendly, and spring is a present prepared *for you*.

A speechless gratitude causes you almost to gasp.

In this way relationship returns. And that relationship in which you discover new feelings, in which you find a new sense of self, *does* feel personal. Spring, though you had experienced seventy such springs before, *can* be your friend, your gift, your sister.

Moreover, the grim asceticism of grief has sensitized you spiritually as well as physically; so your awakening is signaled by the new awareness that all creation is not just a basic necessity "good for food," but like the trees of Eden is also "pleasant to the sight." So what? So the hand of the Creator has given this spring to your spirit as well as your body—and because you can sense his touch in the season, the season must feel as personal to you as his love.

And so what? So you are no longer a cold observer, numb to nature, the inhabitant of a watch-work universe.

You are a citizen. You are kin.

And here in creation, you are home again.

Now, then: though tomorrow your soul may be cast down again, these moments of graceful relationship shall encourage you, and you may risk commitment to the world around you. Spontaneously you perform small tasks. You work. This is the labor of your hands, your own willing response to relationship, dressing and tilling the garden: signs of your resurrection.

The woman who used to tend a garden—before her divorce took the life out of her—feels compelled, suddenly, to buy seed. A tentative act. She tells no one for fear she will fail or change her mind. But she plants a small plot. She begins to trust in a *future*. She is, with caution, re-entering time. Perhaps the world is not altogether destroyed. Perhaps—

First comes the test; then comes the trust.

Or someone remembers certain assignments he had forgotten on the job. They just pop into his head. Without guilt, but with a notion to accomplish them. And he does. And he feels a small sense of satisfaction.

And grandpa, grieved by retirement, notices that the sink leaks. On Monday he fixes it.

Then every success holds an aura of wonder: *It didn't have to be.* To your friends, my Griever, these are events so small that they surely wouldn't measure resurrection thereby. But to you they are the manifestations of grace. You know, now, their truer proportion: life in spite of death. Relationship in spite of separation. And as this fourth act of grief evolves, you shall less and less debase yourself with the thought, *I could never have done this on my own.* Rather, you shall ennoble yourself with glory: *God loves me, even me, in the small and incidental things!*

The Internal Relationship Renewed

So there comes a day when you want to be clean. You bathe. You do laundry. You buy new clothes. On Tuesday you dress as if it were Sunday. You get a manicure.

Once these might have been seen as gestures of denial; in the fourth act, however, they are choices for a future. The past *is*: that is, it has been clearly and consciously confronted. But the past is also *past*, and that it should even *feel* past is a miracle, since you thought despair would go on forever.

Time is friendly again, precisely because every present moment may now be new. The natural succession of days (which never ceased, but which you couldn't trust during grief's worst periods) strikes you with a miraculous insight: *now* is not *then*; and you live *now*. With every new *now* you are being reborn!

Therefore you wash your face. For three reasons you wish to be clean: (1) you never did like being dirty; (2) you are free, in each new day, to make genuine choices for that particular day; and (3) you like the body in which you awoke this morning; you want to honor and to comfort it.

Say it: you like the self that God created, the person whom Jesus redeemed.

And now you may understand re-creation in redemption. God has freed you from the yoke of the past; he does not hold your past against you. No, you will never forget the events of separation and grief; but the *weight* of these events has been removed; and there occur, now, moments of an almost physical lightness, when your body seems to spring from the ground, when you appreciate the simple motion of bone and muscle, when you nearly giggle with the gladness of *self*, of being and of knowing that you are.

Tomorrow you may feel lethargic and heavy again. Yes, yes, the rising is fitful. But this moment is no less real for that. Laughter, when there seems no cause for laughter, is a sign of insanity—or else of resurrection. The two are not dissimilar.

I know a woman who suffers from Huntington's Disease. She's losing control of her motor functions and, like her mother before her, will die of this affliction. She has grieved the inevitability for a very long time. But lately, in the fourth act of grief, she sometimes giggles with sheer delight. "I am the lily," she told me one night. "I live, and soon I'll die. But I live right now. Right now I am alive. And I am better than the lily, because I *know* I am alive." The woman yowled and yawed and jerked to pronounce these words; yet when she did, she was sweeter than fields of lilies, lovelier than a sky of stars.

And Gloria Ferguson, when Tommy sang carols for her, was clearly forgiven her sins against her son. She hugged him and wept. She was free. She needed no more to detest herself. And in the day of her liberation she went home and changed the sheets of her bed—not because she deserved a reward, but because babies should sleep on clean sheets.

Both Gloria and the woman dying of Huntington's Disease (each because of the depth of her grieving!) have both been set free from the grave weight of accumulated time. One of them has shucked the past; the other is unconcerned for the future. Both are stunned by the broad scope of the Eternal Now. Both know something of eternity *now*, for now always is; now is always. In them are the signs of life again, and signs too of the final resurrection.

The Communal Relationship Renewed

"Wait" was the word to your friends and your colleagues, those with whom you maintained relationship. Yet while you suffered the sadness of death, *Wait*:

Stay with her.

Don't judge her.

Don't preach.

Simply, *be* hope while she is hopeless by upholding both ends of the relationship: even so are you the image of Christ for her, Jesus, who chooses to be everything to our nothing—

"Wait."

Now the waiting is nearly over; but before they know it, you know it—by the quiet awareness of their presence, by a remembering of all they've been doing these weeks and months, and by the renewal of gratitude within you, even before you're sure how to express it.

One day, as your sister leaves, you whisper, "Thanks," and you mean it.

One day, with a sudden daring, you reach and touch an honorable cheek—and lo: your friend doesn't vanish. The comforter does not run away with loathing. Nor does he pat your hand with a patronizing superiority. Instead, he smiles and accepts the gesture as natural. Why, then, in his eyes *you* are natural.

One day you are able to look directly in another's eyes. And to listen to somebody else's talk with interest. To have a two-way talk. To return relationship. And lo: you are alive.

And if all these changes were subtle and spontaneous at first, soon you begin to trust them in yourself. Soon you take thought for them: you *choose* to support the relationship out of your own abilities and kindness and emotion, out of the wholeness of your being. You remember that it is someone's birthday. *You* send a card and a gift. Welcome, sister, to the community again, to its life and to your health.

You go out one evening with dear friends for plain entertainment.

How many of these relationships did your sorrow strain to the breaking? How many folks did you scorn or berate or neglect or command without pity? Whose sympathy did you insult? Whose sins did you refuse to forgive? Whom did you in your rages attack? Now you can name the names and see the faults of your recent grieving. Remembering comes like a fire. So the fourth act of grief is not without its own intrinsic pain: like blood returning to frost-bitten flesh, guilt comes hot and hurting.

Well, take consolation in several shining truths:

—This is the pain not of dying but of rising. You are not slipping backward to sorrow. Rather, the soul that returns to life will likewise return to responsibility for herself and for her actions.

—This pain is able to know that the love of your friends is not due to you. It has been sorely tried. It has survived. It is a treasure— because it has been no barter at all, but an unqualified gift. Such love will not suddenly leave you now. Therefore, take consolation in these consequential truths:

—The love that endured your grieving has *already* forgiven your sins. You can in the fourth act of grieving, if you wish, confess and receive an open, spoken absolution. You can, I say; you are cheerfully able: because you are also assured, by such love, of the forgiveness to follow. I encourage you to the confession. It will feel more cleansing than baths or new clothes, a most marvelous proof of new life.

—This love defines you now. How you seem in the eyes of them that love you—well, that is how you *are*, beloved and therefore lovely. That is *who* you are: as a gift. Being itself begins to be revealed to you as a gift.

—This love must have another source than the merely human; for you know better than anyone now how severely you strained its substance and its virtue. Then whom do you see in the faces of them that remained while you were a bane and a danger? Of course.

The Christ.

The friends around you were merely sweet mediums, the living images of Jesus. It was he who companioned you all the way. Of course.

But seeing him now is a sign of your resurrection. Relationship within relationship, the holy within the mundane, grace upon grace, my Savior! Ah, my Lord!

And having been served, you are able to serve, and that is life, because your relationships return to their nature of mutual interaction: but your service has found new competence. *You* are truer, *it* is better: passion has taught you compassion, a deeper and freer involvement in the experiences of others.

Gloria Ferguson can pray for the sake of others with a finer fervor than anyone I know. She begs heaven with faith, with a mother's aggression, with the righteousness of Christ and the boldness of the seraphim, with fire and wind and tears, without embarrassment. She holds God to his promises. She is a thundering buffalo. She is a lamb. She is the daughter whom the father took back again. She knows the mansion and its Lord. She knows. By hard experience she knows.

And this is her service, therefore:

When I am sad, I go to Gloria. "Sister, pray for me?"

Yes. Yes. It is her gift to pray.

22 The Primal Relationship Renewed

E verything is reversed. When the Primal Relationship broke, so did all the others. Death caused death. But now life reveals Life, and tucked within the renewal of every other relationship is proof and truth of the renewal as well as of our relationship to the Creator.

Well, that renewal began in Jesus. It was initiated long ago, on the cross. Always, always it is God who starts things and we who benefit.

But we don't realize the renewal of this Primal Relationship until we experience it, and the long toil of grief is such an experience. In nature, then, the great God smiles. In our selves the Spirit breathes. And in others Jesus dwells and loves and comes to us.

He who outfaced death, humble and low, dying all of the dyings; he who triumphed over Hell itself; he it is who holds me now; for he caught me when the branches broke, and he never let me go.

In him, then, we have peace. *Shalom*: health and the wholeness of life again, the promise he made the day before he went down to the Pit: "Peace I leave with you; my peace I give to you; not as the world gives do I give to you. Let not your hearts be troubled, neither let them be afraid."

"In the world you have tribulation; but be of good cheer, I have overcome the world."

This "Peace" of his life.

All is restored, even as God had intended from the beginning (even as we boldly described our Creator's intentions at the beginning of this book).

But now the health of the Primal Relationship—the love of it—is no longer maintained by our obedience. This is the crucial difference, because it assures us that the relationship will never again be broken, shall continue even into eternity. Its health is now maintained by *Christ's* obedience, to which we cling like children in faith, the which we follow like lambs in faith. In faith. In simple faith.

LIFE WHILE WE LIVE THIS LIFE

After grief we begin again—at the very beginning, as it were, in a sort of an Eden.

Our Communal Relationships may be knit with the love of God rather than the love of self. Christ becomes the tie that binds us one to another. And when we express love at all, we express him, we represent him, we draw upon him, we share him, and therefore we share unshakable Truth and Life with those we cherish.

Now comes the ability, miraculous in human beings, to relate to others without consideration for ourselves, that self which once we deified, which therefore tyrannized our people. Our desires sweetly diminish; and if they are noticed and satisfied, why, that's a gift full worthy of hallelujah and thanksgiving—but it is no longer a right and a demand.

Now comes the ability to forgive as we have been forgiven. Now we can deal with our fellows in forbearance of a truly heavenly quality.

For now *we* are the images of Jesus unto others, and the Word of God is the source of all our words.

Our Natural Relationships now can honor the earth with wisdom and care, can bless and serve the creation God put into our hands for safe-keeping.

My mother once gave me a golden jade ring. I keep it well; I keep it as jade and gold are meant to be kept—because I love my mother. For love of her I learn of rings and keep this one a treasure. When I touch it, I touch the love of my mother. How else shall I touch it, then, but lovingly?

God gave us the earth, and shan't we keep it well—learning of soil and rivers and air, of all of its creatures in order to keep them as God meant them to be kept—simply because we love the Creator? When we touch any natural thing, we touch the love of God. How else shall we touch it, but lovingly?

And won't we receive in the touch, therefore, citizenship in the whole of the universe?

We are free. We stride the skies. Our spirits ascend wherever the beautiful Savior reigns. The stars, that bright sand on the shores of eternity, are sisters to us. They are the hosts of heaven. Angels bearing tidings of love. We, though limited, in Christ are as large as the cosmos.

Hush, child. Hush: thou art no stranger any more.

Sleep peacefully. This is thine abode.

Thou art home.

And so our Internal Relationships are both truthful and unembarrassed.

I am a small packet of talents. Walt: a person of wondrous worth. No, not because I am a lovely little deity, but because the Deity loves me.

God's love maketh lovely even that which once was ugly in sin. So it does not matter what your ex-spouse said to you in the heat of some previous battle; whether the criticism was, at that time, right or wrong doesn't matter; right now it is wrong; you are renewed in the love of the Lord. You are beautiful.

And we needn't be troubled by the fact of our finitude. We become content in the particular self that God created and that Jesus redeemed—knowing that Father, Son, and Holy Spirit, one God, is Infinity enough for us.

Once my grandfather said to me, "Can you see the deer?"

I said, "No."

"Two deer," he said, pointing from the boat to a wooded shore, "looking back at us, can you see them?"

I said, "No." I was short. I was three years old. We were in an excursion boat, traveling down river.

"Okay," he said, "come here."

He led me to the back of the boat and hoisted me high into the air. He leaned back, so that I could see above the canopy. I looked down at water churned by the propeller. I was not afraid. My grandfather held me. I looked up and over the canopy and saw two deer looking back at us. I was not surprised. My grandfather held me. What I could not do for myself, he did.

Even so the Infinite God will lift us to the height and to the heights—and into heaven.

If God is God, it is no more an anguish that we are not gods. And this is an excellent Self after all. I am grateful to have been given it.

AND LIFE HEREAFTER

Softly, without raising her head, Gloria whispered to me, "Where is he?"

I misunderstood her. I thought she meant Jesus, and I said, "Here. He has always been with you—"

"No, Pastor," she said, looking at me now. "Where is Sonny Boy? Where is *he*?"

Before I could answer, the Senior Citizens broke into song and distracted Gloria and gave me a respite from the question. But I didn't forget it.

And I answer it now: "He is with the Lord."

But I want to refine that answer until it truly comforts you, Gloria. It is not meant cheaply. It comes after long thought.

Listen: when Sonny Boy left this life, he left creation as God gave it unto us. He left all things and the space that contains things. He left history and the time that contains history. He departed *time*, Gloria, immediately and entirely to be with God.

You and I are still inside of time. We still move in tiny ticks of seconds through long months and the interminable years. Through days and days we creep toward the Last Day, when all of us will meet God, the living and the dead together, because on that Day the dead will be raised to life, and Sonny Boy too.

From our perspective, that's a long *time* away.

But Sonny Boy has popped free of time.

From *his* perspective, there is no time any more. He doesn't have to wait. He is there already! For him it is already the Great Gettin'-Up Morning—and he's up! He is raised from the dead. And we are there too. And we are meeting each other in the joy of the saved. And when you and I have died, all that is *now* for Sonny Boy will be *now* for us as well, as if no time at all had intervened. He is with the Lord.

But we have a while to wait yet before we experience the *now* he knows. But he's not waiting.

Between you and Sonny Boy, Gloria, you are the lonelier one. All your sorrow has been for yourself while still you are stuck in time. He's the glad one. From his perspective he has never been apart from you. The instant he rises from the dead, so do you.

It's a mystery. We shall not all sleep (which sleeping makes time a mere blink to the sleeper). But we shall all be changed. In a moment. In the twinkling of an eye. At the last trumpet.

For the trumpet will sound the long and the sudden note, and the dead will be raised imperishable, and we shall be changed. This mortal shall put on immortality. Then shall be brought to pass the saying that is written,

DEATH IS SWALLOWED UP IN VICTORY

O death, where is thy sting?
O grave, where is thy victory?
The sting of death is sin; and the strength of sin is the law. But thanks be to God, who gives us the victory through our Lord Jesus Christ.

Therefore, my beloved Gloria, be steadfast, immovable, always abounding in the work of the Lord, forasmuch as you know that your labor is not in vain. No, not in the Lord.

Amen.

EPILOGUE

End at the Beginning

Yet before she goes to Costa Rica, Talitha has found a job. She says that she wants to purchase her clothes in Central America, where things are sure to be cheaper. (She knows so much more than I do.) So she's raising a little cash for the journey.

My daughter, so blithe and so bold and so blind! I, for my part, am astounded by the design of all things.

This book is essentially finished. All of its stories have been written as you've just read them. Where, then, did my daughter go forth to get work for her tough little self? To the Salvation Army. In the Senior Citizen's Drop-In Center. Assisting Gloria Ferguson.

Neither one of them knew that I had already married them in the pages of this book.

But God knew.

And God will shock us by turning our small imaginings into amazing realities.

Well, if I can't outrun the Lord, I had better follow as close as I can. It was time I told Gloria what I have written here.

The Center has moved to new facilities since the year the Citizens sang carols for Gloria. It's above the ground now, sunlit: gloom is banished.

Mr. Sullivan is dead. So is Callie. But there is no lack of elderly. Always they note my arrival in the new waiting room as if I were an intruder; and always I have to tell them why I came: to get Talitha.

Talitha, on the other hand, is their child and no stranger.

Last month, then, when she came and told me to wait, three old folks repeated her words to make sure I understood.

"Read a magazine," the kid said.

"READ MAGAZINES!" echoed hawks and crones and ravens, her friends.

"Sit down," she said. "Relax. You're always so tense."

"TENSE!"

"I gotta straighten the sitting room. Oh, and these," she said, pointing at a bag of tomatoes, "are from Miz Glory. You should thank her." Suddenly she frowned at me. "Jeans!" she squawked. "You should turn the cuff up on jeans. Like this." She knelt down and turned my cuffs up. "Poor Dad. No style."

"STYLE!" her friends shouted, and she was gone.

I turned the cuffs down again and went looking for Gloria.

Talitha, of course, has style.

Gloria was in a stainless-steel kitchen, baking frozen pizzas, sticking some in, pulling some out, passing pieces over a counter to her Seniors.

"Don' worry 'bout that child," she said.

"What?"

"Don' fret for your baby, all full of herself these days. She'll be humbled."

"Oh. You mean Talitha."

"That's the one. The girl's a furnace of good cheer around here. Renders the Seniors happy and weary at once."

Gloria's raven-black hair is shot with white. Her face is round, her body rounder than it was, her complexion somewhat dusted by long experience. There is no less love between us; but because we are both older, there are fewer words. Less need for words. She knows what I'm thinking, mostly.

Her children have children as old as Talitha. The other day she said, *Pastor, I've given them all to God. I'm free. And freedom is wisdom, and wisdom is counseling me now. Don't fret for your baby. She will be fine.*

"Gloria?" I was standing aside of her labor, out of the way. "I've written a book about you. Is that okay?"

"You what?" she said. "You writing what?"

"A book. I'm telling a difficult story, which can be good for all people, tidings to all people. Um, but it's your story. Is that okay?"

She slipped a pizza past me. "What's to tell? My secrets?"

I said, "Yes."

She stopped and faced me directly. "What?"

"Do you remember Sonny Boy Hopson?"

Her face softened, but she kept her eyes on me. "All the time."

"Well, that's the story. I'm describing the time of his dying and the time that came afterward—especially the feelings, Gloria. Your feelings. All of them." I paused a moment. She tilted her chin up and raised her eyebrows a degree—even as she did in the old days. But she kept looking at me. "Some of the feelings were hard and bad. Some were downright horrible. Some were good. I'm telling all of them."

She said quietly, "Why?"

"Why am I writing the book?"

"Why tell my feelings?"

"Because it's through our feelings that God works to change things. Because you *had* to have those feelings even to know how close God was to you and to Sonny Boy, always holding you both, you here and Sonny Boy hereafter."

There were pizzas waiting on the counter, pizzas in the oven. No matter. Gloria reached up and pulled down the metal divider between the kitchen and the sitting room. She went over and closed the door, then she returned to a chair and sat with her head down.

I had roused the memories. In fact, I could name them one by one as they passed in the darkness of her mind. We are old friends, Gloria and I, with little need for words. And when she closed her eyes I knew she was hearing the sentence again: *Baby, I'm goin' on in here to die, now.*

"But you survived," I said. "Even by those feelings, Gloria, God raised you up again."

With her eyes still closed she said, "But why do you have to tell them out loud? In a book?"

"For Talitha," I said.

She looked up at me. "What?"

"For anyone who doesn't know what you know," I said. "Especially for the people I love. For Talitha—who thinks she knows everything, but who is going to be humbled, as you say. No one can keep death away; and so many people don't know that. Well, and then they don't know the goodness of the hard feelings, the grieving that comes with death after all; but you do. Gloria, in my book you will be their teacher."

Just then, the kitchen door banged open and Talitha herself strolled in. As is her custom at any entrance, she was ready to talk.

But Gloria lifted a hand. "Sit down, baby," she said. "Be quiet. Your daddy and I are talking."

The child sat without a sound, and I marveled at the might in Gloria's arm.

Still holding the arm up, she said, "You want this child to know my story?"

I nodded. There was much my daughter should learn from my old friend.

Talitha blinked back and forth between us.

"Okay," Gloria said. "Okay. For this child all full of herself, write it, tell it all." She lowered her arm. "But for Sonny Boy's sake, don't end at the ending."

Talitha said, "Dad, what story—"

"Hush up, baby," Gloria commanded without looking at her. "End in the middle," she said to me. She leaned forward, earnest in the request. "End at the beginning. Pastor, folk should remember the best about Sonny Boy—and the best was when he was dancing."

All at once Gloria stood up and walked over to Talitha. She said, "I want you to promise to read this story when it's in a book."

Talitha said, "What story?"

"Honey, never mind now. Promise me."

Talitha nodded.

Gloria walked toward me. "End," she said, "by telling the times he stood up on Saturday night at Fly's and smiled. Tell how all the people went quiet then, knowing what was comin'. Tell about his beautiful white teeth, and how he tapped his toe once, and the room said, Yes, and the people said, *Yes*, and the music said, *Sonny Boy, Sonny Boy—go!* Then tell how he'd slide his toe across the floor and raise his arms and break into a dazzle of dancing, fast and crafty and good, and the people'ud beat the tables, the people'ud laugh for joy—

because that's what Sonny Boy did with his dancing; he gave the people joy. Tell how he would throw back his head and roar with laughter, enjoying the thing he was doing: dancing. Sonny Boy dancing. Sonny Boy beautiful. Sonny Boy good.

"That's what I'm remembering these days," said Gloria, "that he danced the waltz with me. And the waltz became a two-step. And all of the people watched us. And I loved him. And he loved me.

"That," she said, "is how you should end the story. With dancing."

And so I do, dear Gloria. With dancing.

Oh, my sister, but it is you who are dancing too, brighter than all of the angels in heaven. And into your lovely heart I lay the words to which you move:

> For thou hast changed for me my mourning into dancing:
> thou hast put off my sackcloth,
>   and girded me with gladness
> To the end that my glory may sing praise to thee
>   and not be silent.
>
> O Lord my God, I will give thanks unto thee for ever.

❧

Mourning
into Dancing
was typeset on a
Mergenthaler Linotron 202/N
by the Photocomposition Department
of Zondervan Publishing House; Sue Koppenol, compositor.
The text is set in 11 point Goudy Old Style,
a face designed by Frederic Goudy.
Printed by R. R. Donnelley
of Harrisonburg,
Virginia.